IN THE NAME
ALLAH
THE ALL-COMPASSIONATE, ALL-MERCIFUL

ISLAM
AND
MANAGEMENT

Title: ISLAM AND MANAGEMENT
Author: Dr. Naceur Jabnoun
English Edition 1 (2001)
English Edition 2 (2005)
Edited by: Yousuf Reaz
Layout: IIPH, Riyadh, Saudi Arabia
Filming & Cover Designing: Samo Press Group

Revised Edition

ISLAM
AND
MANAGEMENT

Dr. Naceur Jabnoun

INTERNATIONAL ISLAMIC PUBLISHING HOUSE

© International Islamic Publishing House, 2005

King Fahd National Library Cataloging-in-Publication Data

Al-Qarni, Aaid
The happiest woman in the world. / Aaid al-Qarni ; translated
by Huda al-Khattab .- Riyadh, 2005

...p ; 22 cm

ISBN Hard Cover: 9960-850-89-7
ISBN Soft Cover : 9960-850-90-0

1- Women in Islam   I-Huda al-Khattab (translator)   II-Title

219.2 dc   1424/7273
                    1424/7274

ISBN Hard Cover: 9960-850-89-7   Legal Deposit no. 1424/7273
ISBN Soft Cover : 9960-850-90-0   Legal Deposit no. 1424/7274

International Islamic Publishing House (IIPH)
P.O.Box 55195 Riyadh 11534, Saudi Arabia
Tel: 966 1 4650818 — 4647213 — Fax: 4633489
E-Mail: iiph@iiph.com.sa — www.iiph.com.sa

*Please take part in this noble work by conveying
your comments to IIPH through e-mail,
fax or postal-mail address.*

LIST OF CONTENTS

PART - VII

A VALUE BASED MANAGEMENT MODEL
A GUIDE TO MUSLIM MANAGERS

PUBLISHERS NOTE

All praise belongs to Allah, the All-Compassionate, the All-Merciful. Blessings and Peace be upon His last Prophet Muhammad, his family members and all those who follow his foot steps till the end of this world.

Islam is a comprehensive code of life revealed by the All-Merciful Creator for the guidance and betterment of the humanity here and the Hereafter. No aspect of life has been bereft of proper guidance.

Man being social, needs organization for the achievement of goals and success is dependent on quality management. Qur'an and the last of the Prophets have given practical guidelines on the matter. Muslims of the early days attained grand successes in their worldly life following the teachings of Islam. They were rather leaders in the field of quality management.

Dr. Naceur Jabnoun has come out with the third improved edition of his research work worthy of attention from all and sundry, people in the field of management and general readers. He has given the 'Islamic perspective on management and some important management lessons from the teaching of Islam.' This is the second enlarged edition of his book with more materials for better understanding and appreciation. May Allah accept his efforts.

Muhammad ibn 'Abdul-Muḥsin Al Tuwaijri
Managing Director, IIPH
International Islamic Publishing House, Riyadh, Saudi Arabia.
1426 A.H. / 2005 C.E.

FOREWORD

Islam is an universal religion followed by over one billion people living in different areas of the world. The literal meaning of Islam is the submission to the will of God. Islam has been one of the world's major movements of civilization. The Islamic civilization has made singular and profound contributions in the arts and sciences.

The teachings of Islam seek to protect people from harm and mischief — and serve their interest through the effective use of God-given resources. These objectives must be achieved within the framework of justice, dignity, and benevolence. The teachings of Islam provide a philosophy and a plan for people to live by.

Keeping the above in perspective, the authors purpose is to enhance the field of management by weaving into that discipline, concepts, and principles, of Islam. The book contains information, organizational cultures and conflicts. The material on the convergence of plans viewed from the systems perspective adds strength to the writing. The linking of long-term objectives and organizational actions provides an excellent overview of how planning is linked to the actual execution of strategies to accomplish desired ends.

Leadership is presented as a service to those individuals being led. Rewards and punishment are related to the ideas of personal motivation. Justice in the workplace along with the ideas of equity is given due coverage in this innovative text. Throughout the book the author provides model of the concepts presented. The important point is made that Islam commends conflicts as a means of checks and balances along with discussions of the causes, consequences, and management of conflict. The material on Total Quality Management provides an excellent relationship of the linkages of TQM with other key initiatives expressed in the book.

On balance this book is worthwhile book, which brings together concepts and processes from Management and Islam - two forces which have altered the relationships within the world's society.

Dr. David I. Cleland
Ernest E. Roth Professor and
Professor of Engineering Management
School of Engineering
University of Pittsburgh

INTRODUCTION

Quality management is key to organizational success, and as a certain management style shows its effectiveness, more people tend to explore and learn about it. For example, great interest exists among managers from around the world to learn about Japanese management because of the great success of Japanese companies. Throughout history various schools of management have succeeded one after another in attracting the attention of the worlds management readers. In this book, we will try to shed some light on a relatively obscure management school that far outperformed, more than its contemporaries, and left indelible marks on the minds of innumerable researchers, leaders and managers that followed. The success of early Muslims was achieved so rapidly, yet many of its legacy are lasting until today. This historically unique success induced Micheal Hart[1] to consider Prophet Muhammad (Blessings and Peace be upon him) as the most influential man in history.

This book presents an Islamic perspective on management and delineates some important management lessons from the teachings of Islam. Some readers might ask what the Islamic perspective on management means and what distinguishes this managerial perspective from what is found in current management literature? Is there a deficiency in current management principles, and what further knowledge can be offered by trying to study

---

[1] Micheal Hart, *"The 100: Ranking of the Most Influential Persons in History"* golden Book center, K1 (1979), p. 33.

management from an Islamic perspective? In essence, the distinction of the Islamic perspective is that, unlike the common concepts of management, it encompasses the dimensions of belief in Allah, the Exalted, and in the Hereafter. These added dimensions have innumerable ramifications on the actions and interactions of individuals, organizations, and societies. Ethics play a major role in the Islamic perspective of management. Furthermore, the Islamic teachings represent an inexhaustible source of knowledge that is overlooked by modern management scholars. Believing in revelation, its purity, and its perfection induces us to consider it as a major source of knowledge. The Qur'an proclaims itself to be generous as in the following verse:

﴿إِنَّهُ لَقُرْءَانٌ كَرِيمٌ ۝﴾   (سورة الواقعة ٥٦ : ٧٧)

❮It is indeed a generous Qur'an.❯ (Qur'an 56: 77)

Many scholars of the Qur'an have explained the above verse by the fact that Qur'an keeps giving new guidance, knowledge, and perspective to people at different times and geographical locations.

The word *āyāt* translated as verses, also means signs. This means that the Qur'an is a book of signs, or evidences of the Creator for the people who reflect. Therefore, a major implication of the belief in God is the inclusion of revelation as the primary source of knowledge. The appreciation of this belief can result in significant developments in the area of management. Moreover, the belief in the Hereafter instills the belief in individual accountability for ones deeds. This belief in accountability induces the variable of self-control in the behaviour of Muslims.

On the other hand, while the contributions of contemporary management are so numerous, many of its conclusions were derived from empirical studies that were carried out within a certain cultural framework. These conclusions are generally not universal, and are more applicable to the societies in which the experiments were carried out. The differences in culture induce variations in the managerial style. Moreover, some of the contemporary managerial concepts are based on certain premises of thought that are foreign to the Muslim state of mind. The management theories that are strictly and contradictory to the teachings of Islam are, for that matter, limited, and they are often controversial among the western scholars as well. This means that studies on the Islamic approach to management will provide more additions to the field of management than it will lead to abrogation.

Another major issue in the study of management from an Islamic perspective is that of the sources of information, or the choice of what some people call the roots of Islamic management. Some authors have introduced the roots of Islamic jurisprudence as the sources of Islamic management. Though the roots of Islamic jurisprudence include revelation, this approach is not appropriate because it reflects that these authors are confining knowledge to jurisprudence, or that they were at least confining the sources of knowledge to the roots of jurisprudence. This approach overlooks the important fact that, in areas such as management, the primary concern is not to debate what is lawful or *ḥalāl* and what is unlawful or *ḥarām*. In contrast, the major concern of management research from the Islamic perspective is to provide new ways and means of problem solving and of better allocating the resources that Allah made subservient to mankind. Moreover, the findings of this kind of research need not be unanimously agreed upon, and they need not be compulsory for any body. In his book Management and Administration in Islam,

Al-Buraey allocated an entire chapter to the roots of Islamic administration. Al-Buraey cited the Qur'an, the administration of the Prophet (Blessings and Peace be upon him), the administrations of his four righteous successors, as basis of Islamic administration. Al-Buraey cited a couple of letters written by 'Umar and 'Ali (may Allah be pleased with them) to their governors as foundations of Islamic administration. To further expound upon the concepts of Islamic administration, Al-Buraey also referred to the writings of leading Islamic scholars and pioneers of Islamic administration. By choosing such sources, Al-Buraey had not made the mistake of confining himself to the relatively narrow avenue of Islamic Jurisprudence.

This book is based on the belief that the teachings of Islam provide perfect guidelines and instructions for the success of mankind. In other words, the teachings of Islam represent a perfect plan that, if implemented, will certainly lead to success in this world and in the Hereafter. Considering the teachings of Islam as a plan, we have attempted to deduce some distinctive managerial lessons from them. This means that we have attempted to derive some management concepts from the way the Islamic teachings are structured and integrated. The other major source of management knowledge is the direct teachings of Islam, which are included in the Qur'an and in the tradition of Prophet Muhammad (Blessings and Peace be upon him). Other sources of knowledge include the leadership styles of Prophet Muhammad (bpuh) and his successors, the writings of Muslim as well as non-Muslim scholars who, through their intellectual and field work, have been able to understand a lot of governing rules of the human behaviour that Allah asked us to study and reflect upon. We are not restricting our sources to any class of writers, or to any generation of writers. Knowledge and wisdom are valuable commodities that we have to dig for all over the world and throughout history so long as we have the analytical capability to evaluate them and check their relevance. Prophet Muhammad (Blessings and Peace be upon him) said:

> "Wisdom shall be sought by Muslims, wherever they find it they are the ones most deserving of it." (Ibn Mājah)

Based on the above learning schemes, some important and original managerial concepts are presented in this book. The original concepts discussed here pertain to planning, controlling, and motivating. In these areas, some new models that can provide powerful tools for improved managerial performance are presented. Other topics covered in this book include organizing and conflict management, which are also original and offer ample enriching ideas to managers from all walks of life. The discussion on conflict presented here reveals the fact that Islam encourages functional conflicts in the form of processes of checks and balances. This book reserves a relatively long chapter to organizational culture and its highly important implications for effectiveness. The culture of the Companions of the Prophet is discussed as an example that led to a historically unique success. The most unique concept presented in this book is probably the concept of trust in God or *tawakkul*, which is addressed during the discussion on planning. Finally, this book includes a brief, yet enriching, presentation of the leadership of 'Umar ibn al-Khaṭṭāb (may Allah be pleased with him). A new control model was developed based on the practices of 'Umar. The model is suitable for just-in-time philosophy.

This book maintains a small size and is not arranged as the usual management books, i.e., according to the major management processes, although the topics covered in the later will all be addressed. This book is composed of six parts. The first part consists of two chapters. The first chapter, which is the second chapter in the book, introduces the importance of collectiveness and the need for organizing resources and efforts.

The third chapter discusses the concept of organizational culture and it's relation to effectiveness. It also delineates the major characteristics of the culture of the Companions of the Prophet Muhammad (Blessings and Peace be upon him).

The second part of this book pertains to the planning process and is covered from chapter four to chapter thirteen. Chapter four presents a definition of mission, and outlines the mission of Muslims and its relevance to Muslim organizations. Chapter five presents the concept of objective or long term target and its importance. The peculiar relationships between the long-term objective of Islam and the various actions that lead to it are highlighted together with the planning lessons that can be learned from them. Chapter six deals with the concept of goal and its relationship with the concepts of mission and objective. Chapter seven covers the subject of feasibility and presents its components. The eighth chapter addresses the important issue of participative management. Chapter nine deals with some of the most unique concepts of management in Islam, which we included under the general concept of system approach, but in reality extend beyond it. The beautiful coherence between the various goals and actions in the teachings of Islam will be outlined together with some application of conventional systems approach. Chapter ten deals with the concept of gradualism as used in the teachings of Islam and as practiced by Prophet Muhammad (bpuh). Chapter eleven highlights the flexibility of the Islamic teachings. The twelfth chapter outlines the concept of contingency planning at both the micro and macro levels, and its application in the teachings of Islam. Chapter thirteen covers the issue of consistency and continuity in implementing plans within their projected time horizons. This chapter also explains some of the reasons behind the early cancellation of new projects. The last chapter of this part deals with the important concept of *tawakkul* or putting ones trust in Allah, the Exalted. This section includes the reasons behind *tawakkul* and how critical it is in Muslim behaviour.

The third part of this book deals with the process of organizing in addition to a new chapter on Human resource Management. Chapter fifteen addresses the important concepts of authority and responsibility. This chapter includes a fairly elaborate discussion of delegation. Chapter sixteen deals with the concept of accountability. This chapter will also include a presentation of the control process. Finally, chapter seventeen deals with organizational structure while chapter eighteen is on Human Resource Management.

Part four of this book is reserved for the process of leading. This part is comprised of two chapters. Chapter nineteen addresses the issue of leadership and the required qualities of a good leader before shedding some light on leadership development. Chapter twenty includes an elaborate discussion of motivation. This chapter demonstrates the high relevance of the planning process to motivation and shows how to plan for increased motivation. The second section of this chapter deals with reward and punishment. The third section includes some Islamic teachings that serve as spiritual measures of motivation. The last section presents justice as the cornerstone of workers satisfaction.

Part five deals with some aspects of individual and group behaviour. More specifically, it covers competition and conflict. Chapter twenty one gives a general description of two classes of competition. Chapter twenty two covers the topic of conflict management. It will first present functional conflicts, which were encouraged in the teachings of Islam. Then it will present dysfunctional conflicts, their causes, their consequences, and their management.

Part six presents the enriching leadership style of 'Umar ibn al-Khaṭṭāb (may Allah be pleased with him). This part consists of one chapter only. The first section of this chapter is an introduction of 'Umar. First, his background is outlined. Then, we delineate his personality traits. Finally, we highlight some of the achievements of 'Umar. The second section of this chapter concerns the leadership characteristics of 'Umar. First, the participative management programmes established by 'Umar will be delineated. Following the discussion on participative management, we will outline 'Umar's practice of total quality management. Then, we will cover the control process practiced by 'Umar. Based on 'Umar's control process a new control model is developed. This model is suitable for organizations that pursue total quality management and just-in-time philosophy. Finally the administrative innovations of 'Umar will be highlighted.

PART — I

COLLECTIVENESS AND ORGANIZATIONAL CULTURE

COLLECTIVENESS

Islam is a universal religion for all mankind. It is, therefore, not restricted to any nation, race, or gender. Moreover, human beings are social by nature. They need to cooperate with one another in order to be able to survive. Islam stresses cooperation and the sense of collectiveness. As a matter of fact, Islam cannot be practiced by any individual in isolation. Islam is indeed a collective religion. The Qur'an either addresses the Muslims as a group or addresses all mankind. Reading the Qur'an, we find a multitude of expressions like O! you who believe... or O! Mankind...

Islam requires Muslims to be united together and warns against division:

$$﴿وَٱعۡتَصِمُواْ بِحَبۡلِ ٱللَّهِ جَمِيعٗا وَلَا تَفَرَّقُواْۚ ... ١٠٣﴾$$

(سورة آل عمران ٣: ١٠٣)

﴾And hold fast, all together to the rope of Allah, and be not divided among yourselves...﴿ (Qur'an 3: 103)

Muslims have to work in organized groups, for the collective effort of a group of people is always better and more effective than the arithmetic sum of their individual efforts.

"The hand of Allah is with the group." (Tirmidhi)

This hadith further lends support to the importance of collectiveness.

The collective work of a group, should, however, be aimed at achieving a certain goal, otherwise it loses its *raison d'être*.

When Allah, the Almighty, ordered Muslims to form a group or an organization from among them. He specified the purpose of the organization, which was calling for good, enjoining right, and forbidding evil. Allah, the Exalted, said:

﴿وَلْتَكُن مِّنكُمْ أُمَّةٌ يَدْعُونَ إِلَى ٱلْخَيْرِ وَيَأْمُرُونَ بِٱلْمَعْرُوفِ وَيَنْهَوْنَ عَنِ ٱلْمُنكَرِ ...﴾ (١٠٤) (سورة آل عمران ٣: ١٠٤)

﴿Let there arise out of you a band of people inviting to all that is good, enjoining what is right, and forbidding what is evil...﴾ (Qur'an 3: 104)

Stoner and Freeman[1] defined an organization as two or more individuals that work together in a structured way to achieve a specific goal or set of goals. In the 15th century, Al-Qurṭubi[2] stated in his explanation of the Qur'an that the *ummah* or community is an organised group that has a direction. Al-Kilani[3] defined the word *ummah* as a group of people with a mission and he suggested that a nation without a mission couldn't call itself an *ummah*.

Daft[4] defined an organization as a group of people working together to achieve common goals. Stressing the importance of goals, Morehead and Griffin[5] stated:

---

[1] Stoner and Freeman, *"Management,"* 5th ed., Prentice Hall, N. Jersey (1994), P. 4.

[2] *At-Tafsīr*, vol. 2, P. 127.

[3] Al-Kilani M.E., *"Ikhrāj al-Ummah al-Muslimah,"* Dār al-Ummah, Qatar, (1991), P. 117.

[4] Daft, Richard, *"Organization theory and design,"* 2nd ed., (St. Paul Minn.: West 1986), P. 9.

[5] Moorehead, G. and Griffin, R. W., *"Organizational Behavior,"* 3rd ed., Moorehead/Griffin, P. 525,

"The definition of purpose gives the organization reasons to exist; in effect it answers the question "What business are you in.""

With this understanding of the importance of the purpose, we can conclude that collective work, or organized work, is a means of the purpose, and that it is not an end in itself. An organization pools together resources and skills that would otherwise be incapable of producing the desired results. Gibson, Ivancevich, and Donnelly[6] stated:

"Organizations exist for one reason: They can accomplish things that we cannot accomplish individually. Thus, whether the goal is to make a profit, provide an education, foster religion, improve health care, put a man or woman to the moon, get a candidate elected, or build a stadium, organizations get the job done. Organizations are characterized by their goal-directed behaviour. They pursue goals and objectives that can be achieved more efficiently."

While organizations are created to achieve a goal or a set of goals, and while they are made of a group of people, they in turn affect the behaviour of the people and their future goals. This is because organizations create a setting in which we spend most of our lives.[7]

Organizations have provided great services to humanity. Most of the services and products that are available to us are outcomes of organizations. Education, transportation, food, clothing, appliances, housing, and entertainment are all outcomes

---

[6] Gibson, Ivancevich and Donnelly, Organizations, Business Publications Inc., (1985) p. 7,

[7] Urwich, *"That Word Organization,"* Academy of Management Review, Jan. (1976) Pp. 89-91.

of organizations. Without organizations, humanity would not be able to afford the comforts that it is enjoying now. Generally, the more people get organized, the more productive a country becomes. It is partnership financing, for example that gave Germany its economic lead. Nevertheless, there are many organizations that have caused a lot of harm to humanity. Such organizations include fascist and racist organizations, drug traffickers, and other criminal organizations. Islam forbids individual or collective cooperation for a wrong goal. Islam commands us to cooperate together only on beneficial endeavours. Allah, the Exalted, said:

$$ \text{﴿... وَتَعَاوَنُوا عَلَى ٱلْبِرِّ وَٱلتَّقْوَىٰ وَلَا تَعَاوَنُوا عَلَى ٱلْإِثْمِ وَٱلْعُدْوَٰنِ وَٱتَّقُوا ٱللَّهَ} $$
$$ \text{إِنَّ ٱللَّهَ شَدِيدُ ٱلْعِقَابِ ۝﴾ (سورة المائدة ٥ : ٢)} $$

◆...Help one another unto righteousness and pious duty. Help not one another unto sin and transgression, but keep your duty to Allah. Lo! Allah is severe in punishment.◆ (Qur'an 5: 2)

Organizations should have plans or some specific courses of actions to achieve their objectives and goals. Further, pursuing plans require the organizations to have certain internal processes and certain authority relationships. The pillars of any collective effort are authority, responsibility, and accountability. However, the real foundation of any organization is its culture. The topic of organizational culture will be addressed in the next chapter.

QUESTIONS

1. Islam is a collective religion. Discuss.

2. When Allah ordered the Muslims to form a group or organization, He specified the purpose of the organization. Explain that purpose.

3. State the pillars of any collective effort.

ORGANIZATIONAL CULTURE

In this chapter, we will define organizational culture, outline its importance for effectiveness, and delineate the critical role of leaders in making the organizational culture. Then, we will present the culture of the Companions of the Prophet as an exemplary culture that induced a historically unique success.

1 - Culture

Kilman[8] stated that the likelihood that an organization will achieve success in a dynamic setting is not determined just by the strategy-structure and the reward system that make up its visible features. Rather, every organization has an invincible quality, a certain style, a character, a way of doing things that ultimately determines whether success will be achieved. Ironically, what cannot be seen or touched can be more powerful than the dictates of any one person or any formally documented system. To understand the soul of an organization, therefore, requires a discussion of corporate culture.

Organizations are composed of different people who are unique in many respects. This uniqueness is usually reflected in the organizations themselves.[9] Organizations are said to have

---

[8] Kilman, R. H., *"Managing beyond the Quick Fix,"* Jossey-Bass Inc., (1989) Pp. 49-50.

[9] Baron, R. A. Greenberg, J. *"Behaviour in Organizations,"* Allyn and Bacon, Boston (1989) p. 297.

unique cultures. Culture is a system of shared values and beliefs that produce norms of behaviour.[10] Although there has been abundance of literature on organizational climate and culture since the second quarter of this century, this topic has gained wider audience after the great success of Japanese companies. In the 1980s, many books on organizational studies and management such as *The Art of Japanese Management* (Pascal and Athos 1981)[11], *Corporate Cultures* (Deal and Kennedy)[12] and especially, *In Search of Excellence* (Peters and Waterman 1982)[13] have become best sellers. Commenting on the success of such books throughout the 1980s, Denison[14] stated:

"These books present a different picture of management than that usually offered by strategists, financiers, and marketers who have traditionally run American corporations. Rather than assume, as many have, that the large corporations are simply black boxes that respond to external markets and regulatory forces and can be run closely on financial criteria, these authors have concentrated on what might be called the behaviour side of management and organization. They argued that the difference between a

---

[10] Linda Smircich, *"Concepts of Organizational Analysis,"* Administrative Science Quarterly, Sept. (1983) p. 342.

[11] Pascal, R. T. and athos, A.G., *"The Art of Japanese Management: Applications for American Executives,"* New York: Simon and Schuster, (1981).

[12] Deal, T. A. and Kennedy, A. A. *"Corporate Culture,"* Reading, M. A.: Adison-Wesley, (1982).

[13] Peters, T.J., and Waterman, R. h, *"In Search of Excellence,"* Harper and Row, New York, (1982).

[14] Denison, D., R. *"Corporate Culture and Organizational Effectiveness,"* John Wiley and Sons, New York, (1990), p. 1.

successful and not-so-successful organization rests with the values and principles that underlie their organization."

2 - Effectiveness

There is no consensus about the measures of effectiveness. However, it is generally understood that the effectiveness of an organization encompasses efficiency, satisfaction, participation, and adaptiveness. Cultural theory of organizational effectiveness takes as its foundation the notion that the values, beliefs, and meanings that underlie a social system are the primary source of motivated and coordinated activity. In fact, culture is a very critical determinant of organizational effectiveness.

Barney[15] argues that firms with positive cultures sustain a competitive advantage to the extent that their cultures are not easily imitated by other industries. Nevertheless, culture can only be a positive factor if it is matched with the strategy of the organization. Managers have to either fit the strategy to the culture or fit the culture to the strategy. In most cases, it is easier to form a strategy that fits the culture than to form a culture that fits a strategy. The organizational culture usually reflects the values, beliefs, and norms shared by the greater society. However, because different organizations are composed of different people, they usually have different cultures. Furthermore, while culture can be considered a major source of motivated and coordinated activities, the latter do affect the culture as well. As a matter of

---

[15] Jay B. Barney, "*Organizational Culture, Can it be a source of competitive advantage,*" Academy of Management Review, July (1986), Pp. 656-665,.

fact, we can find a lot of commonality between the attitudes of individuals working in the same field. Sales personnel share a similar attitude, which is different from that of production personnel, or that of quality control personnel. Similarly, organizational cultures are usually influenced by the adopted strategy.

More importantly, the leadership of an organization influences organizational cultures. Leaders should realize that they are considered as role models and that their behaviour is reflected on the culture of their organization. Kets and Miller[16] stated that some researches suggest that organizational cultures are extensions and reflections of personalities of chief executives. They also added that suspicious executives would create paranoid cultures. Similarly, leaders with positive attitude will help foster a positive culture. The real problem is that most leaders do not perceive themselves as makers of culture or as agents of cultural change. Denison stated that, though most managers do not see themselves as culture makers, this role is unavoidable because leadership and managerial actions inevitably create or reinforce key values. He further concluded that the most important step in becoming an effective culture manager is to consider building a culture as an explicit role with a set of objectives rather than simply a by-product of business.[17]

The most important role in building a culture is usually the role of the founders. Founders are the ones who usually possess a comprehensive vision of the future of the organization, its

---

[16] Kets F. R. and Miller, D. *"Personality, Culture and Organization"* Academy of Management Review, April (1986) Pp. 266-279.

[17] Denison D., R. *"Corporate Culture and Organizational Effectiveness,"* John Wiley and Sons, New York (1990) p. 196.

dominant culture, its mission, its objectives, and its strategy. Moreover, founders usually do the preliminary hiring in the organization. This hiring is usually conditioned by the prospective culture that the founders would like to instill. Further, because the founders are the first members of an organization, they usually transmit their values and attitudes to new recruits who usually have to conform to the existing culture. Once established, the culture created by the founders will be hard to change.

The success of early Muslims is largely due to their culture. The pre-Islamic culture included elements that were compatible with Islam and others which were totally contradictory to it. Islam abrogated the negative components of the pre-existing cultural values and replaced them with new ones. The cultural change that accompanied the inception of Islam had resulted in a complete, coherent, and pure set of values. As discussed above, the leaders have a major role in creating a culture, and the presence of the Prophet (Blessings and Peace be upon him) had certainly played a pivotal role in forming the culture of his Companions. Stressing the importance of the change and purification of the values and the manners, Prophet Muhammad (Blessings and Peace be upon him) said:

> "I have only been sent to complete (and) complement the pure and good manners." (Bukhāri)

The pre-Islamic Arabs had some values like generosity and courage that were compatible to those propounded by Islam. Likewise, there were some values and practices that were against the very foundations of Islam such as idol worshipping and low image of men among others. Hence the necessity for the purification, completion and complementary of there cultural values and practices as expounded in the above hadith.

3 - The Culture of the Companions of the Prophet

The culture of the Companions of the Prophet was the strongest reason behind their success. These Companions possessed many positive values even before embracing Islam. The pre-Islamic positive values included courage, generosity, and directness. Islam maintained these values and reinforced them considerably. Besides, Islam integrated these values into a larger value and belief system, which has a precise structure and direction.

1) Tawḥīd

The culture of the Companions of the Prophet can be considered as a culture of belief in one God. In fact, this component of unity of God is the essence of the culture. The Companions of the Prophet believed in one God Who has no partner, therefore, all the lords that were worshipped before Islam had to be rejected. The Companions believed that Allah is The Creator of the universe, The Sustainer of all beings, The Exalted in Might, The All Powerful, The Most Merciful, The Most Gracious, The Exalted in Wisdom and Knowledge, The Eternal, The One Who Begets not and Who is not begotten. Allah, the All-High, States:

﴿قُلْ هُوَ ٱللَّهُ أَحَدٌ ۝ ٱللَّهُ ٱلصَّمَدُ ۝ لَمْ يَلِدْ وَلَمْ يُولَدْ ۝ وَلَمْ يَكُن لَّهُۥ كُفُوًا أَحَدٌ ۝﴾ (سورة الإخلاص ١١٢: ١-٤)

❖Say: He is Allah, the One and Only, Allah the Eternal, Absolute, He begets not, Nor is He begotten. And there is none like unto Him.❖ (Qur'an 112: 1-4)

﴿أَللَّهُ لَا إِلَـٰهَ إِلَّا هُوَ ٱلْحَىُّ ٱلْقَيُّومُ لَا تَأْخُذُهُۥ سِنَةٌ وَلَا نَوْمٌ لَّهُۥ مَا فِى ٱلسَّمَـٰوَٰتِ وَمَا فِى ٱلْأَرْضِ مَن ذَا ٱلَّذِى يَشْفَعُ عِندَهُۥٓ إِلَّا بِإِذْنِهِۦ يَعْلَمُ مَا بَيْنَ أَيْدِيهِمْ وَمَا خَلْفَهُمْ وَلَا يُحِيطُونَ بِشَىْءٍ مِّنْ عِلْمِهِۦٓ إِلَّا بِمَا شَآءَ وَسِعَ كُرْسِيُّهُ ٱلسَّمَـٰوَٰتِ وَٱلْأَرْضَ وَلَا يَـُٔودُهُۥ حِفْظُهُمَا وَهُوَ ٱلْعَلِىُّ ٱلْعَظِيمُ ﴿٢٥٥﴾﴾

(سورة البقرة ٢: ٢٥٥)

﴾Allah! There is no god but He, the Ever-Living, the Self-Subsisting by whom all subsist, Eternal, No slumber can seize Him, nor sleep. His are all things in the heavens and on earth. Who is there that can intercede in His presence except as He permits? He knows what is before [His creatures] and what is behind them. Nor shall they compass aught of His knowledge except as He wills. His throne does extend over the heavens and the earth, and He feels no fatigue in Guarding and preserving them. For He is the Most High, The Supreme [in Glory].﴿ (Qur'an 2: 255)

All the above-mentioned verses speak of Allah's attributes. These attributes have profound impact on the lives of the believers. It is from these attributes and the Companions' firm belief in them that their unique culture and its elements evolved.

This belief in one God Who is the Most Powerful and Who is the Sustainer of this Universe, freed the Companions of the Prophet of any fear from anything other than their Lord. It gave them a sense of confidence that made them more generous and more courageous.

2) Unity of purpose

Worshipping Allah means all actions we undertake should be for the sake of Allah. Whatever we do with the intention of pleasing Allah is considered *'Ibādah* (worship). Focusing our life on one single purpose (*tawhīd*) makes us very efficient. All our actions and intentions become so coherent. Having more than one supreme goal will tear our capabilities apart and ultimately impede our success. We cannot be praying and fasting for Allah while doing business for our greed. Praying for Allah would diminish our greed and boosting our greed will reduce our worship. *Tawhīd* means full commitment to Allah and none but Allah. Muslims should make sure not let their intentions and efforts be divided between this life and the Hereafter. It is true that Muslims can and should enjoy the bounties of Allah, but this enjoyment should be for the sake of Allah in order to secure the Allah's reward, and to ensure unity of purpose.

﴿مَّا جَعَلَ ٱللَّهُ لِرَجُلٍ مِّن قَلْبَيْنِ فِي جَوْفِهِۦ ...﴿۞﴾﴾

(سورة الأحزاب ٣٣ : ٤)

﴿Allah has not made for any man two hearts in his body...﴾
(Qur'an 33: 4)

3) Belief in the Hereafter and reward and punishment

The culture of the Companions of the Prophet is also characterized by the belief in the Hereafter during which they will face reward in Paradise or punishment in Hell. This firm belief in the Hereafter and in reward and punishment created an attitude of self-control among the Companions. Indeed, they were feeling accountable for every tiny action they took. The Hereafter comprised the long-term objective of the Companions who strived hard to enter Paradise and to avoid Hell. This means that the belief in the Hereafter represented a great measure for motivating the Companions of the Prophet to do righteous deeds and to avoid any wrong doings.

The belief in the Oneness of God and the Hereafter entails the belief in the unity of the creation and destiny of mankind. In fact, the pillars of the Islamic faith include the belief in other revelations and Prophets such as Abraham, Moses, and Jesus (May Allah's Peace be upon them all). This is evident in the following verse of the Qur'an:

﴿قُولُوٓاْ ءَامَنَّا بِٱللَّهِ وَمَآ أُنزِلَ إِلَيْنَا وَمَآ أُنزِلَ إِلَىٰٓ إِبْرَٰهِـۧمَ وَإِسْمَٰعِيلَ وَإِسْحَٰقَ وَيَعْقُوبَ وَٱلْأَسْبَاطِ وَمَآ أُوتِيَ مُوسَىٰ وَعِيسَىٰ وَمَآ أُوتِيَ ٱلنَّبِيُّونَ مِن رَّبِّهِمْ لَا نُفَرِّقُ بَيْنَ أَحَدٍ مِّنْهُمْ وَنَحْنُ لَهُۥ مُسْلِمُونَ ﴾ (سورة البقرة ٢ : ١٣٦)

﴾Say You: We believe in Allah, and the revelations given to us and to Abraham, Ismael, Isac, Jacob, and the tribes, and that given to Moses and Jesus, and that given to [all] prophets from their Lord. We make no difference between one and another of them and We [bow and] submit to Allah.﴿ (Qur'an 2: 136)

4) Independence

A natural outcome of the culture of *Tawhīd* is, independence. When we believe sincerely in Allah, the Exalted, we become free from our desires and the dictates of others. We become independent from tyranny by virtue of depending on Allah. Caesar of Rome asked Rabie' ibn 'Āmer, a Bedouin Arab; what did you come for? He replied; We came to free the people from the worship of the people to the worship of the Lord of the people and from the tyranny of religions to the justice of Islam and from the narrowness of *Dunia* (world) to the wideness of *Dunia* and *Ākhirah* (Hereafter). Independent people are more likely to take initiatives to solve problems while dependent people would watch the situation worsens until someone asks them to something. Independent people are likely to say no when their managers take unethical decisions. Independent does, therefore, prevent defects and improve decision making. The Companions' depended on Allah Alone who is the Provider and Sustainer for all things. From this independence, results honesty and bravery. They were not afraid of anyone save Allah. Allah, the All-Powerful, says:

$$﴿وَمَا مِن دَآبَّةٍ فِي ٱلْأَرْضِ إِلَّا عَلَى ٱللَّهِ رِزْقُهَا...﴾ ⑥ (سورة هود)$$

$$(٦ : ١١)$$

﴾There is no moving creature on earth but its sustenance depends on [and is provided by] Allah...﴿ (Qur'an 11: 6)

$$﴿إِنَّ لَكَ أَلَّا تَجُوعَ فِيهَا وَلَا تَعْرَىٰ ⑱﴾ (سورة طه ٢٠ : ١١٨)$$

﴾There is therein [enough provision] For you not to go hungry, nor to go naked.﴿ (Qur'an 20: 118)

$$﴿وَفِي ٱلسَّمَآءِ رِزْقُكُمْ وَمَا تُوعَدُونَ ㉒﴾ (سورة الذاريات ٥١ : ٢٢)$$

﴾And in the heaven is your sustenance as [also] that which you are promised.﴿ (Qur'an 51: 22)

﴿إِنَّ ٱللَّهَ هُوَ ٱلرَّزَّاقُ ذُو ٱلْقُوَّةِ ٱلْمَتِينُ ۝﴾ (سورة الذاريات ٥١ : ٥٨)

﴾For Allah is He Who gives [all] sustenance — Lord of Power-Steadfast [for ever].﴿ (Qur'an 51: 58)

﴿إِنَّ رَبَّكَ يَبْسُطُ ٱلرِّزْقَ لِمَن يَشَاءُ وَيَقْدِرُ إِنَّهُ كَانَ بِعِبَادِهِ خَبِيرًا بَصِيرًا ۝﴾ (سورة الإسراء ١٧ : ٣٠)

﴾Verily your Lord does provide sustenance in abundance for whom He pleases, and He provides in a just measure, for He does know and regard all His servants.﴿ (Qur'an 17: 30)

﴿... وَمَن يَتَّقِ ٱللَّهَ يَجْعَل لَّهُ مَخْرَجًا ۝ وَيَرْزُقْهُ مِنْ حَيْثُ لَا يَحْتَسِبُ ۝...﴾ (سورة الطلاق ٦٥ : ٢-٣)

﴾...And for those who fear Allah. He [ever] prepares a way out, and He provides for him from [sources] he never could imagine...﴿ (Qur'an 65: 2-3)

Anyone who believes in the above verses as did the *Ṣaḥāba* (Companions) would be free from relying on any human being for anything from sustenance to clothing and any other basic and non basic need. Rather he will be independent and thus look up to no one for help but Allah, the Exalted. Such a person is likely to be courageous and capable of taking ethical decisions and correcting the wrong.

5) Responsibility and accountability

Responsibility and accountability are attributes that are very important in determining self-control and honesty. These two important attributes stem from the belief in the Hereafter and in reward and punishment. The Prophet (Blessings and Peace be upon him) said:

> "Behold! Each one of you is a guardian, and each one of you will be asked about his subjects. A leader is a guardian over the people and he will be asked about his subjects; a man is a guardian over the members of his household and he will be asked about his subjects; a woman is a guardian over the members of the household of the husband and of his children... Behold! Each one of you is a guardian and each one of you will be asked about his subjects." (Bukhāri)

From the above, it can be seen that Muslims cannot pass on blames to others. They should take responsibility and be accountable for it. Change should come from within first and thus the Muslims should always strive to change themselves and their environment for the better. They should not wait for others such as their leaders or supervisors to make the change. Leaders should also not blame their followers for their failures. They should always blame themselves, review their intentions and strive for the better.

The success of early Muslims stemmed primarily from their sense of responsibility and accountability. They used to feel guilty for any delay, discomfort, or defect related to anything they were responsible for.

6) Participation

The culture of the Companions of the Prophet was a culture of participation through consultation, advice, and forbidding evil and enjoining good. Consultation is mandatory in Islam, and more importantly, it displayed a way of life. The climate of participation that reigned during the time of the Companions was very fertile for innovation, satisfaction, participation, efficiency, and adaptiveness.

Participation take the form of *Shūra* in order to make better decisions, correcting the wrong in order to reduce defects, and advice in order to improve performance.

Shūra is an exercise aimed at reaching a consensus. If consensus is not reached then people have to stick to the majority. Prophet Muhammad (Blessings and Peace be upon him) also said:

"My nation cannot agree upon an error and if a conflict persists be with the majority." (Ibn Mājah)

Commenting on the weakness of a single opinion and the strength of multiple opinions, 'Umar (may Allah be pleased with him) made the analogy between a single opinion and a single string of thread, and multiple opinions and a strong rope.

Advice was also part of Muslims' everyday life. Prophet Muhammad (Blessings and Peace be upon him) summarized the whole religion as advice. He is reported to have said:

"Religion is sincere advice." (Muslim)

Advice in Islam entails enjoining what is good and forbidding what is bad and righting what is wrong. These two concepts are very much stressed in the teachings of Islam.

﴿وَلْتَكُن مِّنكُمْ أُمَّةٌ يَدْعُونَ إِلَى ٱلْخَيْرِ وَيَأْمُرُونَ بِٱلْمَعْرُوفِ وَيَنْهَوْنَ عَنِ ٱلْمُنكَرِ... ﴾ (سورة آل عمران ٣: ١٠٤)

﴿Let there arise out of you a band of people inviting to all that is good, enjoining what is right, and forbidding what is wrong [evil]...⟩ (Qur'an 3: 104)

Righting the wrong is a duty on every Muslim. Prophet Muhammad (Blessings and Peace be upon him) said:

"Whosoever see wrong, should correct it." (Muslim)

The duty of correcting the wrong is even more emphasized when the perpetrator possesses a great deal of power and authority. On the other hand, leaders are supposed to be anxious for being corrected. Abu Bakr (may Allah be pleased with him), the first successor of the Prophet (bpuh), said:

"I have been given authority over you and I am not the best among you, if I do well help me and if I do wrong put me right."

Muslims, men and women, have frequently corrected their rulers. This process of righting the rulers dissipated after the first generation of Muslims as the culture was influenced by integration with other cultures notably those of the Arab Bedouins, the Romans, and the Persians.

Participation and righting the wrong did not mean that the Companions were not disciplined. In fact, the society of the Companions was analogous to that of soldiers. They were very obedient to their leader, Prophet Muhammad (bpuh). They used to argue with him so much on non-revelation matters, but once they arrived at a decision, they were all very keen on executing the commands. Disagreeing with the decision had nothing to do with its implementation.

7) Justice

Justice is a competitive advantage that affects the balance and income statement. When we are not fair in our recruitment, we send better job candidates to our competitors. We are not fair towards our employees, we fail to retain them. When we offer projects to the wrong contractors we lose in time, quality, and cost, while we sending the better contractors to work for our competitors.

The cornerstone of the culture of the Companions was justice, one of the major goals of Islam, as we will see later.

﴿إِنَّ اللَّهَ يَأْمُرُ بِالْعَدْلِ وَالْإِحْسَٰنِ وَإِيتَآيِ ذِى الْقُرْبَىٰ وَيَنْهَىٰ عَنِ الْفَحْشَآءِ وَالْمُنكَرِ وَالْبَغْيِ يَعِظُكُمْ لَعَلَّكُمْ تَذَكَّرُونَ ۝﴾ (ســورة النحل ١٦ : ٩٠)

﴿Allah commands justice, benevolence, and liberality to kith and kin, and He forbids all shameful deeds, and injustice and transgression: He instructs you, that you may receive admonition.﴾ (Qur'an 16: 90)

Justice is a very natural outcome of the behaviour of caring, loving, mercy and sharing, for the one who loves would not be unjust. When people have a sense of direction and when they have their needs satisfied, there will be no excuse for injustices. To take care of those who still transgress the concept of justice was reinforced by a total adherence to the rule of law, which did not distinguish between people according to their status. Prophet Muhammad (Blessings and Peace be upon him) said:

> "If Faṭima, the daughter of Muhammad, stole I would certainly cut her hand." (Aḥmad)

"All people are equal as the teeth of the comb." (Aṭ-Ṭabarāni)

"The only basis for preference between an Arab and a non-Arab, a white and a black, and a male and a female is piety." (Ibn Isḥāq)

Below is an example of an incidence that shows that there is no distinction among people in the Islamic rule of law.

One time, ʿAli (may Allah be pleased with him), the fourth successor of the Prophet (bpuh), found his shield with a Christian man. Both ʿAli, who was then the leader of the Muslims, and the Christian man, went to Judge Shurayḥ. ʿAli said, "This is my shield, I did not give it and I did not sell it." Shurayḥ asked the defendant: "What do you say about the statement of the leader of the believers (head of the nation)." The latter replied, "The shield is just mine and I do not consider the leader of the believers to be a liar." Judge Shurayḥ turned to ʿAli asking him: "O leader of the believers, do you have any proof?" ʿAli smiled and said: "Shurayḥ is correct, I have no proof." The judge dismissed the case. The Christian man took the shield walked out a few steps, then came back and said, "I believe that this is a judgment of prophets. The leader of the believers sues me to his judge who dismisses the case! I bear witness that there is no god but Allah and that Muhammad is His servant and messenger. The shield is yours O' leader of the believers, I took it when I followed your army in Ṣiffīn. ʿAli said: "Now that you became a Muslim, it is yours."[18]

---

[18] Sayyid Quṭb, *"Universal Peace and Islam"*, Dār ash-Shuruq, Egypt (1983) p. 129.

Justice is more difficult when we deal with people we like or dislike

$$﴿يَٰٓأَيُّهَا ٱلَّذِينَ ءَامَنُوا۟ كُونُوا۟ قَوَّٰمِينَ لِلَّهِ شُهَدَآءَ بِٱلْقِسْطِ وَلَا يَجْرِمَنَّكُمْ شَنَـَٔانُ قَوْمٍ عَلَىٰٓ أَلَّا تَعْدِلُوا۟ ٱعْدِلُوا۟ هُوَ أَقْرَبُ لِلتَّقْوَىٰ وَٱتَّقُوا۟ ٱللَّهَ...﴾ ⑧$$

(سورة المائدة ٥ : ٨)

﴿O you who believe! Stand out firmly for Allah, as witnesses to *fair* dealing, and let not the hatred of others to you make you swerve to wrong and depart from justice. Be just, that is next to piety...﴾ (Qur'an 5: 8)

8) Dignity, respect and privacy

Islam emphasizes the dignity of mankind irrespective of their race, gender or religion.

$$﴿وَلَقَدْ كَرَّمْنَا بَنِىٓ ءَادَمَ وَحَمَلْنَٰهُمْ فِى ٱلْبَرِّ وَٱلْبَحْرِ وَرَزَقْنَٰهُم مِّنَ ٱلطَّيِّبَٰتِ وَفَضَّلْنَٰهُمْ عَلَىٰ كَثِيرٍ مِّمَّنْ خَلَقْنَا تَفْضِيلًا ⑦٠﴾$$

(سورة الاسراء ١٧ : ٧٠)

﴿We have honoured the children of Ādam, provided them with transport on the land and the sea, given them for sustenance things good and pure and conferred on them special favours above a great part of Our Creation.﴾ (Qur'an 17: 70)

The above verse did not restrict dignity and honour to any group of people. The only qualification required for dignity is to be a human being. Recognizing the dignity of people means respecting them. This respect includes customers, employees, investors and all stakeholders. Respecting stakeholders translates into fulfilling our promises to them, listening to their concerns, and trying to satisfy them. Respecting people mean also respecting their privacy. Indeed, Islam places important emphasis on the privacy of man. This is evident in the Prophet's teaching that if one visits another, he must knock thrice at his host door and if he did not receive any leave to enter, he must leave. With regards to dignity, it is one of the basic elements of life that must be safeguarded.

The right of privacy was also emphasized in the teachings of the Qur'an through the prohibition of spying. Allah, the Exalted, said:

﴿يَٰٓأَيُّهَا ٱلَّذِينَ ءَامَنُوا۟ ٱجْتَنِبُوا۟ كَثِيرًا مِّنَ ٱلظَّنِّ إِنَّ بَعْضَ ٱلظَّنِّ إِثْمٌ وَلَا تَجَسَّسُوا۟

... ﴾ (سورة الحجرات ٤٩ : ١٢)

⟨O you who believe avoid suspicion as much [as possible] for suspicion is in some cases a sin and spy not on each other...⟩ (Qur'an 49: 12)

9) Trust

The discussion on privacy to the issue of trust is essential for any business transaction. Indeed if there is no trust at all no business transaction can ever take place no matter how much efforts we can put in closing loopholes. On the other hand increased trust leads to saving transaction time and cost that could be otherwise spent in negotiating and legal fees.

The above verse (*āyah*) implies a relation between being suspicious and spying. Indeed spying is an outcome of suspicion. People who don't trust one another might resort to spying and counter-spying something-which leads to the waste of time, efforts and mental focus. Trust prevailed in the relationships between the Companions. Mutual trust existed between the leaders and their followers, and among the followers. The openness and directness of the Companions supported this trust. Prophet Muhammad (Blessings and Peace be upon him) also said:

"A leader who is suspicious of his people will lead them to mischief." (Abu Dawūd)

10) Dialogue

The culture of the Companions of the Prophet can also be described as a culture of dialogue. There was no time during the life of the Prophet (bpuh) when dialogue has ever seized between Muslims and their enemies, the pagans of Quraysh, nor was there any time at which the dialogue seized between the Muslims and the Jewish tribes of Madīnah. The value of dialogue was shared by all members of the society of the Companions irrespective of their age, gender, race, or ethnic origin. The Qur'an contained so many verses (*āyāt*) dealing with matters related to people of different religions. Allah, the All-High, All-Glorious, said:

﴿قُلْ يَٰأَهْلَ ٱلْكِتَٰبِ تَعَالَوْا۟ إِلَىٰ كَلِمَةٍ سَوَآءٍ بَيْنَنَا وَبَيْنَكُمْ أَلَّا نَعْبُدَ إِلَّا ٱللَّهَ وَلَا نُشْرِكَ بِهِۦ شَيْـًٔا وَلَا يَتَّخِذَ بَعْضُنَا بَعْضًا أَرْبَابًا مِّن دُونِ ٱللَّهِ فَإِن تَوَلَّوْا۟ فَقُولُوا۟ ٱشْهَدُوا۟ بِأَنَّا مُسْلِمُونَ ۝﴾ (سورة آل عمران ٣: ٦٤)

❮Say: O People of the Book! Come to common terms as between us and you: That we worship none but Allah: That we associate no partners with Him; that we erect not from among ourselves, lords and patrons other than Allah. If then they turn back, say you: Bear witness that we are Muslims [submitting to the will of God]. (Qur'an 3: 64)

$$\text{﴿قُلْ يَا أَيُّهَا ٱلْكَافِرُونَ ۞ لَا أَعْبُدُ مَا تَعْبُدُونَ ۞ وَلَا أَنتُمْ عَابِدُونَ مَا أَعْبُدُ ۞ وَلَا أَنَا عَابِدٌ مَّا عَبَدتُّمْ ۞ وَلَا أَنتُمْ عَابِدُونَ مَا أَعْبُدُ ۞ لَكُمْ دِينُكُمْ وَلِيَ دِينِ ۞﴾}$$

(سورة الكافرون ١٠٩ : ١-٦)

﴿O you who reject Faith! I worship not what you worship. Nor will You worship that which I worship. And I will not worship that which you have been wont to worship. Nor will you worship that which I worship. To you be your way [religion] and to me mine﴾ (Qur'an 109: 1-6)

The above verses are examples of some of the dialogue between the believers and non-believers. Implicit in them is, the importance of politeness and the freedom of choice that Allah has bestowed upon man.

In some other verses Allah addressed all mankind. For instance in the following verse Allah, the Exalted, commanded all mankind to get to know one another:

$$\text{﴿يَا أَيُّهَا ٱلنَّاسُ إِنَّا خَلَقْنَاكُم مِّن ذَكَرٍ وَأُنثَىٰ وَجَعَلْنَاكُمْ شُعُوبًا وَقَبَائِلَ لِتَعَارَفُوا إِنَّ أَكْرَمَكُمْ عِندَ ٱللَّهِ أَتْقَاكُمْ إِنَّ ٱللَّهَ عَلِيمٌ خَبِيرٌ ۞﴾}$$

(سورة الحجرات ٤٩ : ١٣)

﴿O mankind! We created you from a single [pair] of male and female, and made you into nations and tribes, that you may know one another [not that you may despise one another]. Verily the most honoured of you in the sight of Allah is [he who is] the most righteous of you and Allah has full knowledge and is well acquainted [with all things].﴾ (Qur'an 49: 13)

Moreover, there are ample verses in the Qur'an relating the various discussions between many Prophets such as Noah, Abraham, Moses, and Jesus (May Allah's Peace be upon them all) and their respective disbelievers'.

The norm of dialogue existed among the pagan Arabs even before Islam, as they were known for their openness and directness. Islam came and further reinforced this norm with the foe let alone the friend. Currently, the concept of dialogue has been mixed with capitulation and surrender. Dialogue was never considered as surrender in the Islamic heritage, rather it was considered as a way of life. Surrender is undesirable whether it occurs through dialogue or not, but surrender should not be attributed to dialogue.

11) Cost efficiency

It is just impossible to invest or to pay zakāh without saving money. It is also impossible to save money which have some cost efficiency. The Companions were taught by their leader, the Prophet (Blessings and Peace be upon him) to be cost efficient. The Prophet's teaching to his Companions is that they should use the minimum amount of water necessary even if they are taking their ablution in the river show this.

Luxury was not part of life of the Companions of the Prophet. Many of them could not afford it, and those who could, were not interested in indulgence. Islam encourages moderate spending for ones comfort. Extravagance is strongly condemned in Islam. Allah, the Exalted, says:

﴿ إِنَّ ٱلْمُبَذِّرِينَ كَانُوٓا إِخْوَٰنَ ٱلشَّيَٰطِينِ ۖ وَكَانَ ٱلشَّيْطَٰنُ لِرَبِّهِۦ كَفُورًا ﴾ ۝

(سورة الإسراء ١٧ : ٢٧)

﴿Verily spendthrifts are brothers of Satan and Satan is to his Lord ungrateful.﴾ (Qur'an 17: 27)

Finally, because the Companions lived in the desert, they were not used to the comfort of urban Rome, or Persia. The difficulties they experienced in their daily lives made them capable of enduring hardship. It also fostered in them strength, patience, and perseverance. These qualities contributed in making the Companions great soldiers.

12) Time efficiency

While time means money in the West, it means 'Life' in Islam. Whatever time we lose is lost from our limited life for which we are accountable. The Prophet (bpuh) said:

"Man will be asked about his life, how he spent it, his youth, how he used it and his money, how he earned it and how he spent it." (Tirmidhi)

The Prophet (bpuh) also said:

"Take advantage of five before five: Your youth before your aging, your health before your sickness, your wealth before your poverty, your free time before your busy time, and your life before your death." (Tirmidhi)

The *Ṣaḥāba* (Companions) hardly had free time during their lives. Their life was a continuous jihād (struggle). Their descendants, the *Tabey'īn* - the Followers - were also very busy but not like their fathers. The *tabey ʿīn* were known for scheduling their time effectively between three main activities, seeking knowledge, formally worshipping Allah and working.

13) Caring and sharing

Caring is necessary for the success of any organization. Be it a family or an MNC. Letting a teammate down is letting the whole team down. We shall care about our clients, subordinates and colleagues. Caring leads to helping and sharing. When we help our colleagues when they are going through some difficulties, we are actually helping or organization by getting the job well done and by promoting a culture of mutual support.

The culture of the Companions was also a culture of caring and sharing. It was a culture of mercy towards fellow human beings as well as with the animals and nature. Islam established a real sense of collectiveness and community among the Companions of the Prophet who felt like one body that feels the pain whenever one of its members suffers. Prophet Muhammad (Blessings and Peace be upon him) said:

> "The believers are like one man, if his head is in pain his whole body suffers and if his eye is in pain his whole body suffers." (Bukhāri)

The Prophet (bpuh) further said:

> "None among you will believe until he loves for his brother what he loves for himself." (Bukhāri)

> "He did not believe. He did not believe, the Prophet said, He did not believe, he who slept with a full stomach knowing that his neighbour is hungry." (Al-Ḥākim)

The above hadiths show the emphasis that the Prophet (bpuh) placed on unity and brotherhood among the believers. The sense of brotherhood was not just a simple teaching of Islam; rather it was a living reality. When Muslims migrated from Makkah and left all their belongings behind them, their hosts in Madīnah shared all their wealth with them. This happened after the Prophet (bpuh) established brotherhood between each migrant and each citizen of Madīnah. In fact, the caring and empathy of Muslims went beyond sharing to sacrificing. Muslims were giving up what they urgently needed for themselves. Describing the Companions, Allah, the Exalted, said:

﴿وَالَّذِينَ تَبَوَّءُو ٱلدَّارَ وَٱلْإِيمَٰنَ مِن قَبْلِهِمْ يُحِبُّونَ مَنْ هَاجَرَ إِلَيْهِمْ وَلَا يَجِدُونَ فِى صُدُورِهِمْ حَاجَةً مِّمَّآ أُوتُواْ وَيُؤْثِرُونَ عَلَىٰٓ أَنفُسِهِمْ وَلَوْ كَانَ بِهِمْ خَصَاصَةٌ وَمَن يُوقَ شُحَّ نَفْسِهِۦ فَأُوْلَٰٓئِكَ هُمُ ٱلْمُفْلِحُونَ ۝﴾

(سورة الحشر ٥٩ : ٩)

﴿But those who before them, had homes and had adopted the faith show their affection to those as came to them for refuge, and entertain no desire in their hearts for things given to the latter, but give them preference over themselves, even though poverty was their [own lot]. And those saved from the covetousness of their own souls - they are the ones that achieve prosperity.﴾ (Qur'an 59: 9)

The caring and sharing attitude was motivated by the belief in Allah and the attachment to His reward and the fear of His punishment. Allah, the All-Powerful, said:

﴿وَيُطْعِمُونَ ٱلطَّعَامَ عَلَىٰ حُبِّهِۦ مِسْكِينًا وَيَتِيمًا وَأَسِيرًا ۝ إِنَّمَا نُطْعِمُكُمْ لِوَجْهِ ٱللَّهِ لَا نُرِيدُ مِنكُمْ جَزَآءً وَلَا شُكُورًا ۝ إِنَّا نَخَافُ مِن رَّبِّنَا يَوْمًا عَبُوسًا قَمْطَرِيرًا ۝﴾

(سورة الإنسان ٧٦ : ٨ـ١٠)

❝And they feed, for the love of Allah, the indigent, the orphan and the captive. [Saying], "We feed you for the sake of Allah Alone. No reward do we desire from you or thanks. We only fear a Day of distressful wrath from the side of our Lord."❞ (Qur'an 76: 8-10)

14) Mercy towards humans, animals and the environment

Islam also requires its followers to be merciful towards everything on this earth. Prophet Muhammad (Blessings and Peace be upon him) said:

"Be Merciful with those on the earth, you have the Mercy of the One Who is in the heaven (Allah)." (Tirmidhi)

Islam values the creatures of God, which include besides the honoured human being, the animals and the environment. As for animals, Prophet Muhammad (bpuh) said:

"A woman will be punished in Hell-Fire because she confined a cat. She neither fed it, nor did she allow it to roam on the land in search of food." (Muslim)

When asked whether helping an animal is rewarded in Islam, Prophet Muhammad (bpuh) replied:

"There is reward in helping every living soul." (Ibn Mājah)

Muslims, in history, created Islamic endowments or *Awqāf* for the sole purpose of sheltering and feeding cats and other animals. Muslims have also been prohibited from cutting trees, polluting wells, and burning books during the time of war (i.e. protecting both the environment and civilization of even the enemies). The care that Muslims have to show toward all creatures stems from the belief that every thing belongs to Allah and that humans are the vicegerents of Allah in the universe. This means that people have the right to use the environment but they have no right to abuse it.

15) Eagerness to learn

Among the most important characteristics of the culture of the Companions, was their eagerness to learn. People in Makkah were predominantly illiterate. Those who knew how to read and write were very few. Prophet Muhammad (Blessings and Peace be upon him) himself was unlettered. The first word revealed to the unlettered Prophet (bpuh) was, however, 'read.' Allah, the Exalted, says:

﴿اقْرَأْ بِاسْمِ رَبِّكَ الَّذِى خَلَقَ ۝ خَلَقَ الْإِنسَـٰنَ مِنْ عَلَقٍ ۝ اقْرَأْ وَرَبُّكَ الْأَكْرَمُ ۝ الَّذِى عَلَّمَ بِالْقَلَمِ ۝ عَلَّمَ الْإِنسَـٰنَ مَا لَمْ يَعْلَمْ ۝﴾

(سورة العلق ٩٦ : ١-٥)

﴿Read! In the name of your Lord and Cherisher, Who created -created man, out of a mere clot of congealed blood: Read! And your Lord is Most Bountiful, - He Who taught with the pen - taught man that which he knew not.﴾ (Qur'an 96: 1-5)

The revelation of the above verses (*āyāt*) and the fact that they were the first Qur'anic verses to be revealed created an educational revolution among the Muslims. Education, which had not been among the major concerns of people, suddenly became very important. Muslims, men and women, started to learn how to read and write and the literacy level increased rapidly. Seeking education became synonymous to a religious duty. Prophet Muhammad (Blessings and Peace be upon him) said:

"Seeking knowledge is a must for every Muslim — male and female." (Ibn Mājah)

Incentives were given to people to learn and to teach. War prisoners were granted freedom upon teaching Muslims how to read. Further, students were exempted from fighting. The eagerness of the Companions of the Prophet to learn can also be explained by the fact that people tend to be more appreciative of things that are new to them or that they do not possess.

The Qur'an also inspired Muslims to search in areas such as geology, astronomy, biology, and history by providing significant pointers about them and by suggesting to strengthen the faith by improving the understanding of the creation of Allah, the Exalted. Further, the Qur'an contains many instructions for people to reflect and research. Allah, the All-Glorious, says:

﴿إِنَّ فِى خَلْقِ ٱلسَّمَٰوَٰتِ وَٱلْأَرْضِ وَٱخْتِلَٰفِ ٱلَّيْلِ وَٱلنَّهَارِ وَٱلْفُلْكِ ٱلَّتِى تَجْرِى فِى ٱلْبَحْرِ بِمَا يَنفَعُ ٱلنَّاسَ وَمَآ أَنزَلَ ٱللَّهُ مِنَ ٱلسَّمَآءِ مِن مَّآءٍ فَأَحْيَا بِهِ ٱلْأَرْضَ بَعْدَ مَوْتِهَا وَبَثَّ فِيهَا مِن كُلِّ دَآبَّةٍ وَتَصْرِيفِ ٱلرِّيَٰحِ وَٱلسَّحَابِ ٱلْمُسَخَّرِ بَيْنَ ٱلسَّمَآءِ وَٱلْأَرْضِ لَأَيَٰتٍ لِّقَوْمٍ يَعْقِلُونَ ۝﴾ (سورة البقرة

(٢ : ١٦٤)

❧Behold! In the creation of the heavens and the earth; In the alternation of the night and the day; In the sailing of ships through the oceans for the profit of mankind; in the rain which Allah sends down from the skies, and the life He gives therewith to an earth after it is dead; in the beasts of all kinds that He scatters through the earth; in the change of the winds and the clouds that are made subservient between the sky and the earth, are indeed signs for a people that are wise.❧ (Qur'an 2: 164)

﴿... يُغْشِى ٱلَّيْلَ ٱلنَّهَارَ إِنَّ فِى ذَٰلِكَ لَآيَٰتٍ لِّقَوْمٍ يَتَفَكَّرُونَ ۝﴾

(سورة الرعد ١٣ : ٣)

❧...He draws the night as a veil over the day. Behold, verily in these things, there are signs for those who reflect.❧ (Qur'an 13: 3)

﴿وَفِىٓ أَنفُسِكُمْ أَفَلَا تُبْصِرُونَ ۝﴾ (سورة الذاريات ٥١ : ٢١)

❧And also in your own selves: Will you not see.❧ (Qur'an 51: 21)

﴿قُلْ سِيرُوا۟ فِى ٱلْأَرْضِ فَٱنظُرُوا۟ كَيْفَ بَدَأَ ٱلْخَلْقَ ... ۝﴾

(سورة العنكبوت ٢٩ : ٢٠)

❧Say: Travel through the earth and see how Allah did originate creation...❧ (Qur'an 29: 20)

﴿أَوَلَمْ يَسِيرُوا۟ فِى ٱلْأَرْضِ فَيَنظُرُوا۟ كَيْفَ كَانَ عَٰقِبَةُ ٱلَّذِينَ مِن قَبْلِهِمْ ... ۝﴾ (سورة الروم ٣٠ : ٩)

❧Do they not travel through the earth, and see what was the end of those before them?...❧ (Qur'an 30: 9)

In summary, the culture of the Companions of the Prophet was focused on the belief in Allah and in the belief in the Hereafter. This belief makes their efforts focused and subsequently efficient. The culture of the *ṣaḥāba* (Companions) was based on the unity of mankind and the unity of their destiny. It was, therefore, a culture of dialogue, openness, and cooperation. It was also a culture of participation which was achieved through consultation, advice, and righting the wrong and enjoining the good. On the other hand, it was a culture of discipline and efficiency and order. It was also a culture of unity, caring, and sharing. It was a culture of justice for all. It was a culture characterized by a thirst for knowledge. Finally, it was a culture of thrift in using the resources of Allah, collective commitments, courage, strength, endurance, and perseverance.

This culture was the real secret behind the astonishing success in the achievement of the goals and objectives of Muslims within the framework of their mission. It was the real reason behind their effectiveness. This culture provided consistency and allowed for adaptiveness. It also secured total involvement of the Companions and resulted in great satisfaction among them.

﴾... رَّضِيَ ٱللَّهُ عَنْهُمْ وَرَضُوا۟ عَنْهُ ...﴿ ۝ (سورة البينة ٩٨ : ٨)

﴾...Allah is well pleased with them and, they are well pleased with Him...﴿ (Qur'an 98: 8)

'Umar (may Allah be pleased with him), the second successor of the Prophet (bpuh), understood quite well the value of this culture and he tried his best to maintain it and to further reinforce it. 'Umar was afraid that the Companions who conquered Iraq would lose some of their attitudes when they start enjoying the comfortable life of urban Persia. As a result, he ordered them to build the new city of Kufa to serve as a base for them. Nevertheless, because of the huge number of Muslim converts especially among the bedouins who had little knowledge of Islam, and because of the integration of Muslims with various other cultures, the Muslim culture lost some of its depth, intensity, and purity. This culture, however, did not totally disappear. This was, thanks to comprehensive mandatory programmes, and projects reinforced and the set of beliefs and values shared by Muslims. These programmes encompassed the teachings of Islam, which are consistent with the human nature. These teachings are not just behaviourally feasible, but are a source of satisfaction and comfort to their practitioners. The aims of the teachings of Islam are to serve the interest of the people, to protect them from any harm or mischief, and to free them from any yokes. These goals of the teachings of Islam are clearly presented in the following verse of the Qur'an:

﴿ٱلَّذِينَ يَتَّبِعُونَ ٱلرَّسُولَ ٱلنَّبِيَّ ٱلْأُمِّيَّ ٱلَّذِى يَجِدُونَهُۥ مَكْتُوبًا عِندَهُمْ فِى ٱلتَّوْرَىٰةِ وَٱلْإِنجِيلِ يَأْمُرُهُم بِٱلْمَعْرُوفِ وَيَنْهَىٰهُمْ عَنِ ٱلْمُنكَرِ وَيُحِلُّ لَهُمُ ٱلطَّيِّبَـٰتِ وَيُحَرِّمُ عَلَيْهِمُ ٱلْخَبَـٰٓئِثَ وَيَضَعُ عَنْهُمْ إِصْرَهُمْ وَٱلْأَغْلَـٰلَ ٱلَّتِى كَانَتْ عَلَيْهِمْ فَٱلَّذِينَ ءَامَنُوا۟ بِهِۦ وَعَزَّرُوهُ وَنَصَرُوهُ وَٱتَّبَعُوا۟ ٱلنُّورَ ٱلَّذِىٓ أُنزِلَ مَعَهُۥٓ أُو۟لَـٰٓئِكَ هُمُ ٱلْمُفْلِحُونَ ۝ ﴾ (سورة الأعراف ٧: ١٥٧)

❧Those who follow the Apostle, the unlettered Prophet, that they find mentioned in their own [Scriptures] - In the Torah and the Gospel - For he [Muhammad] commands them what is just and forbids them what is evil; He allows them as lawful what is good and prohibits them from what is bad [harmful]. He releases them from their heavy burdens and from the yokes that are upon them...❧ (Qur'an 7: 157)

The teachings of Islam also aim at the attainment of justice, benevolence, and dignity. Allah, the All-High, says:

﴿إِنَّ ٱللَّهَ يَأْمُرُ بِٱلْعَدْلِ وَٱلْإِحْسَٰنِ وَإِيتَآئِ ذِى ٱلْقُرْبَىٰ وَيَنْهَىٰ عَنِ ٱلْفَحْشَآءِ وَٱلْمُنكَرِ وَٱلْبَغْىِ يَعِظُكُمْ لَعَلَّكُمْ تَذَكَّرُونَ ۝﴾

(سورة النحل ١٦ : ٩٠)

﴿Allah commands justice, the doing of good [benevolence], and liberality to kith and kin, and He forbids all shameful deeds, and injustice and transgression: He instructs you, that you may receive admonition.﴾ (Qur'an 16: 90)

We can formulate the goals of the teaching of Islam as:

1. Serving the interest of mankind,

2. Avoiding harm and mischief, and

3. Freeing people from any kind of yokes.

These goals should be attained together or within the framework of:

1. Justice,

2. Benevolence, and

3. Dignity.

The teachings of Islam can be considered as a comprehensive strategic plan that rests on five pillars. These pillars which are referred to as the pillars of Islam are:

1. Bearing witness that there is no god but Allah and that Muhammad is his messenger.

2. Establishing *Ṣalāh* (Prayer) which has to be performed five times a day.

3. Paying *Zakāh* which is a specified alms to be given to the poor.

4. Fasting the month of Ramaḍān.

5. Making pilgrimage to Makkah for whoever can afford it.

The above pillars of Islam are the major programmes that maintain and safeguard the culture of Muslims. The most important of these pillars is the obligatory prayer, which is repeated five times a day. The prayer is a constant reminder to those who practice it about their Creator and the Hereafter. It is also an ever-repeated opportunity for people to repent from any minor mistakes.

On the other hand, paying *Zakāh* fosters a sense of caring and sharing. It trains people to give and to sacrifice. Fasting the month of Ramaḍān is a great exercise of self-control and self-discipline. Muslims are not supposed to eat or drink from sunrise to sunset during the whole month. In this manner, they can also have a feeling about the predicament of the poor people and they will, hence, be more inclined to help others. Prophet Muhammad (Blessings and Peace be upon him) was extremely generous and he was even more generous during the month of Ramaḍān.

Finally, going for pilgrimage to Makkah, to the House built by Abraham (Peace be upon him), establishes the historical tie between Muslims and the sacrifices of the father of the prophets, Abraham, and his descendant Muhammad (Blessings and Peace be upon him), and their determination to assume their mission. Pilgrimage is a great opportunity for reviving faith and the values of justice, mercy, and benevolence. It is also a chance to foster a sense of unity and equity among Muslims from all over the world. During this season Muslims from all over the world, with different social status, leave their belongings and go to Makkah to perform identical duties while wearing the same simple clothes.

The pillars of Islam are the main protectors of the Muslim culture. These pillars have maintained a great portion of the culture of the Companions. Moreover, the whole culture has been revived on many occasions throughout history after some leaders and intellectuals have been able to reinforce its remnants. On the other hand, the absence of these pillars could lead to a gradual collapse of the culture. Currently, as many Muslims are not practicing these pillars, they are getting gradually deprived from the culture that led to the historically unique success of the early Muslims.

Muslim organizations must also have programmes to develop and nurture a good culture for culture cannot be taken for granted. As people can become unethical and degenerate morally, organizations can develop a wrong culture.

Exercises

1. What are the elements that make an organization effective?

2. Who are the founders or an organization's culture?

3. The lack of Unity of purpose rendered Muslims inefficient. Discuss!

4. What was the culture of the Companions of the Prophet and how had it contributed to their success?

5. List the goals of the teachings of Islam and the framework within which they are attainable.

PART — II

PLANNING

MISSION

This chapter presents the general mission of Muslims as outlined in the teachings of the Qur'an. Then, the lessons that an organization can draw from this mission are presented.

Mission is defined as the "business," an organization is in.[1] Mission is generally a statement of attitude, outlook, and orientation rather than of details and measurable targets.[2]

The mission statement generally includes the product or service, the market, and the type of operations adapted by a firm.

King and Cleland[3] outlined the following objectives of a mission by defining:

1. To ensure unanimity of purpose within the organization.

2. To provide a basis for motivating the use of the organization's resources.

3. To develop a basis, or standard for allocating organizational resources.

4. To establish a general tone of organizational climate, for example to suggest a businesslike operation.

---

[1] Cleland and King, "*System Analysis and Project Management*," Mc Graw Hill, N.Y., (1983) p. 61.

[2] Pearce, J. A. Ii, et al. "*The Company's Mission as a Guide to Strategic Action*", "*Strategic Planning and Management Handbook*" edited by King and Cleland, (1987) p. 72.

[3] King W. R., and Cleland, D. I., "*Strategic Planning and Policy*," Van Nostrand Reynold, N. Y., (1978).

5. To serve as focal point for those who can identify with the organization's purpose, and direction and to deter those who cannot, from participating further in the Organization's activities.

6. To facilitate the translation of objectives and goals into work structure involving the assignment of tasks to responsible elements within the organization.

7. To specify organizational purposes into goals in such a way that cost, time and performance parameters can be assessed and controlled.

The mission of Muslims in this world is to worship Allah, and be His vicegerents on this earth by submitting to His will, as is evident in the following verses of the Qur'an:

$$﴿قُلْ إِنَّ صَلَاتِي وَنُسُكِي وَمَحْيَايَ وَمَمَاتِي لِلَّهِ رَبِّ ٱلْعَٰلَمِينَ ۝ لَا شَرِيكَ لَهُۥ ۖ وَبِذَٰلِكَ أُمِرْتُ وَأَنَا۠ أَوَّلُ ٱلْمُسْلِمِينَ ۝﴾ (سورة الأنعام ٦ : ١٦٢-١٦٣)$$

﴿Say: Truly my prayer and my service of sacrifice, my life and my death are [all] for Allah, The Cherisher of the worlds: No partner has He: This I am commanded and I am the first of those who submit to His Will.﴾ (Qur'an 6: 162-163)

In another verse of the Qur'an, Allah, the Almighty, says that both jinn and mankind have only been created to worship Him.

$$﴿وَمَا خَلَقْتُ ٱلْجِنَّ وَٱلْإِنسَ إِلَّا لِيَعْبُدُونِ ۝﴾ (سورة الذاريات ٥١ : ٥٦)$$

﴿I have only created jinn and humankind so that they worship Me.﴾ (Qur'an 51: 56)

Furthermore, in other verses, Allah explained that the function of man is to be His vicegerent. Such verses include the following:

$$﴿وَإِذْ قَالَ رَبُّكَ لِلْمَلَٰئِكَةِ إِنِّي جَاعِلٌ فِي ٱلْأَرْضِ خَلِيفَةً ...﴾ ۝﴿$$

(سورة البقرة ٢ : ٣٠)

﴿Behold, your Lord said to the angels; I will create a Vicegerent on earth...﴾ (Qur'an 2: 30)

$$﴿وَهُوَ ٱلَّذِى جَعَلَكُمْ خَلَٰئِفَ ٱلْأَرْضِ...﴾ ۝﴿$$ (سورة الأنعام ٦ : ١٦٥)

﴿It is He Who has made you vicegerents of the earth...﴾ (Qur'an 6: 165)

In analyzing the above verses, Aḥmad Ṣaqr (1979: 29) stated that worship means not only the pillars of Islam, but it also includes among the many other aspects of life: eating, sleeping, studying, searching into the universe, scientific investigation, doing business, attaining knowledge and participating in sport activities. It also includes earning money to nourish and sustain one's, family. All human endeavours and activities, as long as the intention is the attainment of the pleasure of Allah, are part of worship.[4]

While both jinn and mankind were created to worship Allah, mankind is favoured over jinn by being Allah's vicegerent on earth. Al-Buraey[5] outlines that this vice-gerency is not

---

[4] Quoted in Al-Buraey, M. *"Management and Administrative Development in Islam,"* (1990) p. 112.

[5] Ibid.

restricted to a special group of people; rather it is the mission of every human being:

"This mission of being the deputy of God is not a monopoly of apostles and messengers who are sent to guide people, nor is it confined to kings, governors, or high officials who are elected or appointed to administer the affairs of their nations. It is a mission open to every human being. Every individual is responsible for people and things in his own sphere of influence."

Historically, different Muslim organizations had their own missions. These missions were essentially dealing with the worship of Allah. This worship was however pursued differently as work worship can be pursued through different forms. Muslim organizations were at least making sure that their missions were consistent with the general mission of Islam [i.e. the vicegerence and the worship of Allah (God)]. For an organization's mission to be consistent with the mission of Allah, Muslim organizations should ask themselves whether or not their plans are considered as acts of worship. As such, they should make sure not to contravene the laws of Allah by committing *ḥarām* (illegal acts).

Currently, every Muslim organization needs to have a clear mission statement to use as a frame of reference in planning, implementing, and controlling its activities. The mission statement of a business sub-unit should be consistent with the mission of the parent business. All these mission statements can start by indicating the common denominator, which is "the worship of Allah through...", then they should add what distinguishes them from other organizations in their other industries, followed by what distinguishes them from other organizations within their industry.

By assuming its mission, an organization should attain a certain long-term purpose. This long-term purpose is defined as the objective of the organization. The next chapter will include the definition of the general objective of Muslims and its implications for contemporary organizations.

Exercises

1. What are the objectives for defining a mission?

2. What are the basic missions of Muslims in this world? Give examples from the Qur'an.

3. What is your own mission?

OBJECTIVE

To address the concept of objectives and goals, we will start by mentioning the inception of the discipline of goals in the tenth century by the Muslim philosopher Muhammad ibn 'Ali at-Tirmidhi in his book, *"Prayer and its Objectives."* In this book, Tirmidhi created a model presenting a sequence of the reasons for, or the causes of prescribing prayer. The real landmarks in this discipline, however, are the works of the Islamic scholar Al-Juwayni (Eleventh century) in his book, *"The Proof in the Roots of Islamic Law,"*[6] and his student, the famous Muslim philosopher, Al-Ghazāli[7] who developed a full model for all the teachings of Islam in his book *"Al-Muṣṭafa."* Finally, the culmination of this discipline is found in *"Al-Muwafaqāt"* which was written by Ash-Shāṭibi[8] in Spain in the fifteenth century. The modeling by objectives of the teachings of Islam, comprised in the discipline of the goals of Islamic Jurisprudence, could be an asset for the modern discipline of Strategic planning. The generally agreed upon goals of the teachings of Islam will be presented in the next chapter. The remainder of this chapter will focus on the concept of objective.

---

[6] Al-Juwayni Abu al-Ma'ali, *"The Proof in the Roots of Islamic Law"* reviewed by Dīb, A. A., Dār al-Anṣār, Cairo, (1982).

[7] Al-Ghazāli, Abu Ḥamid, *"Al-Muṣṭasfa,"* Dār al-Fikr, Beirut.

[8] Ash-Shāṭibi, Abu Isḥāq, *"Al-Muwafaqāt,"* reviewed by 'Abdullah Draz, Dār al-Ma'arifa, Beirut.

Objective is defined as the long-term target that people seek to achieve. Some authors use the term goal for the long-term target instead of the term objective as used in this book. The Islamic perspective of objectives includes both this world and the Hereafter. The long-term target of Muslims is in the Hereafter, and is nothing else but entering Heaven and avoiding Hell.

﴿كُلُّ نَفْسٍ ذَآئِقَةُ ٱلْمَوْتِ وَإِنَّمَا تُوَفَّوْنَ أُجُورَكُمْ يَوْمَ ٱلْقِيَٰمَةِ فَمَن زُحْزِحَ عَنِ ٱلنَّارِ وَأُدْخِلَ ٱلْجَنَّةَ فَقَدْ فَازَ وَمَا ٱلْحَيَوٰةُ ٱلدُّنْيَآ إِلَّا مَتَٰعُ ٱلْغُرُورِ ۝﴾ (سورة آل عمران ٣: ١٨٥)

﴿Every soul shall have a taste of death and only on the Day of Judgment shall you be paid your full recompense. Only he who is saved from the fire and admitted to the Garden will have attained success: For the life of this World is but goods and chattels of deception.﴾ (Qur'an 3: 185)

In another verse, Allah, the Exalted, says,

﴿إِنَّ ٱلَّذِينَ كَفَرُوا۟ بِـَٔايَٰتِنَا سَوْفَ نُصْلِيهِمْ نَارًا...۝﴾ (سورة النساء ٤: ٥٦)

﴿Those who reject our signs, We shall soon cast them into the fire...﴾ (Qur'an 4: 56)

﴿...وَتُنذِرَ يَوْمَ ٱلْجَمْعِ لَا رَيْبَ فِيهِ فَرِيقٌ فِى ٱلْجَنَّةِ وَفَرِيقٌ فِى ٱلسَّعِيرِ ۝﴾ (سورة الشورى ٤٢: ٧)

﴿...And warn [them] of the Day of Assembly, of which there is no doubt: [When] some will be in the Garden and some will be in the blazing Fire.﴾ (Qur'an 42: 7)

﴿إِنَّ ٱلْأَبْرَارَ لَفِى نَعِيمٍ ۝ وَإِنَّ ٱلْفُجَّارَ لَفِى جَحِيمٍ ۝﴾

(سورة الانفطار ٨٢ : ١٣-١٤)

﴾As for the righteous, they will be in Bliss; And the Wicked - they will be in Fire.﴿ (Qur'an 82: 13-14)

﴿وَٱلَّذِينَ ءَامَنُوا۟ وَعَمِلُوا۟ ٱلصَّٰلِحَٰتِ سَنُدْخِلُهُمْ جَنَّٰتٍ تَجْرِى مِن تَحْتِهَا ٱلْأَنْهَٰرُ خَٰلِدِينَ فِيهَآ أَبَدًا لَّهُمْ فِيهَآ أَزْوَٰجٌ مُّطَهَّرَةٌ وَنُدْخِلُهُمْ ظِلًّا ظَلِيلًا ۝﴾

(سورة النساء ٤ : ٥٧)

﴾But those who believe and do deeds of righteousness, We shall soon admit to Gardens, with rivers flowing beneath their eternal home; therein shall they have companions pure and holy. We shall admit them to shades, cool and ever deepening.﴿ (Qur'an 4: 57) ·

﴿وَتِلْكَ ٱلْجَنَّةُ ٱلَّتِى أُورِثْتُمُوهَا بِمَا كُنتُمْ تَعْمَلُونَ ۝ لَكُمْ فِيهَا فَٰكِهَةٌ كَثِيرَةٌ مِّنْهَا تَأْكُلُونَ ۝ إِنَّ ٱلْمُجْرِمِينَ فِى عَذَابِ جَهَنَّمَ خَٰلِدُونَ ۝﴾ (سورة الزخرف ٤٣ : ٧٢-٧٤)

﴾Such will be the Garden of which you are made heirs for your [good] deeds [in life]. You shall have therein abundance of fruit from which you shall have satisfaction. The sinners will be in the punishment of Hell, to dwell therein [for ever].﴿ (Qur'an 43: 72-74)

The objective of entering Paradise and avoiding Hell can only be achieved by adequately pursuing the mission of the worship and the vicegerents of Allah. The fact that the objective of Muslims is twofold, i.e. including both Paradise and Hell, indicates that Islam utilizes both the appeal of reward and the fear of punishment in motivating people. The objective of entering Paradise and avoiding Hell is clearly defined. Indeed, both Paradise and Hell were extensively described in the teachings of Islam.

What is so unique about the teachings of Islam is that every action a person does is directly related to the long-term objective. These direct links to the Hereafter are expressed in numerous verses (*āyāt*) of the Qur'an. These actions do not have to connect to the ultimate objective through intermediate goals only.

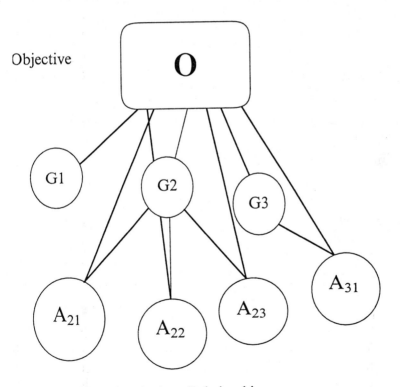

Figure 1. Objective-Actions Relationship

The direct links between the ultimate objective and the various actions are represented in Figure 1. One can see that actions A21, A22, A23, are conducive to G2 (which can be considered as the final action to accomplish a certain goal leading to the objective O), but there are still direct links between them and the higher objective. The links between the objective and the actions are more stressed in the teachings of Islam than the links among the various sequentially dependent actions. The links between the ultimate objective and the various actions go beyond the usual feedback process to a direct cause and effect relationship. Every action, no matter how small it is, has a corresponding reward or punishment in the Hereafter. 'Ali (may Allah be pleased with him), the fourth successor of the Prophet (Blessings and Peace be upon him), reflected on the role of the clouds saying: The objective of the clouds is not the rain, rather it is the fruits. In this statement, 'Ali, through wisdom, explained in a direct manner the relationship between the clouds and their end result, which are fruits. The intermediate steps of the process of fruit production, that involve the clouds, are the rain and the irrigation of the trees. Establishing the direct cause and effect relationship between the long-term goal and the various immediate actions is an added value to these actions. It is very instrumental in motivating people to carry out these actions effectively.

Figure 1., relates very well to the case of the three construction workers who were all doing the same job. One of these workers was asked what he was doing; he said he was laying bricks. This corresponds to the lowest level of action in the figure. When the second worker was asked what he was doing, he replied that he was building a wall. This corresponds to the intermediate level goals in the figure. Finally, when the third worker was asked the same question, he replied that he was building a house. This corresponds to the highest level objective, in the figure. It is clear that the third worker was more motivated because he saw more meaning in what he was doing than the other two workers were. Managers should convince workers that they are all building a house or contributing to the end goal rather than making them feel that they are just laying bricks or performing some hardly significant task.

The teachings of Islam emphasize the long-term objective as opposed to any intermediate goal. The real success expressed in the teachings of Islam shall be the farthest possible in time whether in the Hereafter or in this world. Immediate achievements will not be of any help if the end result will be a failure. In fact, in many cases, immediate gains result in long-term losses. Qur'an has strongly stressed the end results both in this world and in the Hereafter. The Arabic term of *'aquibah* or *'uqbā* which can be translated into end result are repeated very frequently in the Qur'an. They can be found in various forms in the following verses (*Sūrah Aal-i 'Imrān* 3: 137), (*Sūrah al-An'am* 6: 11, 135), (*Sūrah al-Aa'rāf* 7: 84, 86, 103, 128), (*Sūrah Yunus* 10: 39, 73), (*Sūrah Hūd* 11: 49), (*Sūrah Yoosuf* 12: 109), (*Sūrah an-Nahl* 16: 136), (*Sūrah Ta Ha* 20: 132), (*Sūrah al-Hajj* 22: 41), (*Sūrah al-Naml* 27: 14, 51, 69), (*Sūrah al Qasas* 28: 37, 40, 83), (*Sūrah ar-Rūm* 30: 9, 10, 42), (*Sūrah Luqmān* 31: 22), (*Sūrah Fātir* 35: 44), (*Sūrah as-Saffāt* 37: 74), (*Sūrah Ghāfir* 40: 21, 72), (*Sūrah al-Zukhruf* 43: 25), (*Sūrah Muhammad* 47: 10), (*Sūrah at-Talāq* 65: 9), (*Sūrah al-Hashr* 59: 17), (*Sūrah ar-Ra'd* 13: 22, 24, 35, 42), and (*Sūrah ash-Shams* 91: 15). These verses address both ends in this world and in the Hereafter. Further, Prophet Muhammad (Blessings and Peace be upon him) said:

"Deeds are based on the ends." (Bukhāri)

This should not be taken to imply the phrase, "the end justify the means". There is no such thing in Islam. Both the means and ends must satisfy the Islamic principle of *halāl* (legal). The above hadith means that success is only relevant when it is a long-term one, an end result.

Some Arabic language idioms similarly emphasize the importance of the end results. Such idioms include; Matters are according to their ends and he laughs a lot who laughs the last. Recent studies have confirmed the importance of long-term goals and how immediate gains can ultimately be very detrimental. The Boston Consulting Group has made the following statement regarding the British-Motorcycle Industry.[9]

"The result of the British industries historic focus on short-term profitability has been low profits and no losses in the long term. The long term result of Japanese industries historic focus on market share and volume often at the expense of short term profitability, has been the precise opposite: high and secure profitability."

At the individual level for example, a student may have to choose between working and furthering his study. For a student who decides to work, he is focusing on the short-term for working would give immediate financial returns. While studying further could delay financial return it would likely be more beneficial in the long run both financially and intellectually.

---

[9] Boston Consulting Group, "*Strategic Alternatives for the British Motorcycle Business*," Vol. 1, p. 4, London department of Industry, Her majesty stationary office, (1975).

Someone may also be faced with the choice of having a high paying job versus having a skill-improving job. The skill-improving job can be considered as a future investment while the high paying job as short-term satisfaction. This is because one may not be able to maintain the high paying job for always, however one's skills are always with him. If the person decides on the high paying job, he might find himself jobless because he may not have the necessary skills to take up another job.

One can infer from the above discussion that every organization shall have a clearly defined objective. This objective should be consistent with its own mission. If the organization is part of a bigger organization, its objective has also to be consistent with the general mission and objective of its parent organization. The direct cause and effect relationships between the various activities of a business and its objective should be clearly established and the focus on the objective should be very strong.

The objective of an organization can only be achieved after going through some milestones. These milestones are some specific targets along the way leading to the objective. These milestones are usually called goals. The concept of goals will be discussed in the next chapter.

Exercises

1. What is the Islamic perspective on objectives?

2. Illustrate and explain the Objective - Actions relationship.

GOALS

Goals are defined in much management literature as the intermediate targets or as some specific targets to be sought at some specific times. Goals are therefore, the timely specified milestones leading to some objective.[10] As such, they should reflect a certain output of the strategy or the general direction in which the objectives are pursued.[11] On the other hand, goals are achieved through programmes, which are made of a variety of projects and activities. King and Cleland made the following summary about goals:[12]

1. Goals are specified steps along the way to the accomplishment of broad objectives.

2. Goals are established to reflect the expected outputs from strategies.

3. Goals are directly achieved through programmes.

4. Strategies are implemented through programmes.

The time horizon of goals depends on the scope we are dealing with. So, for a retail store example, the goal might be to achieve a certain sales figure at the end of a fiscal year. Looking at Muslims in their greater space or greater domain of definition that

---

[10] King, W., R. and Cleland, D., I., "*The Choice of Strategic Management*," in strategic planning and Management Handbook, edited by King and Cleland, (1987) p. 64.

[11] Ibid.

[12] Ibid. p. 68

encompasses both this life and the Hereafter, one can consider life as the time horizon for the goals of Islam. Scholars of the discipline, "The Goals of Islamic Jurisprudence", broadly defined the goals of the teachings of Islam as serving the interest of the people and protecting them from any harm or mischief.[13] They also classified these goals into three categories.

The first category is called the absolutely indispensable goals, the second category is called the necessary goals, and the third category is called the complementary goals. It is further explained that the necessary goals serve and complement the indispensable goals while the complementary goals serve and complement the necessary goals.[14]

According to many scholars, the indispensable goals are: The protection of religion, the protection of peoples' honour and dignity, the protection of their lives, the protection of their wealth, and the protection of their faculty of intellect. Other scholars formulate the goals of the teachings of Islam as justice, benevolence, and liberality, in addition to the abrogation of injustice, shameful deeds, and transgression. These goals are included in the following verse (āyah) of the Qur'an:

﴿الَّذِينَ يَتَّبِعُونَ الرَّسُولَ النَّبِيَّ الْأُمِّيَّ الَّذِي يَجِدُونَهُ مَكْتُوبًا عِندَهُمْ فِي التَّوْرَاةِ وَالْإِنجِيلِ يَأْمُرُهُم بِالْمَعْرُوفِ وَيَنْهَاهُمْ عَنِ الْمُنكَرِ وَيُحِلُّ لَهُمُ الطَّيِّبَاتِ وَيُحَرِّمُ عَلَيْهِمُ الْخَبَائِثَ وَيَضَعُ عَنْهُمْ إِصْرَهُمْ وَالْأَغْلَالَ الَّتِي كَانَتْ عَلَيْهِمْ فَالَّذِينَ...﴾ ﴿١٥٧﴾   (سورة الأعراف ٧ : ١٥٧)

---

[13] Ibn 'Abdus-Salām, A., "*Legal Maxims in the Interest of Mankind*," Reviewed by 'Abdur-Raouf T., Dār al-Jeel, Cairo., p. 8.

[14] Ar-Raysouni, Aḥmad "*The Theory of Goals*," IIIT., Virginia, (1992) p. 26.

❨Those who follow the apostle, the unlettered Prophet that they find mentioned in their own [Scripture] - In the Torah and the Gospel - For he [Muhammad] commands them what is just and forbids them what is evil. He allows them as lawful what is good and prohibits them from what is bad [harmful]. He releases them from their heavy burdens and the yokes that are upon them...❩ (Qur'an 7: 157)

We would formulate these goals as serving the interest of the people, protecting them from any harm and mischief, and liberating them from their yokes within the framework of justice, benevolence, and dignity. This is evident in the following verse (*āyah*) from the Qur'an:

❨إِنَّ ٱللَّهَ يَأْمُرُ بِٱلْعَدْلِ وَٱلْإِحْسَـٰنِ وَإِيتَآئِ ذِى ٱلْقُرْبَىٰ وَيَنْهَىٰ عَنِ ٱلْفَحْشَآءِ وَٱلْمُنكَرِ وَٱلْبَغْىِ يَعِظُكُمْ لَعَلَّكُمْ تَذَكَّرُونَ ❨٩٠❩❩ (سُورة النحل ١٦ : ٩٠)

❨Allah commands justice, Benevolence, and liberality to kith and kin, and He forbids all shameful deeds, and injustice and transgression: He instructs you, that you may receive admonition.❩ (Qur'an 16: 90)

Research on compensation has revealed that workers look at their compensation on the basis of whether they are being justly compensated particularly relative to their colleague. The goal of Benevolence ensures the spirit of caring and sharing as well as brotherhood. Furthermore it complements the goal of justice for it is the just that are benevolent. Liberality of kith and kin will lead to an environment that will ensure development, progress and prosperity for it warrants social security. Given the benefits that accrues from the above factors, it is not surprising that Islam has them as its goals for it is a religion that is but a mercy to mankind.

In order to pursue its objective, it is incumbent upon every organization to have a series of goals (specific targets at specific times) that will consequently enable it to achieve this objective within the framework of its own mission. In planning to achieve its objective, a Muslim organization has also to make sure that any work package, it plans to perform, be consistent with the general mission and objective of Muslims. This should be an uninterrupted feedback process.

The major goals of Islam are achieved through the achievement of the other categories of goals which are in turn achieved through certain programmes, projects, and actions outlined in the teachings of Islam. The three categories of goals, mentioned above, as well as the programmes, projects, and actions required to achieve them are consistent with the above-described general mission and objective of Islam.

From the above discussion, an organization can learn to define some major goals to be achieved in a relatively long term. Then, other sets of intermediate goals that are conducive to the major goals should be determined. Finally the necessary programmes, projects, and actions for achieving these goals have to be clearly described.

For example, an organization may have as its objective a twenty-percent increase in profits from last years. In order to achieve this, it sets up the goal of achieving an average two-percent increase monthly. To achieve its monthly sales target, it launches an aggressive advertising campaign to increase sale and revamped its production process to decrease cost and improve schedule. However, the above programme, goal and objective can be achieved only if they are clearly communicated to the overall organization, provided that they are acceptable to them. This acceptance can be ensured by the corporate culture in place.

Before implementing the actions leading to its goals, an organization should establish a direct cause and effect relationship between its planned actions and its long-term objective. From the above example, this cause and effect relationship would be represented by an analysis of the impact of advertising on profits. This is more effective than just exercising a simple feedback process.

Many organizations develop goals and objectives and start working towards achieving them, but ultimately realize that these goals and objectives are infeasible. Based on the teaching of Islam, the concept of feasibility in the planning process will be addressed in the next chapter.

Exercises

1. Outline King and Cleland's summary of goals.

2. What are the goals of the teachings of Islam?

3. Based on the chapter, what are the absolutely indispensable goals in Islam as prescribed by the Scholars of *Maqāṣid ash-Sharī'ah*?

4. What are the necessary and complementary goals in Islam?

5. How are the major goals achieved?

FEASIBILITY

This chapter establishes the indispensable need for making sure that the desired goals of an organization be feasible. It also derives the components of feasibility based on the teachings of Islam.

The achievements of the general goals of Muslims are within their reach. The Qur'an clearly states that people are only demanded to do what is within their capacity. The Qur'an clearly states that Allah, the Exalted, places on people no burden that they cannot bear.

﴾لَا يُكَلِّفُ ٱللَّهُ نَفْسًا إِلَّا وُسْعَهَا لَهَا...﴿ ﴿٢٨٦﴾ (سورة البقرة ٢ : ٢٨٦)

﴾On no soul does Allah place a burden greater than it can bear...﴿ (Qur'an 2: 286)

It would not make sense to address Islam as a religion of mercy if it requires people to be over burdened in order to comply with Allah's commands. If the creator is not requiring from His creatures' activities that are beyond their capability, then organizations in pursuing their objective of pleasing Allah, should not ask their employees to perform tasks that are beyond them.

In another verse, Allah shows that even *Taqwa* is demanded according to people's capabilities.

﴾فَٱتَّقُوا ٱللَّهَ مَا ٱسْتَطَعْتُمْ...﴿ ﴿١٦﴾ (سورة التغابن ٦٤ : ١٦)

﴾So fear Allah as much as you can...﴿ (Qur'an 64: 16)

Another verse of the Qur'an dealing with spending, clarifies that everybody should spend according to his means and that Allah puts no responsibility on any person beyond what he was given:

$$\left\{\text{لِيُنفِقْ ذُو سَعَةٍ مِّن سَعَتِهِۦ وَمَن قُدِرَ عَلَيْهِ رِزْقُهُۥ فَلْيُنفِقْ مِمَّا ءَاتَىٰهُ ٱللَّهُ لَا يُكَلِّفُ ٱللَّهُ نَفْسًا إِلَّا مَآ ءَاتَىٰهَا سَيَجْعَلُ ٱللَّهُ بَعْدَ عُسْرٍ يُسْرًا ۝}\right\}$$ (ســـورة الطلاق ٦٥ : ٧) '

❝Let the man of means spend according to his means: and the man whose resources are restricted, let him spend according to what Allah has given him. Allah puts no burden on any person beyond what He has given him. After a difficulty Allah will soon grant relief.❞ (Qur'an 65: 7)[15]

Having illustrated that the mission of mankind had been made feasible by Allah, the All-High, we now try to find the elements that constitute this feasibility. The first element of feasibility is the set of default values or *"Fitrah"* that Allah bestowed human beings with. These values provide a predisposition for a child to be a Muslim. In fact Prophet Muhammad (bpuh) indicated that every baby is born as Muslims. We should therefore make sure that the jobs we assign to people are consistent with their personal values to ensure the feasibility of accomplishment of our goals. Allah has also sent revelation to provide guidance to mankind and assist them in clinging to their *"Fitrah"* or inborn values. This illustrates the importance of priding direction to ensure the feasibility of achieving goals.

---

[15] The end of this verse implies that what is not feasible now may become feasible at sometime in the future.

Furthermore Islam teaches that, as Allah created people, He has given them senses and the faculty of intellect that made it capable of acquiring knowledge and skills. This shows that the importance of the abilities to acquire skills in the ensuring the job feasibility.

﴿وَٱللَّهُ أَخْرَجَكُم مِّنۢ بُطُونِ أُمَّهَٰتِكُمْ لَا تَعْلَمُونَ شَيْـًٔا وَجَعَلَ لَكُمُ ٱلسَّمْعَ وَٱلْأَبْصَٰرَ وَٱلْأَفْـِٔدَةَ لَعَلَّكُمْ تَشْكُرُونَ ٧٨﴾ (سورة النحل ١٦ : ٧٨)

﴿It is He who brought you forth from the wombs of your mothers when you knew nothing; and He gave you hearing and sight and intelligence and affections: that you may give thanks [to God].﴾ (Qur'an 16: 78)

Since human beings are the Vicegerents of Allah on this earth, Allah provided them with the necessary resources by making everything on earth subservient to them.

﴿هُوَ ٱلَّذِى خَلَقَ لَكُم مَّا فِى ٱلْأَرْضِ جَمِيعًا...٢٩﴾

(سورة البقرة ٢ : ٢٩)

﴿He it is Who has created for you all that is on the earth...﴾ (Qur'an 2: 29)

﴿هُوَ ٱلَّذِى جَعَلَ لَكُمُ ٱلْأَرْضَ ذَلُولًا فَٱمْشُوا۟ فِى مَنَاكِبِهَا وَكُلُوا۟ مِن رِّزْقِهِۦ وَإِلَيْهِ ٱلنُّشُورُ ١٥﴾ (سورة الملك ٦٧ : ١٥)

﴿It is He who has made the earth obedient and manageable for you, so you traverse through its tracts and enjoy of the sustenance which He furnishes: but unto Him is the resurrection.﴾ (Qur'an 67: 15)

Every duty comes with responsibility and accountability and the post of Vicegerent is no different. Everything in the heavens and on the earth may be made subservient for man, nevertheless, he is also accountable for how he made use of them hence the remainder in the last part of the above verse that to Allah is the resurrection. In the same way, employees are responsible and accountable for the resources placed at their disposal for the attainment of an organization's goals and thus objectives and Allah will ask them about their performance.

The Qur'an specifies that not only did Allah create every thing on this earth for men, rather He revealed to mankind that He had made everything in the earth and in the heavens subservient to them.

> ﴿اللَّهُ الَّذِى خَلَقَ السَّمَـٰوَٰتِ وَالأَرْضَ وَأَنزَلَ مِنَ السَّمَآءِ مَآءً فَأَخْرَجَ بِهِ
> مِنَ الثَّمَرَٰتِ رِزْقًا لَّكُمْ وَسَخَّرَ لَكُمُ الْفُلْكَ لِتَجْرِىَ فِى الْبَحْرِ بِأَمْرِهِ
> وَسَخَّرَ لَكُمُ الأَنْهَٰرَ ۝ وَسَخَّرَ لَكُمُ الشَّمْسَ وَالْقَمَرَ دَآئِبَيْنِ وَسَخَّرَ
> لَكُمُ الَّيْلَ وَالنَّهَارَ ۝ وَءَاتَىٰكُم مِّن كُلِّ مَا سَأَلْتُمُوهُ وَإِن تَعُدُّوا نِعْمَتَ
> اللَّهِ لَا تُحْصُوهَآ ... ۝﴾ (سورة إبراهيم ١٤ : ٣٢-٣٤)

❧It is Allah Who has created the heavens and the earth and sends down rain from the skies, and with it brings out fruits wherewith to feed you; it is He Who has made the ships subject to you, that they may sail through the sea by His command; And the rivers [also] has He made subject to you. And He has made subject to you the sun and the moon, both diligently pursuing their courses; and the Night and the Day has He also made subject to you. And He gives you of all that you ask for but if you count the bounty of Allah, never will you able to number them...❧ (Qur'an 14: 32-34)

Allah's bounty to man is uncountable. It covers all the aspects of man's life from health to sustenance, transportation to scientific discoveries among others. Man is to be grateful for such gifts by utilizing them according to Allah's wish.

$$﴿وَسَخَّرَ لَكُم مَّا فِى ٱلسَّمَـٰوَٰتِ وَمَا فِى ٱلأَرْضِ جَمِيعًا مِّنْهُ إِنَّ فِى ذَٰلِكَ لَأَيَـٰتٍ لِّقَوْمٍ يَتَفَكَّرُونَ ۝﴾ (سورة الجاثية ٤٥ : ١٣)$$

﴿And He has subjected to you, as from Him all that is in the heavens and on the earth: behold, in that are signs indeed for those who reflect.﴾ (Qur'an 45: 13)

Just as Mankind and the jinn are created for a purpose that is to worship Allah, these bounties of Allah to mankind should also serve the purpose of worship.

Everything in this Universe is made for the use of people, however, people cannot dream of taking advantage of it without learning and understanding how it functions, and without some kind of transformation or production process of its materials.

There is no way of getting any reward without doing the right job. This process of learning, understanding, planning for an attainable goal, and then implementing the plan is prerequisite for the help of Allah. It is what helping the cause of Allah in the following verse (*āyah*) means.

$$﴿يَتأَيُّهَا ٱلَّذِينَ ءَامَنُوٓاْ إِن تَنصُرُواْ ٱللَّهَ يَنصُرْكُمْ ... ۝﴾ (سورة محمد ٤٧ : ٧)$$

﴿O you who believe, If you help [the cause of] Allah, He will help You...﴾ (Qur'an 47: 7)

The above verse tells Muslims that it is not only feasible for them to be successful in this world, but Allah, the creator of the heavens and the earth, will help them provided they do their part. This also teaches people that they should never underestimate themselves because Allah has provided them with the faculty of intellect, made the universe subservient to them and promised them help. Islam also teaches that the fact that some people are Muslims will not help them if they do not do their work. The Qur'an states:

$$\text{﴿لَّيۡسَ بِأَمَانِيِّكُمۡ وَلَآ أَمَانِيِّ أَهۡلِ ٱلۡكِتَٰبِۗ مَن يَعۡمَلۡ سُوٓءًا يُجۡزَ بِهِۦ...﴾}$$

$$\text{(سورة النساء ٤ : ١٢٣) ﴿١٢٣﴾}$$

﴿It is not up to your wishes nor is it up to the wishes of the people of the book whoever does wrong will be requited accordingly...﴾ (Qur'an 4: 123)

In Islam, reward is contingent upon doing the good deeds.

$$\text{﴿مَنۡ عَمِلَ صَٰلِحٗا مِّن ذَكَرٍ أَوۡ أُنثَىٰ وَهُوَ مُؤۡمِنٞ فَلَنُحۡيِيَنَّهُۥ حَيَوٰةٗ طَيِّبَةٗۖ}$$
$$\text{وَلَنَجۡزِيَنَّهُمۡ أَجۡرَهُم بِأَحۡسَنِ مَا كَانُواۡ يَعۡمَلُونَ ٩٧﴾}$$

$$\text{(سورة النحل ١٦ : ٩٧)}$$

﴿Whosoever does right, whether male or female, and is a believer, him surely We Shall quicken with good life, and We shall pay them a recompense in proportion to the best of what they used to do.﴾ (Qur'an 16: 97)

Finally Allah, the Almighty, assigned a mission, an objective, and goals for people. In the mean time, He equipped them with the necessary capabilities to perform their mission and to achieve their objective and goals. People possess the faculty of intellect or the necessary skill to perform their duty. They also have the whole earth and universe subservient to them, which is, they have the necessary resources to perform their duty.

Based on the above discussion, the students of Islam can learn that organizations should only choose among feasible alternative goals in their operations. Pursuing an unfeasible goal is considered to be wasting the resources that Allah has given. Feasibility encompasses both the skills and the resources. The absence of one of these components renders the job unfeasible.

After developing its feasible alternative plans, an organization has to choose which one to adopt. The decision process can yield better results if it is done through consultation or *shūra*. The following chapter will address this important Islamic concept.

Exercises

1. ❨You who believe, If You help [the cause of] Allah, He will help You.❩ (Qur'an 47: 7). Discuss the above verse in the context of feasibility.

2. What is the Islamic principle of establishing a goal?

3. What are the elements of job feasibility?

PARTICIPATIVE MANAGEMENT

Participative management is the continuous involvement of people in decision making. It is a culture rather than a programme. It is an Islamic duty for a leader to consult his/her subordinates. This consultation is called in Islam *Shūra*. It is stated in the Qur'an that the believers who will be rewarded in the Hereafter are those who conduct their affairs with *Shūra* or consultation.

﴿وَٱلَّذِينَ ٱسْتَجَابُوا۟ لِرَبِّهِمْ وَأَقَامُوا۟ ٱلصَّلَوٰةَ وَأَمْرُهُمْ شُورَىٰ بَيْنَهُمْ وَمِمَّا رَزَقْنَٰهُمْ يُنفِقُونَ ۝﴾ (سورة الشورى ٤٢ : ٣٨)

❋Those who hearken to their Lord and establish regular prayer; who [conduct] their affairs by mutual consultation; who spend out of what We bestow on them for sustenance.❋ (Qur'an 42: 38)

In another verse, Allah, the Exalted, ordains His Prophet Muhammad (Blessings and Peace be upon him) to apply *Shūra*.

﴿فَبِمَا رَحْمَةٍ مِّنَ ٱللَّهِ لِنتَ لَهُمْ وَلَوْ كُنتَ فَظًّا غَلِيظَ ٱلْقَلْبِ لَٱنفَضُّوا۟ مِنْ حَوْلِكَ فَٱعْفُ عَنْهُمْ وَٱسْتَغْفِرْ لَهُمْ وَشَاوِرْهُمْ فِى ٱلْأَمْرِ فَإِذَا عَزَمْتَ فَتَوَكَّلْ عَلَى ٱللَّهِ إِنَّ ٱللَّهَ يُحِبُّ ٱلْمُتَوَكِّلِينَ ۝﴾ (سورة آل عمران ٣ : ١٥٩)

❋It was by the mercy of Allah that you were lenient with them [O Muhammad], for if you had been stern and fierce of heart they would have dispersed from round about you. So pardon them and ask forgiveness for them and consult with them upon the conduct of affairs. And when you are resolved then put your trust in Allah. Lo! Allah loves those who put their trust [in Him]. ۞ (Qur'an 3: 159)

Four reasons have been highlighted by Muhammad ibn al-Ḥasan al-Murādi as to why a leader should involve his followers in decision making. These reasons are:

"First, the inadequacy of the knowledge of the one seeking council for making decision. Second, his fear of committing mistakes in assessing the situation even when he is not lacking in knowledge. Third, the possibility that despite his intelligence and skills, the emotions of love and hate could prevent him from making the right decisions.... Finally, when the person consulted is a partner, or supporter in an action, his engagement in the decision would encourage him to render his utmost effort and support, because the decision reflects his choice."[16]

Shūra is aimed at building a consensus that will benefit the community or the business that has to make the decision. In case no consensus is reached, voting is resorted to. Prophet Muhammad (Blessings and Peace be upon him) said:

"My nation cannot agree upon an error and if a conflict persists be with the majority." (Ibn Mājah)

Commenting on the above saying, Izetbegovic[17] said that the opinion of the majority is an expression of higher common mind. This is because it yields better outcomes than a single person's opinion. Izetbegovic added, "This is a declaration of a democratic process." Participative management is also critical for

---

[16] Al-Murādi Pp. 61-62.

[17] Izetbegovic, A. A, *"Islam Between East and West,"* 2nd ed. American Publications, Indianapolis, (1990).

motivation. People are generally more motivated to execute the decisions which they were a part in making.

Shūra is however not democracy. Unlike democracy, it does not assume that conflicts are inevitable. It therefore requires people to strive for achieving consensus. While consensus may render the decision making process lengthy, it certainly ensures better implementation. Democracy on the other hand, is a mechanism of solving conflicts through the majority rule. It might be more efficient than *Shūra* but it does not guarantee full commitment of the losing party/s. Democracy, on the other hand, is, much better than autocratic rule for it does not completely ignore the opinion of the people. Table 1 compares the use of dictatorship, democracy and *Shūra* in strategic decision making.

Table 1. Approaches to Strategic Decision Making:

	Dictatorship	Democracy	*Shūra*
Time to decide	Short	Moderate	Long
Decision quality	Low	Fair	High
Quality of implementation	Low	Fair	High

One should however understand that achieving consensus is not practical in operational decisions. In fact individual decision coupled, if needed, with consultations of experts is the best operational decision approach. Individual decision should not be mixed with dictatorship. In fact we can only establish a real consensus when we have independent people that are capable of having their own opinions and making their own decisions. Otherwise if we just have dependent people that cannot stand on their own, we will have a dictatorship presented in the form of consensus or democracy.

As the decision gets more and more strategic, there is increased need for consensus. Between the operational and strategic extremes of a continuum, we may settle for a majority rule. Figure 2. shown the continuum relating type decision and decision approach

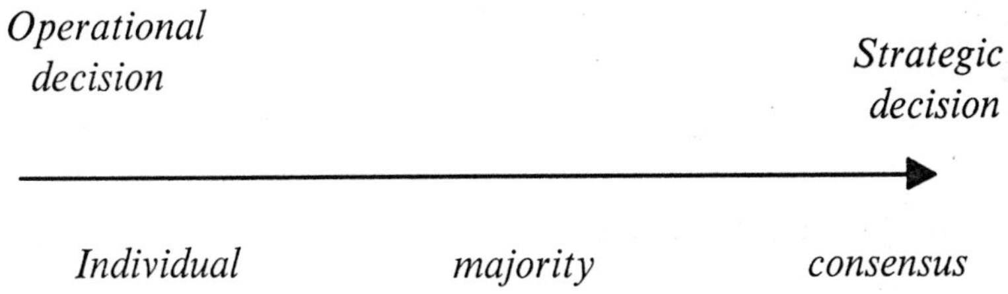

*Operational
decision*

*Strategic
decision*

⎯⎯⎯⎯⎯⎯⎯⎯⎯⎯⎯⎯⎯⎯⎯⎯⎯⎯⎯⎯⎯▶

Individual   *majority*   *consensus*

Figure 2. Decision Types and Decision Approaches

Shūra had been a culture during the time of Prophet Muhammad (Blessings and Peace be upon him) and his successors after him as mentioned before. No major decision had ever been made without consultation. In many occasions, Prophet Muhammad's opinion was adopted as it received major support. On other occasions such as during the battle of Uḥud, other opinions received the majority and were subsequently adopted. On the occasion of the battle of Uḥud, Prophet Muhammad (bpuh) wanted to stay in his town Madīnah when he heard that the pagans of Makkah were about to attack him. But the Prophet (Blessings and Peace be upon him) finally decided to go to the mountain of Uḥud instead, because the majority of his Companions preferred facing their enemy there. In spite of the fact that consultation was a culture during his time, 'Umar (may Allah be pleased with him), the second successor of Muhammad (bpuh), created a number of programmes to reinforce this culture. These programmes include the creation of an annual conference for all Muslims during pilgrimage and the establishment of an agency of complaints. Muslim scholars state that consultation shall not be forsaken for any reason.[18]

The scope of consultation should be as wide as possible. 'Umar was so keen on listening to different opinions that he was seeking the opinions of juveniles on critical matters. In one of his sayings, Prophet Muhammad (bpuh) summarized the whole religion as advice, which can be obtained only through consultation:

"Religion is sincere advice." (Muslim)

The culture of participation of the Companions of the Prophet resulted in high level of satisfaction and involvement. It also induced numerous administrative innovations notably during the time of 'Umar. These innovations included building the cities of Baṣra and Koofa in Iraq, and the creation of new departments such as the department of payroll and the department of documentation where information was gathered and managed. In today's world, businesses are realizing the importance of participative decision making, and the businesses that consult their workers are doing much well than those that do not. Denison argued that participative management could contribute significantly to the long-term success of the organization[19],[20].

---

[18]. Awwa, M. S., *"On the Political System of an Islamic State"* Cairo, (1980) Pp. 335-336.

[19] Dension, D.R., *"Bringing Corporate Culture to the bottom line,"* Organizational Dynamics, Autumn Pp. 4-22.

[20] Ibid.

A stronger statement that probably comes closer to the Islamic understanding was made by Sashkin,[21] who stated that participative management is effective and, in fact, morally necessary in organizations.

Those who are involved in decision-making or those who are part of consultation should seek to serve the interest of the whole organization. Focusing on the interest of one part of the organization at the expense of another can eventually hurt all the parts. Moreover, the decision-makers should consider the behaviour of all the stakeholders within the environment of their organization. This approach, known as systems approach, is presented in the next chapter.

Exercises

1. Define participative management.

2. What is the objective of participative management?

3. What were the outcomes of the culture of participation of the Companions of the Prophet particularly during 'Umar's time?

4. What is the Islamic principle of consultation?

5. What is the difference between *Shūra* and democracy

6. There has been debate in the literature on the difference between consultation and *Shūra*. Can relate this debate to the continuum shown in figure 2?

---

[21] Sashkin Marshall, *"Participative Management is an Ethical imperative,"* Organizational Dynamics, Spring 1984 Pp. 4-22.

SYSTEMS APPROACH

Gibson[22] et al. defines system approach as a theory based on the notion that organizations can be visualized as systems. Stone and Freeman[23] stated that:

"The system approach to management views the organization a unified, purposeful system composed of interrelated parts. This approach gives managers a way of looking at the organization as a whole and as apart of a larger external environment. In so doing, systems theory tells us that the activity of any segment of an organization affects in various degrees, the activity of every other segment."

The systems approach consists of certain pillars. The first pillar is to consider the organization as a whole. This pillar can be better explained by the following saying of Prophet Muhammad (Blessings and Peace be upon him).

"The believers are like one man if his head is in pain his whole body suffers and if his eye is in pain his whole body suffers." (Bukhāri)

Thus the organization must first be viewed as one unit consisting of many parts with each part supporting and complementing the other parts in the unit. If one exercises one leg

---

[22] Gibson et. Al. *"Organizations"* 5th ed., Business Publications Inc., Texas, (1985) p. 30.

[23] Stoner and Freedman, *"Management,"* 5th ed. Prentice Hall, N. Jersey, (1992) p. 31.

and not the other, he will end up limping. Similarly, working for one department in an organization and not the others would only reduce the effectiveness of the organization.

The second pillar of systems approach is to consider the organization as a part of a larger environment. In this respect, Muslims believe in the unity of mankind, and in the necessity of their interrelations. The Qur'an, addressed all mankind in many verses.

﴿يَـٰٓأَيُّهَا ٱلنَّاسُ إِنَّا خَلَقْنَـٰكُم مِّن ذَكَرٍ وَأُنثَىٰ وَجَعَلْنَـٰكُمْ شُعُوبًا وَقَبَآئِلَ لِتَعَارَفُوٓاْ إِنَّ أَكْرَمَكُمْ عِندَ ٱللَّهِ أَتْقَىٰكُمْ إِنَّ ٱللَّهَ عَلِيمٌ خَبِيرٌ ﴿١٣﴾﴾ (سورة الحجرات ٤٩: ١٣)

﴿O mankind! We created you from a single [pair] of a male and a female, and made you into nations and tribes, that you may know one another [not that you may despise one another]. Verily, the most honoured of you in the sight of Allah is [he who is] the most righteous of you and Allah has full knowledge and is well acquainted [with all things].﴾ (Qur'an 49: 13)

In the above verse, the Qur'an highlights the diversity of mankind. However, in such diversity is mercy and is not meant for people to be enemies but to know and understand one another.

The Qur'an also stresses the premise of diversity, and honours the dignity of all people regardless of their religion, race, or ethnicity.

﴿لَآ إِكْرَاهَ فِى ٱلدِّينِ ... ﴾ (سورة البقرة ٢: ٢٥٦)

﴿Let there be no compulsion in religion...﴾ (Qur'an 2: 256)

﴿وَلَقَدْ كَرَّمْنَا بَنِى ءَادَمَ وَحَمَلْنَٰهُمْ فِى ٱلْبَرِّ وَٱلْبَحْرِ وَرَزَقْنَٰهُم مِّنَ ٱلطَّيِّبَٰتِ
وَفَضَّلْنَٰهُمْ عَلَىٰ كَثِيرٍ مِّمَّنْ خَلَقْنَا تَفْضِيلًا ٧٠﴾ (سورة الإسراء ١٧ : ٧٠)

◈We have honoured the children of Ādam,
transported them in the land and in the sea, given
them for sustenance things · good and pure and
conferred on them special favours above a great part
of Our creatures.◈ (Qur'an 17: 70)

Muslims were being informed about their larger
environment even when they were very few oppressed people
in Makkah.

﴿غُلِبَتِ ٱلرُّومُ ١ فِىٓ أَدْنَى ٱلْأَرْضِ وَهُم مِّنۢ بَعْدِ غَلَبِهِمْ سَيَغْلِبُونَ ٣
فِى بِضْعِ سِنِينَ لِلَّهِ ٱلْأَمْرُ مِن قَبْلُ وَمِنۢ بَعْدُ وَيَوْمَئِذٍ يَفْرَحُ
ٱلْمُؤْمِنُونَ ٤﴾ (سورة الروم ٣٠ : ٢-٤)

◈The Roman Empire has been defeated. In a land close by:
But they after this defeat of theirs will soon be victorious.
Within a few years. With Allah is the decision in the past
and in the future: On that day shall the believers rejoice.◈
(Qur'an 30: 2-4)

In Islam, the larger system encompasses the whole world
and is extended to the Hereafter. Muslims are considered as a
system whose mission is the worship and are the vicegerents of
Allah, whose objective is to enter Paradise and avoid Hell. This
system should consider its environment and deal with it in a
manner consistent with the guidance of Allah and the general
objective of creation. Muslim tribes or groups (which can be
considered as countries in today's terminology) were considered

as subsystems that could have their agenda in their regional and international environments provided that this agenda was in accordance with the general mission and objective of Islam. Further, businesses and families were considered as sub-subsystems that had their own cultural, political, technological, and economic environments. The operation of every unit within the system should exercise a feedback process within its greater environment and with its general mission, objective, and goals.

The functions of the various units and sub-units of a system should also be coherent and consistent with one another. System coherence is very well manifested in the teachings of Islam where the theology provides the will and the general direction, and the jurisprudence provides the practical implementation. In Islam, the educational, social, moral, economic, political and legal systems function as a whole, and no one can be applied without the other.

Full Integration

If we carefully investigate the teachings of Islam, we find that they make an indivisible package each teaching supporting and is supported by the other teachings. These teachings are interrelated horizontally, vertically, and diagonally. Allah, the Exalted, said:

$$﴿أَفَلَا يَتَدَبَّرُونَ ٱلْقُرْءَانَ وَلَوْ كَانَ مِنْ عِندِ غَيْرِ ٱللَّهِ لَوَجَدُوا۟ فِيهِ ٱخْتِلَـٰفًا كَثِيرًا ﴾$$

(٨٢) ﴿ (سورة النساء ٤ : ٨٢)

﴿Do they not reflect on the Qur'an? Had it been from other than Allah, they would surely have found therein much discrepancy.﴾ (Qur'an 4: 82)

The following example elucidates the full integration of the teachings of Islam. In order to preserve a decent (or conservative) social life, Islam prohibited Muslims from committing adultery, but did not stop at this point. In fact, Islam taught Muslims how to reach that goal. Islam asked every Muslim not to be with a person of the opposite sex in isolation. Muslims were also asked to lower their gaze, and to dress decently. Islam also encouraged marriage. On the other hand, Muslims are supposed to lead a moral life, by praying, fasting, giving charity, and reading the Qur'an. In addition, they are required to be educated about these issues. If they still commit adultery after these prerequisites are satisfied, they would be severely punished. This simple example shows how closely integrated the teachings of Islam are. Goals with no clear sequential dependence such as praying, getting married, and avoiding adultery are still supportive of one another, besides their pooled contribution to the higher objective of Islam. A schematic representation of this concept is illustrated in figure 3.

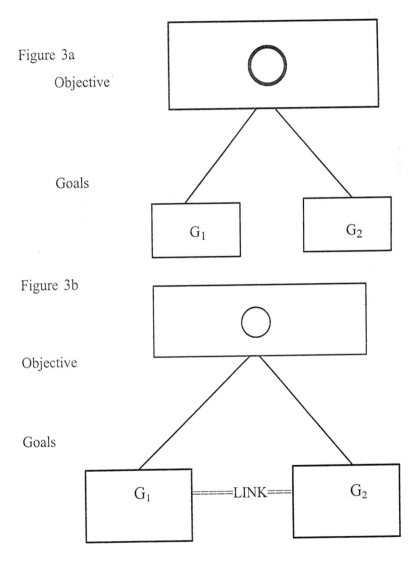

Figure 3a

　Objective

Goals

G_1　　　　G_2

Figure 3b

Objective

Goals

G_1　=====LINK===　G_2

Figure 3. Parallel Goals' Mutual Support

In figure 3a, we see two parallel goals that have a pooled contribution to the higher objective. Figure 3b reproduces the same components of figure 3a, but it also includes a link of mutual support between the two parallel goals.

The example of avoiding adultery is not the only one that can show the integration of the Islamic teaching. Indeed we can reproduce the same argument using any of the Islamic teachings. Another example is the prohibition of stealing. Islam prohibits stealing and in order to implement this prohibition, it first made it the responsibility of the state to ensure that all its residents are assured of the basic necessities of life. People need to be educated about their rights and the rights of others. The pillars of Islam do not protect people from the achievement of such responsibility, anyone who steals will be punished by cutting his or her wrist. This punishment may seem harsh but let us look at its objective. The objective of this rule of law is to preserve the property of the people, which is among the five elements of life, by stopping people from stealing. Furthermore, it ensures honesty and thus justice, that are among the goals of Islam.

The full integration of the various parts of the human body leads to best performance. Running fast requires the whole body to engage in facilitating this exercise and not just the feet. We cannot imagine a sprinter winning a race by putting his hands behind or on his head. The arm movement is almost as important as the leg movement. Organizational action programmes should be supportive of one another to achieve higher effectiveness.

Planning in the teachings of Islam can be visualized as a structure that has to fit within a certain neighbourhood in a certain city in a certain country. The structure has to be designed for a certain weather (including temperature, rain, snow, and wind), certain geological conditions, and certain regulations. Similarly,

Islamic planning accounts for interrelations with both the immediate and general environment of Muslims.

Further, the plan of Islam, or the teaching of Islam, consists of different work packages to be implemented in a certain sequence. Like a physical structure, the plan is supposed to have some pillars without which it cannot stand. The plan must also have some beams that rest on the pillars but that also connect them together, help support the roof, and therefore, strengthen the stability of the pillars themselves. The plan also includes some intermediate goals, which are analogous to joists in a physical structure.

The plan should also have diagonal bracing members to account for possible pressures from environment. The connections between the various work packages of the plan should make them support one another in such manner that they act as one unit. The plan's shape can be visualized as a pyramid (see figure. 4 below, The Integration of the teachings of Islam) or an inverted cone.

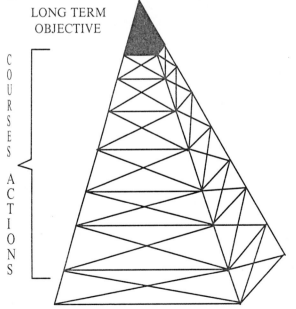

LONG TERM
OBJECTIVE

C
O
U
R
S
E
S

A
C
T
I
O
N
S

The teachings of Islam also specify certain actions that shall never be taken. These actions can be considered as rigid constraints, and can be outlined in the policies of an organization. The rigid constraints are similar to some design errors that could hinder the stability of the structure. This planning concept encompasses the three dimensions of space besides the time dimension. Modern organizations should try to emulate this multidimensional planning concept in order to achieve better effectiveness.

Besides the use of systems approach, Muslims generally adopted a gradual approach in pursuing their goals.

Exercises

1. Outline the pillars of a systems approach and discuss with an illustration, how the pillars are related.

2. How can planning in the teachings of Islam be viewed? Explain.

3. Describe the notion of flexibility in Islam.

PLAN FLEXIBILITY

The teachings of Islam provide a high degree of flexibility and freedom. This allows Muslims to effectively adopt to evolving situations.

Indeed in the teachings of Islam, one sees a great degree of flexibility in the sense that Islam does not give us specific orders that people have to follow in every aspect of their lives.

The verses of *aḥkam* (ordainments) in the Qur'an are only five hundred according to Imam al-Ghazali. Other authors such as Aṣ-Ṣābouni in his book *Badae'u al-Bayān fī tafsiri āyātul aḥkām*,[24] included less than three hundred verses. An investigation of the verses included in this book resulted in the following classification:

❑ Noxiants

❑ Noxiants Related

❑ *'Aqīdah*

❑ *Sha'āer*

❑ *Akhlāq*

❑ Etiquette

❑ Etiquette Related

❑ *Ebahah*

---

[24] Ṣābūni, M. *"Badae'u al-Bayān fī tafsiri āyātul aḥkām,"* Dār-ul Qur'an al-Karīm, Beirut.

Noxiants refer to verses that ask us to avoid doing things while noxiant related refer the outcomes of undertaking the noxiants. Anyone familiar with the verses of noxiants or *ḥarām* knows that these verses aim at preserving *Akhlāq*, deals with issues related the belief in Allah which can also be considered as *Akhlāq with Allah*. *Sha'āer* refers to the pillars of Islam which, as explained in part I, aim at improving and maintaining good manners. On the other hand *akhlāq* refers to general values such as forgiveness and generosity. Etiquette deals with certain manners to be adapted in certain situations, while etiquette related refers to the outcome of violating the etiquette. Finally the *Ebahah* verses clarify that certain practices, that might have been presumed unlawful to be lawful. The above classification shows that the verses of *Aḥkām* can be considered as verses of *Akhlāq*.

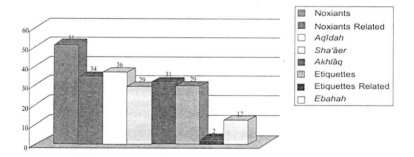

Figure 5. Verses of *Aḥkām*

Finding the number of verses in each category and putting them in a bar charter gives us the figure above.

If we do not consider the verses pertaining to *sha'āer* and *'aqīdah* and further combine the noxiants and the noxiants related, the etiquette and the etiquette related, we find the following figure:

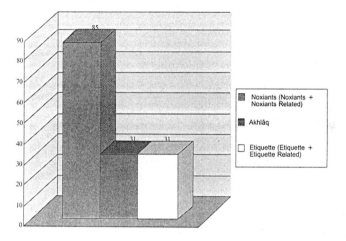

Figure 6. Noxiants, *Akhlāq* and Etiquette

The above figure shows that, aside from *'aqīdah* and *sha'āer*, the verses of *aḥkām* are basically dealing with noxiants, *akhlāq* and etiquette. We have to note, however, that the noxiant are basically dealing with *akhlāq* while the etiquette is basically a specific *akhlāq*. This can lead us to conclude that the verses of *aḥkam* are basically verses of *akhlāq* and that the majority of these verses are written in the for of nixiants. We can think of the teachings of Islam in terms of the noxiants/*akhlāq* model where everything we do is rewarded by Allah so long as it is done for His sake and without going through the noxiants or violating our Islamic *akhlāq*. This model reflects the flexibility of the teachings of Islam that we should try to emulate in our plans. Telling a person to avoid certain actions gives much more freedom than ordering him to perform certain activities. This model provides us with a floor

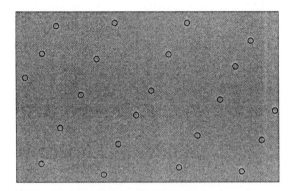

Figure 7. Noxiants/*Akhlāq* Model

    rather than a ceiling. It widens our horizon and allows us to think freely and be more innovative and creative. The green space is huge and the red is limited.

    In the Figure 7, the noxiant/*akhlāq* model is presented. The noxiants are represented by the darker dots.

    As opposed to the flexible noxiant/*akhlāq* model, the above mechanistic model depicts a situation of inflexibility whereby a person is allowed to act only in the dotted area while avoiding the darker space.

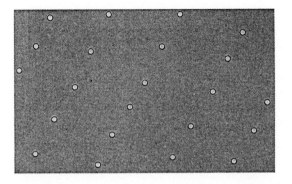

Figure 8. Mechanistic or Specific Order Model

Exercises

1. Describe the noxiants/*akhlāq* model.

2. How does the noxiants/*akhlāq* model reflect the flexibility of the teachings of Islam?

GRADUALISM

Gradualism is a very important Islamic Concept. Indeed the Qur'an was not revealed all at once, rather it was revealed progressively over a period of 23 years, according to people's needs and capabilities. The most illustrative example of gradualism in Islam can be found in the prohibition of alcohol drinking, which was done in three steps as illustrated in the following verses:

In the first verse, the benefits or damages that may accrue from wine drinking, the prohibited behaviour, are stressed to the people concern.

﴿يَسْئَلُونَكَ عَنِ ٱلْخَمْرِ وَٱلْمَيْسِرِ قُلْ فِيهِمَآ إِثْمٌ كَبِيرٌ وَمَنَٰفِعُ لِلنَّاسِ وَإِثْمُهُمَآ أَكْبَرُ مِن نَّفْعِهِمَا ... ﴿٢١٩﴾﴾ (سورة البقرة ٢: ٢١٩)

﴿They ask you about wine and gambling say: In them is great sin and some benefit for men and their sin is greater than their benefit...﴾ (Qur'an 2: 219)

Then the importance of consciousness in prayers is stressed and Muslims were asked not to approach prayer while drunk. This limits the time available for drinking.

﴿يَٰٓأَيُّهَا ٱلَّذِينَ ءَامَنُوا۟ لَا تَقْرَبُوا۟ ٱلصَّلَوٰةَ وَأَنتُمْ سُكَٰرَىٰ حَتَّىٰ تَعْلَمُوا۟ مَا تَقُولُونَ ... ﴿٤٣﴾﴾ (سورة النساء ٤: ٤٣)

﴿O you who believe! Approach not prayers while drunk

until you can understand all that you say...⟩ (Qur'an 4: 43)

Then follows the final prohibition.

﴿يَٰٓأَيُّهَا ٱلَّذِينَ ءَامَنُوٓا۟ إِنَّمَا ٱلْخَمْرُ وَٱلْمَيْسِرُ وَٱلْأَنصَابُ وَٱلْأَزْلَٰمُ رِجْسٌ مِّنْ عَمَلِ ٱلشَّيْطَٰنِ فَٱجْتَنِبُوهُ لَعَلَّكُمْ تُفْلِحُونَ ﴾ (سورة المائدة ٥ : ٩٠)

﴿O you who believe! Intoxication and gambling, [dedication of] stones, and [divination by] arrows are abomination — of Satan's handiwork; eschew such [abomination] that you might be successful.﴾ (Qur'an 5: 90)

Given the dynamic nature of the environment that organizations operate, they are sometimes faced with the need to alter certain norms of behaviour. If such a need arise, it is better that the organization first inform its people the benefits and harmful effect of the norm prohibited. After this awareness has been inculcated in the people, then they can finally prohibit the norm.

Prophet Muhammad (Blessings and Peace be upon him) had ordained Muslims to practice their religion in a gradual manner. Prophet Muhammad (bpuh) said:

"This religion is strong, so deal with it delicately and nicely." (Aḥmad)

Gradualism was also very clear in the call for Islam in Makkah. Makkah is the city of the Ka'bah, which was built as a centre of worship by Prophet Abraham and his son Ishmael (May Allah's peace be upon them all). Even though their ancestors were the followers of Abraham and Ishmael, the residents of Makkah were worshipping idols at the beginning of revelation. However, the Makkans also believed in a higher God. They pretended that the idols would help them and intercede for them with God. This is seen in the following verse.

$$﴿ ... وَٱلَّذِينَ ٱتَّخَذُواْ مِن دُونِهِۦٓ أَوْلِيَآءَ مَا نَعْبُدُهُمْ إِلَّا لِيُقَرِّبُونَآ إِلَى ٱللَّهِ زُلْفَىٰٓ ... ٣ ﴾ (سورة الزمر ٣٩ : ٣)$$

◈...But those who take for protectors others than Allah [say]: We only worship them in order that they bring us nearer to Allah...◈ (Qur'an 39: 3)

The idols worshipped in Makkah were Ḥubal, Naila, Laat, and 'Uzza. The Arabs of Makkah were so committed to idols that every family had one at home. They also used to caress the idols before and after any trip hoping to get their blessings.[25] Further, idol worshipping was an integral part of the Makkan order which was, even then, a site of pilgrimage. Makkah had a tribal society and only certain leading tribes were responsible for making arrangements for the pilgrimage and for taking care of the idols.

Allah, the Exalted, sent the message of Islam through Muhammad (Blessings and Peace be upon him) to all mankind. Islam was not confined to his family nor was it confined to Makkah. Islam is a religion for all humanity as is evident in the following verses (*āyāt*).

$$﴿وَمَآ أَرْسَلْنَٰكَ إِلَّا كَآفَّةً لِّلنَّاسِ بَشِيرًا وَنَذِيرًا وَلَٰكِنَّ أَكْثَرَ ٱلنَّاسِ لَا يَعْلَمُونَ ٢٨ ﴾ (سورة سبإ ٣٤ : ٢٨)$$

◈We have not sent you [O Muhammad] but as a universal messenger to mankind, giving them glad tidings and

---

[25] Al-Banna, F.A., *"Planning in the field of Islamic Administration,"* Cairo, (1985) p. 113.

warning them [against sin] but most people understand not.❩ (Qur'an 34: 28)

﴿قُلْ يَٰٓأَيُّهَا ٱلنَّاسُ إِنِّى رَسُولُ ٱللَّهِ إِلَيْكُمْ جَمِيعًا...﴾ ﴿١٥٨﴾

(سورة الأعراف ٧ : ١٥٨)

❨Say: O mankind! I am sent to you all as a Messenger of Allah.❩ (Qur'an 7: 158)

﴿وَمَآ أَرْسَلْنَٰكَ إِلَّا رَحْمَةً لِّلْعَٰلَمِينَ﴾ ﴿١٠٧﴾ (سورة الأنبياء ٢١ : ١٠٧)

❨We have sent you not, but as a mercy for all creatures.❩ (Qur'an 21: 107)

Farnas al-Banna[26] explained that Makkah was a suitable place for a universal religion because it has been the destination of the pilgrims from different parts of the world since the building of Ka'bah by Abraham and his son Ismael (May Allah's peace be upon them).

In spite of the universality of Islam, Prophet Muhammad (Blessings and Peace be upon him) followed a staged strategy. He was first very selective in choosing whom to preach this new religion among his people. This period of highly selective preaching was denoted as the period of discrete preaching. The only people that the Prophet (bpuh) called to Islam were the ones he trusted the most among his family and friends.

The period of discrete preaching lasted about three years[27] during which time a limited number of people accepted the new

---

[26] Al-Banna, F.A., *"Planning in the field of Islamic Administration,"* Cairo, (1985) p. 115.

[27] Ibn Hisham, *"The Prophetic Bibliography,"* Vol. 1, p. 169.

religion. The first woman to accept Islam was Khadija bint Khuwaylid, the wife of the Prophet (bpuh), and the first man was Abu Bakr, the friend of the Prophet (bpuh), and the first child was 'Ali, the young cousin of the Prophet (bpuh). The first converts went on in their turn to convey the message of Islam to the people they trusted. Abu Bakr, for example, was able to convert a good number of his close friends such as Uthmān ibn Affān who later became the third successor of the Prophet (bpuh), Az-Zubayr ibn al-Awwam, 'Abdur-Raḥmān ibn 'Awf, Sa'ad ibn Abi Waqās, and Ṭalḥa ibn 'Ubaydullah. This stage of preaching was required before the Muslims can be able to call for their religion in a public manner. Using a discrete method neutralized group pressure and gave the preached individuals a chance to make an independent and rational decision. In fact, some scholars of organizational behaviour sometimes advise people to form coalition before they present their ideas in a meeting.

The second stage of preaching was that of public preaching.

$$\text{﴿فَٱصْدَعْ بِمَا تُؤْمَرُ وَأَعْرِضْ عَنِ ٱلْمُشْرِكِينَ ﴾}\quad \text{(سورة الحجر ١٥ : ٩٤)}$$

﴿Therefore expound openly what you are commanded, and turn away from those who join false gods with Allah.﴾ (Qur'an 15: 94)

This stage, in turn, started with a relatively smaller group composed of the relatives of the Prophet (bpuh).

$$\text{﴿وَأَنذِرْ عَشِيرَتَكَ ٱلْأَقْرَبِينَ ﴾}\quad \text{(سورة الشعراء ٢٦ : ٢١٤)}$$

﴿And admonish your nearest Kinsmen.﴾ (Qur'an 26: 214)

This stage was necessary in the preaching process, for discrete preaching is selective and will not reach everybody. The problem is that this period is dangerous because the leading pagans of Quraysh were not to allow this religion to spread out. The beginning of this period resulted in the defamation, torture, and even killings of Muslim men and women. However, the Muslims, who knew fully well that this stage of public preaching was necessary, persisted and persevered. They kept calling to their religion with wisdom and by setting a good example. They endured all the hardships that they were subjected to, and they never responded to any provocation. Their determination won them new converts and many sympathizers. As the suppression of Muslims increased further, Prophet Muhammad (Blessings and Peace be upon him) recommended that some of his oppressed followers migrate to Abyssinia whose leader was known for his fairness and justice. The Prophet (bpuh) and the bulk of his Companions stayed in Makkah where they were subjected to further hardships. The leaders of Quraysh imposed a rigid trade embargo on the Companions of the Prophet and his family for three years. During these years, Muslims underwent some of their toughest times. They had no food to eat whatsoever. They resorted to eating whatever little grass they could find. Further, both the uncle of the Prophet, Abu Ṭālib, who was a great supporter of him, and his wife Khadija, who was the first to believe in him, passed away during these years. This embargo was finally lifted as a number of people in Quraysh felt very sorry for their Muslim friends and relatives and agreed to lift the embargo against the will of some leaders of Quraysh.

After the Prophet (Blessings and Peace be upon him) exhausted this stage by fully conveying his message publicly to all the people of Makkah in a peaceful manner and after a prolonged hardship and restraint, the Prophet (bpuh) started to seek refuge in another town that could be a more fertile ground for his message.

In the tenth year of Islam, Prophet Muhammad (Blessings and Peace be upon him) went to the town of Ṭaif, which is located between Makkah and Madīnah hoping to find a new centre for his call. However, the leaders of Ṭaif rejected him and ordered their slaves and children to slander him and to beat him. Prophet Muhammad (bpuh) returned from his trip with bleeding feet. But this did not discourage him from further seeking the cooperation of other people from other towns. The Prophet (bpuh) continued to call upon the pilgrims who came to Makkah from different regions, and to ask them for support. These efforts were concluded when a group of leaders of yathrib, later named Madīnah after the Prophet (bpuh) migrated to, believed in him and agreed to support him. Then, they went home to call for this new religion. One year later, a delegation from Madīnah gave its allegiance to the Prophet (bpuh). This was the turning point in the Islamic history which paved the way for the migration of the Prophet (bpuh) to Madīnah and the establishment of the first Islamic state, which used a gradual development approach also.

It is very important to note that, while gradualism is an important Islamic concept, it was not applied in every single case. For example, there was no gradualism in the prohibition and rejection of *Shirk*, which is associating partners with Allah. Gradualism is a function of the needs and capabilities of the people. Therefore, if there is a strong need for certain measures, and people are capable of undertaking these measures immediately, there is no need for a gradual approach. Nevertheless, gradualism is generally wise as stated by Athey[28] in his book "Systematic System Approach."

---

[28] Athey, T., *"Systematic System Approach,"* Prentice Hall, N. Jersey, p. 71.

In addition to pursuing a gradual plan of action, Islam also teaches Muslims to prepare contingency plans. Contingency planning as illustrated in the Qur'an is presented in the following chapter.

Exercises

1. Give examples of the concept of gradualism from the Qur'an and Sunnah.

2. Gradualism is a function of the needs and capability of the people. Explain!

CONTINGENCY PLANNING

No one can precisely predict the future. Therefore, no matter how good our forecasting methods are, it is imperative that we plan for alternative events or for uncertainties. Further, even if our forecast is correct, our plan might not be fully feasible, therefore, we have to always prepare alternative plans or have the necessary skills and organizational infrastructure to adjust to different situations. The best way to manage uncertainty is probably by a combination of both. Organizations should be learning ones. This would give them the capability for adaptability and making the best out of every situation. This means that they should not develop specific plans for every activity, division or department. For cases requiring specific plans, contingency plans must also be prepared. The teachings of Islam consist generally of general principles and noxiants thus allowing great flexibility. There are cases however, where Islam gives specific commands as in the case of the rituals of Islam. In this case nevertheless, Islam provided contingent set of actions, which we call contingency planning at the operational level.

Because Islam declares itself as a religion for all the people and for all the times, it has to be a religion that can adjust to different events and situations. Part of this adjustment is achieved through contingency planning, or planning for different scenarios. This can be illustrated at its operational level by the following verses of the Qur'an:

﴿شَهْرُ رَمَضَانَ ٱلَّذِىٓ أُنزِلَ فِيهِ ٱلْقُرْءَانُ هُدًى لِّلنَّاسِ وَبَيِّنَٰتٍ مِّنَ ٱلْهُدَىٰ وَٱلْفُرْقَانِ فَمَن شَهِدَ مِنكُمُ ٱلشَّهْرَ فَلْيَصُمْهُ وَمَن كَانَ مَرِيضًا أَوْ عَلَىٰ سَفَرٍ فَعِدَّةٌ مِّنْ أَيَّامٍ أُخَرَ يُرِيدُ ٱللَّهُ بِكُمُ ٱلْيُسْرَ وَلَا يُرِيدُ بِكُمُ ٱلْعُسْرَ وَلِتُكْمِلُوا۟... ﴾ (سورة البقرة ٢: ١٨٥)

﴿Ramaḍān is [the month] in which was sent down the
Qur'an, as a guidance to mankind, also clear [signs] for
guidance and judgment [between right and wrong] so
everyone of you who witnesses this month should fast it.
But if anyone is ill, or on a journey, the prescribed period
[should be made up] by days later. Allah intends every
facility for you. He does not want to put you to
difficulties...﴾ (Qur'an 2: 185)

The above verse contains a conditional statement (IF)
whereby sick and traveling people have the permission not to fast
and to make up for the miss days later.

Another operational level of contingency planning in Islam
is the provision made for the Ḥajj or pilgrimage and 'Umrah
(visit) to Makkah. The following verse elucidates this.

﴿وَأَتِمُّوا۟ ٱلْحَجَّ وَٱلْعُمْرَةَ لِلَّهِ فَإِنْ أُحْصِرْتُمْ فَمَا ٱسْتَيْسَرَ مِنَ ٱلْهَدْىِ وَلَا تَحْلِقُوا۟ رُءُوسَكُمْ حَتَّىٰ يَبْلُغَ ٱلْهَدْىُ مَحِلَّهُ فَمَن كَانَ مِنكُم مَّرِيضًا أَوْ بِهِۦٓ أَذًى مِّن رَّأْسِهِۦ فَفِدْيَةٌ مِّن صِيَامٍ أَوْ صَدَقَةٍ أَوْ نُسُكٍ فَإِذَآ أَمِنتُمْ فَمَن تَمَتَّعَ بِٱلْعُمْرَةِ إِلَى ٱلْحَجِّ فَمَا ٱسْتَيْسَرَ مِنَ ٱلْهَدْىِ فَمَن لَّمْ يَجِدْ فَصِيَامُ ثَلَٰثَةِ أَيَّامٍ فِى ٱلْحَجِّ وَسَبْعَةٍ إِذَا رَجَعْتُمْ تِلْكَ عَشَرَةٌ كَامِلَةٌ ذَٰلِكَ لِمَن لَّمْ يَكُنْ أَهْلُهُ حَاضِرِى ٱلْمَسْجِدِ ٱلْحَرَامِ وَٱتَّقُوا۟ ٱللَّهَ وَٱعْلَمُوٓا۟ أَنَّ ٱللَّهَ شَدِيدُ ٱلْعِقَابِ ﴾ (سورة البقرة ٢: ١٩٦)

❃And complete the Ḥajj or 'Umrah for Allah. **But if** you are prevented [from completing it], send an offering for sacrifice, such as you may find. And do not shave your heads until the offering reaches the place of sacrifice. **And if** any of you is ill, or has an ailment in his scalp, [necessitating shaving] He should in compensation either fast, or offer *ṣadaqah*, or offer sacrifice; and when you are in peaceful conditions. **If** anyone wishes to continue the 'Umrah on to the Ḥajj, he must make an offering of sacrifice such as he can afford **but if** he cannot afford he should fast three days during Ḥajj and seven days on his return, making them ten days in all. **This is for those** whose household is not [in the precincts of] the sacred Mosque, and fear Allah and know that Allah is strict in punishment.❃ (Qur'an 2: 196)

The above verse contains five contingency statements.

1) Those people who are unable to complete their Ḥajj or 'Umrah are permitted to offer a sacrifice.

2) Those who are sick or have head injuries making shaving their heads necessary, are required to fast, offer *ṣadaqah* or offer sacrifice.

3) Those who cannot afford to offer sacrifice are asked to fast three days during Ḥajj.

4) Those who wish to continue their Ḥajj or 'Umrah during the time of peace should offer sacrifices in accordance to what they can afford.

5) For those who live away from the Sacred Mosque, they are to fast seven says extra when they return home.

Another example of operational contingency planning in Islam is in the area of transactions (contracts):

﴿يَـٰٓأَيُّهَا ٱلَّذِينَ ءَامَنُوٓاْ إِذَا تَدَايَنتُم بِدَيۡنٍ إِلَىٰٓ أَجَلٍ مُّسَمًّى فَٱكۡتُبُوهُۚ وَلۡيَكۡتُب بَّيۡنَكُمۡ كَاتِبٌۢ بِٱلۡعَدۡلِۚ وَلَا يَأۡبَ كَاتِبٌ أَن يَكۡتُبَ كَمَا عَلَّمَهُ ٱللَّهُۚ فَلۡيَكۡتُبۡ وَلۡيُمۡلِلِ ٱلَّذِي عَلَيۡهِ ٱلۡحَقُّ وَلۡيَتَّقِ ٱللَّهَ رَبَّهُۥ وَلَا يَبۡخَسۡ مِنۡهُ شَيۡـًٔاۚ فَإِن كَانَ ٱلَّذِي عَلَيۡهِ ٱلۡحَقُّ سَفِيهًا أَوۡ ضَعِيفًا أَوۡ لَا يَسۡتَطِيعُ أَن يُمِلَّ هُوَ فَلۡيُمۡلِلۡ وَلِيُّهُۥ بِٱلۡعَدۡلِۚ وَٱسۡتَشۡهِدُواْ شَهِيدَيۡنِ مِن رِّجَالِكُمۡۖ فَإِن لَّمۡ يَكُونَا رَجُلَيۡنِ فَرَجُلٌ وَٱمۡرَأَتَانِ مِمَّن تَرۡضَوۡنَ مِنَ ٱلشُّهَدَآءِ أَن تَضِلَّ إِحۡدَىٰهُمَا فَتُذَكِّرَ إِحۡدَىٰهُمَا ٱلۡأُخۡرَىٰۚ وَلَا...﴿٢٨٢﴾ (سورة البقرة ٢: ٢٨٢)

﴿O you who believe! **When** you deal with each other, in transactions involving future obligation in a fixed period of time, reduce them to writing. Let a scribe write down faithfully as between the parties; let not the scribe refuse to write: as Allah has taught him, so let him write. Let him who incurs the liability dictate, but let him fear his Lord Allah and not diminish aught of what he owes. **If** the party liable is mentally deficient, weak, or **if** he were not able to dictate, let his guardian dictate faithfully. And get two witnesses out of your own men. And **if** there are not two men, then a man and two women such as you choose, for witnesses so that if one of them errs, the other can remind her...﴿ (Qur'an 2: 282)

The above verse contains four conditional statements.

1) Transactions resulting into future obligations should be written.

2) The debtor should dictate and if he is mentally unstable, his guardian should dictate.

3) If the debtor is unable to dictate the terms of the contract for other reasons than above, his guardian should dictate.

4) Two men are required to witness the transaction other-wise, a man and two women will suffice.

$$﴿وَإِن كُنتُمْ عَلَىٰ سَفَرٍ وَلَمْ تَجِدُواْ كَاتِبًا فَرِهَٰنٌ مَّقْبُوضَةٌ ۖ فَإِنْ أَمِنَ بَعْضُكُم بَعْضًا فَلْيُؤَدِّ ٱلَّذِى ٱؤْتُمِنَ أَمَٰنَتَهُۥ وَلْيَتَّقِ ٱللَّهَ رَبَّهُۥ ... ﴿٢٨٣﴾ ﴾$$

(سورة البقرة ٢ : ٢٨٣)

﴾If you are on a journey, and cannot find a scribe, a pledge with possession [may serve the purpose]. **And if** one of you deposits a thing on a trust with another, let the trustee [faithfully] discharge his trust, and let him fear his Lord...﴾ (Qur'an 2: 283)

The two conditional statements contained in the above verse relate to the previous verses.

1) Should in case there is no writer on the journey to write the transaction, a possession should be pledge.

2) The one to whom the pledge is given should discharge his trust faithfully.

In the verse below, Allah, the All-High, All-Merciful, makes provision for a believing man who killed another believer by mistake:

$$﴿وَمَا كَانَ لِمُؤْمِنٍ أَن يَقْتُلَ مُؤْمِنًا إِلَّا خَطَـًٔا ۚ وَمَن قَتَلَ مُؤْمِنًا خَطَـًٔا فَتَحْرِيرُ رَقَبَةٍ مُّؤْمِنَةٍ وَدِيَةٌ مُّسَلَّمَةٌ إِلَىٰٓ أَهْلِهِۦٓ إِلَّآ أَن يَصَّدَّقُواْ ۚ فَإِن كَانَ مِن قَوْمٍ عَدُوٍّ لَّكُمْ وَهُوَ مُؤْمِنٌ فَتَحْرِيرُ رَقَبَةٍ مُّؤْمِنَةٍ ۖ وَإِن كَانَ مِن قَوْمٍ بَيْنَكُمْ وَبَيْنَهُم مِّيثَٰقٌ فَدِيَةٌ مُّسَلَّمَةٌ إِلَىٰٓ أَهْلِهِۦ$$

وَتَحْرِيرُ رَقَبَةٍ مُّؤْمِنَةٍ فَمَن لَّمْ يَجِدْ فَصِيَامُ شَهْرَيْنِ مُتَتَابِعَيْنِ
تَوْبَةً مِّنَ ٱللَّهِ وَكَانَ ٱللَّهُ عَلِيمًا حَكِيمًا ﴿٩٢﴾

(سورة النساء ٤ : ٩٢)

⟨Never should a believer kill a believer; but [if it so happens] by mistake, [compensation is due]; if one [so] kills a believer, it is ordained that he should free a believing slave, and pay compensation to the deceased's family, unless they remit it freely. **If** the deceased belonged to a people at war with you, and he was a believer, the freeing of a believing slave [is enough]. **If** he belonged to a people with whom you have a treaty of mutual alliance, compensation should be paid to his family, and a believing slave be freed. **For those** who find this beyond their means, [is prescribed] a fast for two consecutive months by way of repentance to Allah; for Allah has all knowledge and wisdom.⟩ (Qur'an 4: 92)

In general, a believer must not kill another believer. If he does, he will be killed. However, it is possible that a believer might kill another by mistake. If this should happen, instead of being killed, many provisions have been made according to the situation between the tribes of the killer and that of the deceased.

1) The killer is required to free a believing slave and pay compensation to the deceased family according to the general rule. However, he is not obliged to compensate if the family waive it.

2) If the deceased is from a tribe at war with that of the killer, the freeing of a slave is sufficient compensation.

3) On the other hand, if the deceased is from a tribe that has an alliance with that of the killer, he is to compensate the deceased family and free a slave.

4) In case the killer is unable to do the above, he is required to fast for two consecutive months.

In order to achieve its specific goals, a successful organization shall have plans ready for all possible scenarios. Failure to have contingency plans can result in unexpected losses for a business. However, organizations have to make sure that their contingency plans are also conducive to their desired goals and consistent with their mission. Indeed, by reading the above verses, one can notice that the scopes of the teachings and their goal have not changed by accommodating contingent situations. Preparing contingency plans should not allow any deviation from the desired goal.

At the strategic level, contingency planning is manifested in the fact that the teachings of Islam provide guidelines in a variety of different situations that include norms and exceptions. Allah, the Almighty, said:

$$ \text{...وَنَزَّلْنَا عَلَيْكَ ٱلْكِتَٰبَ تِبْيَٰنًا لِّكُلِّ شَىْءٍ وَهُدًى وَرَحْمَةً وَبُشْرَىٰ لِلْمُسْلِمِينَ ﴿٨٩﴾} $$

(سورة النحل ١٦ : ٨٩)

◆...We have sent down to you a book explaining all things, a guide, a Mercy, and glad tidings to Muslims.◆ (Qur'an 16: 89)

Further, Islam called upon Muslims to prepare their utmost for different possible scenarios. Allah, the Exalted, said:

﴿وَأَعِدُّواْ لَهُم مَّا ٱسۡتَطَعۡتُم مِّن قُوَّةٖ وَمِن...﴾ ﴿٦٠﴾

(سورة الأنفال ٨ : ٦٠)

﴾And prepare for them your utmost of strength...﴿
(Qur'an 8: 60)

Preparing the utmost expressed in the above verse is continuous process for our utmost tomorrow should be higher that our utmost today. Since we are living in a more interdependent world, the effects of the external environment on a business are becoming increasingly significant, therefore, preparing contingency plans is becoming more needed. Further, the quick political development in many parts of the world, such as Eastern Europe, is providing businesses with possible new investment opportunities. These investment opportunities can be very profitable for companies that have prepared for such eventualities. Preparing contingency plans for various opportunities requires a sophisticated management information system, a multi-skilled workforce, and flexible production/operation system. These prerequisites can be called infrastructure.

A simple contingency planning model is shown in Figure 9 where a business has a certain objective, say profit maximization, which can be achieved through one or more of the possible goals or opportunities G1, G2, G3. Because the feasibility of these goals is contingent upon some environmental events or actions outside the control of the business, this latter does not know whether it will be able to pursue one or more of these goals. Awaiting such events to unravel, the business prepares the necessary actions that will lead to the achievement of these goals.

Objective

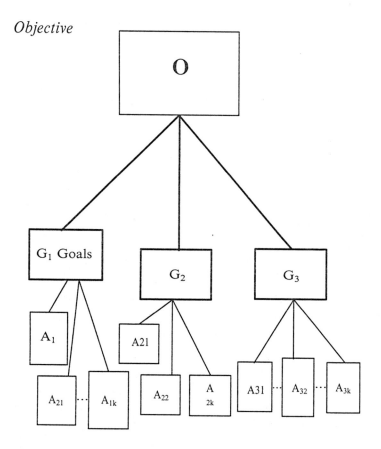

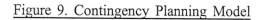
Figure 9. Contingency Planning Model

These actions are All through A1k for goal G1, A21 through A2k for goal G2 and A31 through A3k for goal G3. Whenever there is an opportunity to achieve any of the goals, the organization starts implementing its corresponding actions. Note that, in some cases, the goals could be possible threats rather than opportunities. Again, the ability to pursue the required actions depends on how versatile the skills of the workforce are, how effective the management information system is and how flexible the production/operation processes are.

Finally, it is important to note that future uncertainties can also be dealt with using a proactive approach. This approach is focused on shaping the environment. It necessitates aggressive marketing and advertising projects in order to influence demand, reducing dependence on highly changing environmental conditions, research and development, and lobbying.

After going through the above components of planning, the organization has to start implementing its plans. Many plans get canceled before their projected time horizon because the organization does not have the capability to endure some of the losses the plans might cause for a certain time. Continuity of the implementation is very important especially for new businesses. This concept is presented in the following chapter.

Exercises

1. Discuss the importance of contingency planning.

2. Give some verses in the Qur'an showing contingency planning.

IMPLEMENTATION

After developing their plans, managers should start the process of implementations. At this stage, resources are allocated and scheduled. The availability of the necessary skills and resources is indispensable for the implementation, which will be carried out through the organization structure.

The major question that should be asked at this stage is what could go wrong. In this chapter, we will attempt to discuss cases where the implementation of some plans gets canceled before their planned horizon. We will particularly focus on consistency and continuity in implementing long term plans.

1 - Consistency and Continuity

Short-term profits usually come at the expense of long-term profits. In the short-term companies profits can be earned by mortgaging the future.[29] Pearce stated[30]:

"A firm might be misguided into overlooking the enduring concerns of customers, suppliers, creditors, and regulatory agents. Such a strategy could be profitable in the short run, but over time its consequences are likely to be seriously detrimental."

---

[29] Bernard Taylor, *"An overview of Strategic Style,"* in Strategic and Management hand book, Edited by King and Cleland, (1987) p. 75,

[30] Pearce, J., A II, et. al *"The Company's mission as a guide to Strategic action"* in *Strategic Planning and Management hand book,* (1987) p. 73.

On the other hand, long-term success usually requires some sacrifices in the short term in order for a firm to have a larger market share, for example. It is therefore encouraged that organizations focus on long term benefits in their planning.

Once an organization adopts a long-term plan after clear consideration of its feasibility, and after a careful evaluation of other alternative plans, this organization has to start implementing this plan putting its trust in Allah. In many cases the implementation of such plans gets canceled before its projected time horizon. This is especially true for newly formed businesses that, even though planned for certain losses during the beginning of operation, would not be able to resist incurring them when they happen. This could be caused by extra financial strains incurred outside these businesses, or to the fact that the business could no longer maintain quality personnel at low salaries while most other businesses can afford to pay their personnel higher incomes. This can also be due to a lack of competence in the owners of the business and that they are able to talk the talk but not to walk the walk.

The premature cancellation of the plan is also a sign of the shortcomings of the plan itself because a good plan is one that considers the weakness and strength of the organization, and uses a system approach where the behaviours of all stakeholders within the immediate and general environments of the organization are clearly studied. The planning process shall also include all the members of the organization otherwise, it will be difficult to ask them to be patient in implementing a plan that they did not choose. The weakness of the leadership and its inability to motivate its followers could also cause the cancellation of certain plans. Finally the lack of *tawakkul* or trust in Allah (see chapter

Contingency Planning) could definitely be lethal to the organization.

1) Importance of patience during implementation

The implementation of a plan requires a lot of patience as some unforeseen circumstances may arise leading to frustration and even the abandoning of the plan. There are ample references to patience and perseverance in Islam. Indeed, Islam had asked Muslims to be steadfast, patient, and to help one another maintain patience while doing the righteous work.

﴿إِنَّ ٱلْإِنسَٰنَ لَفِى خُسْرٍ ۝ إِلَّا ٱلَّذِينَ ءَامَنُوا۟ وَعَمِلُوا۟ ٱلصَّٰلِحَٰتِ وَتَوَاصَوْا۟ بِٱلْحَقِّ وَتَوَاصَوْا۟ بِٱلصَّبْرِ ۝﴾ (سورة العصر ١٠٣: ٢-٣)

❅Verily man is in loss. Except such as have faith and do right deeds and join together in the mutual teaching of Truth, and of patience and constancy.❅ (Qur'an 103: 2-3)

2) Conditions for patience

Patience also depends on how much people have learned about the reward, and how much they have understood about the requirements of the plan being pursued.

3) Understanding the reward for patience

Understanding about things for which patience is required is an important condition for patience. This is evident in the following verse (*āyah*):

﴿وَكَيْفَ تَصْبِرُ عَلَى مَا لَمْ تُحِطْ بِهِ خُبْرًا ۝﴾ (سورة الكهف ١٨ : ٦٨)

❅And how can you have patience about things about which your understanding is not complete.❅ (Qur'an 18: 68)

4) Belief in the reward for patience

Further, patience does not only depend on how much people understand the expected reward, but also in how much they believe that they can really attain it. The verse below attest to this.

﴿فَاصْبِرْ إِنَّ وَعْدَ اللَّهِ حَقٌّ ... ۝﴾ (سورة غافر ٤٠ : ٥٥)

❅Patiently then persevere. For the promise of Allah is true...❅ (Qur'an 40: 55)

In another verse Allah, the All-High, All-Glorious, says:

﴿فَاصْبِرْ إِنَّ وَعْدَ اللَّهِ حَقٌّ وَاسْتَغْفِرْ ... ۝﴾ (سورة غافر ٤٠ : ٧٧)

❅So persevere in patience; for the promise of Allah is true...❅ (Qur'an 40: 77)

5) Patience as a condition for reward

In some verses of the Qur'an, some of which are presented below, Allah, the Exalted, has stated patience as a condition for reward. This can be seen as highlighting the importance of patience as well as the fact that it is very difficult to exhibit patience.

﴿سَلَامٌ عَلَيْكُمْ بِمَا صَبَرْتُمْ فَنِعْمَ عُقْبَى الدَّارِ ۝﴾ (سورة الرعد ١٣ : ٢٤)

❨Peace be unto you for that you have persevered in patience!
Now how excellent is the final home.❩ (Qur'an 13: 24)

The above verse shows that those who persevere in this
world with patience will be rewarded in the Hereafter with
excellent homes.

$$﴿... إِنَّمَا يُوَفَّى ٱلصَّٰبِرُونَ أَجْرَهُم بِغَيْرِ حِسَابٍ ۝ ﴾ (سورة الزمر ٣٩: ١٠)$$

❨...Those who patiently persevere will truly receive their
reward without measure.❩ (Qur'an 39: 10)

The above verse shows that the reward for the patient is
uncountable.

$$﴿وَقَالَ ٱلَّذِينَ أُوتُوا۟ ٱلْعِلْمَ وَيْلَكُمْ ثَوَابُ ٱللَّهِ خَيْرٌ لِّمَنْ ءَامَنَ وَعَمِلَ$$
$$صَٰلِحًا وَلَا يُلَقَّىٰهَآ إِلَّا ٱلصَّٰبِرُونَ ۝ ﴾ (سورة القصص ٢٨: ٨٠)$$

❨But those who have been granted [true] knowledge said:
Alas for you! The reward of Allah is best for those who
believe and work righteousness: But this none shall attain
except who steadfastly persevere [in good].❩
(Qur'an 28: 80)

The above verse shows that those who believe and do
righteous work will be rewarded however, one cannot achieve
these unless he patiently perseveres.

$$﴿وَمَا يُلَقَّىٰهَآ إِلَّا ٱلَّذِينَ صَبَرُوا۟ وَمَا يُلَقَّىٰهَآ إِلَّا ذُو حَظٍّ عَظِيمٍ ۝ ﴾$$
$$(سورة فصلت ٤١: ٣٥)$$

❨And none will be granted such goodness except those who
exercise patience and self-restraint, — None but persons of
the greatest good fortune.❩ (Qur'an 41: 35)

The above verse shows that those who are patient are those with the greatest good fortune.

6) Patience a competitive advantage

In a competitive environment, an organization that wishes for success should be able to exercise more patience than its competitors.

$$﴿يَـٰٓأَيُّهَا ٱلَّذِينَ ءَامَنُوا۟ ٱصْبِرُوا۟ وَصَابِرُوا۟ وَرَابِطُوا۟ وَٱتَّقُوا۟ ٱللَّهَ لَعَلَّكُمْ تُفْلِحُونَ ٢٠٠﴾ (سورة آل عمران ٣: ٢٠٠)$$

﴿O you who believe persevere in patience and constancy; in such perseverance; strengthen each other; and fear Allah that you may prosper.﴾ (Qur'an 3: 200)

Patience in an organization can be considered as a competitive advantage.

$$﴿٦٥ ... إِن يَكُن مِّنكُمْ عِشْرُونَ صَـٰبِرُونَ يَغْلِبُوا۟ مِا۟ئَتَيْنِ ... ﴾$$
$$(سورة الأنفال ٨: ٦٥)$$

﴿If there are twenty amongst you, patient and persevering, they will vanquish two hundred.﴾ (Qur'an 8: 65)

$$﴿ٱلْـَٔـٰنَ خَفَّفَ ٱللَّهُ عَنكُمْ وَعَلِمَ أَنَّ فِيكُمْ ضَعْفًا فَإِن يَكُن مِّنكُم مِّا۟ئَةٌ صَابِرَةٌ يَغْلِبُوا۟ مِا۟ئَتَيْنِ ... ٦٦﴾ (سورة الأنفال ٨: ٦٦)$$

﴿For the present, Allah has lightened your [task]. For He knows that there is a weak spot in you: But [even so] if there are a hundred of you patient and persevering, they will vanquish two hundred.﴾ (Qur'an 8: 66)

7) Requirement for patience and perseverance

Patience and perseverance are not easy to exercise. Indeed, they require a great degree of determination that is not possessed by everyone.

$$\text{﴾... وَإِن تَصْبِرُواْ وَتَتَّقُواْ فَإِنَّ ذَٰلِكَ مِنْ عَزْمِ ٱلْأُمُورِ ﴿١٨٦﴾}$$

(سورة آل عمران ٣: ١٨٦)

◆But if you persevere patiently, and guard against evil-then that will be a determining factor in all affairs.◆
(Qur'an 3: 186)

$$\text{﴾فَٱصْبِرْ كَمَا صَبَرَ أُوْلُواْ ٱلْعَزْمِ مِنَ ٱلرُّسُلِ... ﴿٣٥﴾}$$

(سورة الأحقاف ٤٦: ٣٥)

◆Therefore patiently persevere, as did the messengers of inflexible will;◆ (Qur'an 46: 35)

8) Feasibility, a prerequisite for patience

If it is determined that a certain strategy will result in burdens that an organization cannot endure, it will not make sense to adopt it, for both organizations and individuals shall only do what is within their capacities. This is true even in matters pertaining to the worship of Allah:

$$\text{﴾لَا يُكَلِّفُ ٱللَّهُ نَفْسًا إِلَّا وُسْعَهَا ... ﴿٢٨٦﴾}$$ (سورة البقرة ٢: ٢٨٦)

◆On no soul does Allah place a burden greater than it can bear...◆ (Qur'an 2: 286)

﴿فَٱتَّقُوا۟ ٱللَّهَ مَا ٱسْتَطَعْتُمْ...﴾ ﴿١٦﴾ (سورة التغابن ٦٤ : ١٦)

﴿So fear Allah as much as you can;...﴾ (Qur'an 64: 16)

It is certainly much better to progress slowly but steadily than to start a difficult undertaking that is not likely to last and succeed. Prophet Muhammad (Blessings and Peace be upon him) said:

> "The best deeds are the continuous ones even if they were small in size." (Ibn Mājah)

9) The relationship between patience and Tawakkul

Because the degree of patience depends on how much one believes in the reward and its feasibility, it has been closely related to the trust in Allah or *tawakkul*. This is elucidated in the following verses.

﴿... نِعْمَ أَجْرُ ٱلْعَٰمِلِينَ ﴿٥٨﴾ ٱلَّذِينَ صَبَرُوا۟ وَعَلَىٰ رَبِّهِمْ يَتَوَكَّلُونَ ﴿٥٩﴾﴾

(سورة العنكبوت ٢٩ : ٥٨-٥٩)

﴿...Aye:- an excellent reward for those who do [good]!- Those who persevere in patience and put their trust in their Lord.﴾ (Qur'an 29: 58-59)

﴿وَٱلَّذِينَ هَاجَرُوا۟ فِى ٱللَّهِ مِنۢ بَعْدِ مَا ظُلِمُوا۟ لَنُبَوِّئَنَّهُمْ فِى ٱلدُّنْيَا حَسَنَةً وَلَأَجْرُ ٱلْأَخِرَةِ أَكْبَرُ لَوْ كَانُوا۟ يَعْلَمُونَ ﴿٤١﴾ ٱلَّذِينَ صَبَرُوا۟ وَعَلَىٰ رَبِّهِمْ يَتَوَكَّلُونَ ﴿٤٢﴾﴾ (سورة النحل ١٦ : ٤١-٤٢)

❖To those who leave their homes in the cause of Allah, after suffering oppression, We will surely give a good home in this world; But the reward of the Hereafter will be greater. If they only realized [this]. [They are] those who persevere in patience and put their trust in Allah.❖ (Qur'an 16: 41-42)

10) Negative patience

It is very important however, to mention that some managers might abuse the concept of consistency and continuity in order to justify their inability to adapt to new environments. Many businesses are still using some very old technologies and processes, and are, thereby, losing market share and profit opportunities in the name of consistency. Without adaptiveness and development every business will face stagnation and ultimately obsolescence and bankruptcy. Further, if the planning of an ongoing project is determined to be defective, it will not make sense to further pursue it. Many businesses exhibit patience with the wrong projects, which prove to be detrimental in the long run. The Qur'an taught us that patience can be for the wrong goal, and thus it can lead to the greatest loss:

$$﴿وَٱنطَلَقَ ٱلْمَلَأُ مِنْهُمْ أَنِ ٱمْشُوا۟ وَٱصْبِرُوا۟ عَلَىٰٓ ءَالِهَتِكُمْ إِنَّ هَٰذَا لَشَىْءٌ يُرَادُ ۝﴾$$

(سورة ص ٣٨ : ٦)

❖And the leaders among them went on [saying]: "Walk you away, and remain patiently constant to your gods! For this is truly a thing designed [against you]."❖ (Qur'an 38: 6)

The perseverance, patience, and persistence of Prophet Muhammad (Blessings and Peace be upon him) and his Companions in pursuing a policy of restraint for thirteen years in Makkah are excellent examples of consistency and continuity. The Muslims successfully pursued a plan calling to Islam with wisdom and good manners in spite of the many severe provocations they were subjected to. These provocations included beating and killing quite a number of Muslims, boycotting Muslims economically for three years, and even the physical abuse towards the Prophet (Blessings and Peace be upon him) himself.

On the other hand, many seemingly bright and innovative plans adopted by many organizations failed because the latter could not persist in implementing them. The premature cancellation of plans is frequent with both large and small organizations. Smaller organizations usually cancel their plans because of financial restraints. On the other hand, large organizations cancel their plans because of the inability to adjust to some environmental changes. This is especially true in international operations. Some countries or trade blocks often cancel their plans because of their political inability to stand the pressures of some domestic or international interest groups.

The most unique concept in Islamic management is that of putting ones trust in Allah, or *tawakkul*. This concept is defined in the following chapter.

Exercises

1. Give two factors necessary for plan implementation.

2. Why do some plans get canceled before their time horizon?

3. Name three attributes mentioned in the Qur'an necessary in successful implementation of a plan.

4. What are the conditions for patience?

5. What are the Islamic indicators that patience is a competitive advantage?

TRUST IN GOD

After Muslims prepare alternative plans to achieve their desired goals, evaluate their plans, make a decision through consultation, and get engaged in the implementation process, they have to put their trust in Allah who is the only One Who will deliver the outcomes. Putting our trust in Allah is called *tawakkul*. Making *tawakkul* is a sign of belief in Allah. It is a sign of belief in the unseen that is controlled by Allah. Abu Sulaymān[31] said:

"*Tawakkul* is the reliance of the heart on, and its confidence in Allah. He added that *tawakkul* is the belief of the heart in the power, wisdom, and justice of Allah and that all ends are on His disposal."

This trust stems from the belief that Allah is the only One Who will deliver the outcomes. Putting one's trust in Allah or making *tawakkul* reflects the belief in Allah. Muslims make *tawakkul* believing that Allah is the Most Merciful, the Most Graceful, the Exalted in Might, the One with absolute knowledge, wisdom, and justice. *Tawakkul* gives Muslims a sense of optimism that can encourage them avoid excessive risk aversion.

---

[31] Pearce, J., A II, et. al "*The Company's mission as a guide to Strategic action*" in Strategic Planning and Management hand book, (1987) p. 73.

Tawakkul does not mean that one does not do what is necessary to achieve his/her goal and expects Allah to grant him/her success. *Tawakkul* comes after one does his/her best to achieve his/her goal. For example, suppose a student starts studying from the beginning of the semester. He goes to class on time and is always prepared before going to the class. He does all his assignments and projects. Worked hard for a good mid-term score. Then come final exams. He studies well in preparation, prays hard for success, answers the examination questions to the best of his ability and then he has *tawakkul* on Allah. For all outcomes rest on Allah. This is what is meant by *tawakkul*.

Muslims, make *tawakkul* knowing that Allah is the Most Merciful, the Most Graceful, the Exalted in Might, the One with absolute knowledge, wisdom, and justice. *Tawakkul*, thus, gives Muslims a sense of optimism and satisfaction.

1 - Tawakkul and Allah's Attributes

Tawakkul stems from the belief in Allah and His Attributes. This is evident in the following verses.

﴿وَتَوَكَّلْ عَلَى ٱلْعَزِيزِ ٱلرَّحِيمِ ۝﴾ (سورة الشعراء ٢٦ : ٢١٧)

﴿And put your trust on the Exalted in Might, the Merciful.﴾
(Qur'an 26: 217)

﴿... قُلْ إِنَّ ٱلْأَمْرَ كُلَّهُۥ لِلَّهِ ... ۝﴾ (سورة آل عمران ٣ : ١٥٤)

﴿...You say: Indeed this affair is wholly Allah's...﴾
(Qur'an 3: 154)

﴾... وَٱلشَّمْسَ وَٱلْقَمَرَ وَٱلنُّجُومَ مُسَخَّرَٰتٍ بِأَمْرِهِۦٓ أَلَا لَهُ ٱلْخَلْقُ وَٱلْأَمْرُ ... ﴿

(سورة الأعراف ٧: ٥٤)

﴾...And the sun, the moon and the stars [all] governed by laws under His command. Is it not His to create and to govern?...﴿ (Qur'an 7: 54)

﴾... وَلَا يُحِيطُونَ بِشَىْءٍ مِّنْ عِلْمِهِۦٓ إِلَّا بِمَا شَآءَ ... ﴿

(سورة البقرة ٢: ٢٥٥)

﴾Nor shall they compass aught of His knowledge except as He wills.﴿ (Qur'an 2: 255)

﴾... وَمَن يَتَوَكَّلْ عَلَى ٱللَّهِ فَإِنَّ ٱللَّهَ عَزِيزٌ حَكِيمٌ ﴿

(سورة الأنفال ٨: ٤٩)

﴾...If any trust in Allah, behold! Allah is Exalted in Might, Wise.﴿ (Qur'an 8: 49)

2 - Tawakkul a Condition for Reward

Allah ordained Muslims to make *tawakkul* and promised them reward for it. The following verses show this.

﴾... فَإِذَا عَزَمْتَ فَتَوَكَّلْ عَلَى ٱللَّهِ إِنَّ ٱللَّهَ يُحِبُّ ٱلْمُتَوَكِّلِينَ ﴿

(سورة آل عمران ٣: ١٥٩)

﴾...And when you are resolved, then put your trust in Allah. Lo! Allah loves those who put their trust [in Him].﴿ (Qur'an 3: 159)

The above *āyah* (verse) lends support to the above claim that *tawakkul* comes after and not before one strives to achieve ones goal. Organizations must first do everything within their means to achieve their goals and then put their trust in Allah.

$$﴿... وَمَا عِندَ ٱللَّهِ خَيْرٌ وَأَبْقَىٰ لِلَّذِينَ ءَامَنُوا۟ وَعَلَىٰ رَبِّهِمْ يَتَوَكَّلُونَ ۝ ﴾$$

(سورة الشورى ٤٢ : ٣٦)

﴾But that which is with Allah is better and more lasting: [It is] for those who believe and put their trust in their Lord.﴿ (Qur'an 42: 36)

The reward that Allah has in store for mankind is for those who trust Him.

$$﴿... خَٰلِدِينَ فِيهَا ۚ نِعْمَ أَجْرُ ٱلْعَٰمِلِينَ ۝ ٱلَّذِينَ صَبَرُوا۟ وَعَلَىٰ رَبِّهِمْ يَتَوَكَّلُونَ ۝ ﴾$$

(سورة العنكبوت ٢٩ : ٥٨-٥٩)

﴾...To dwell therein forever; - Excellent reward for those who do good. Those who persevere and put their trust in their Lord.﴿ (Qur'an 29: 58-59)

3 - Tawakkul and Belief

The importance of *tawakkul* in Islam is best illustrated in the following two verses where being a Muslim and a believer are respectively made contingent upon making *tawakkul*.

$$﴿وَقَالَ مُوسَىٰ يَٰقَوْمِ إِن كُنتُمْ ءَامَنتُم بِٱللَّهِ فَعَلَيْهِ تَوَكَّلُوٓا۟ إِن كُنتُم مُّسْلِمِينَ ۝ ﴾$$

(سورة يونس ١٠ : ٨٤)

﴾Moses said: O my people! If you [really] believe in Allah,

then in Him put your trust if you are Muslims [submit to Allah's Will].❥ (Qur'an 10: 84)

﴾... وَعَلَى ٱللَّهِ فَتَوَكَّلُوٓاْ إِن كُنتُم مُّؤْمِنِينَ ﴿٢٣﴾ ﴿ (سورة المائدة ٥ : ٢٣)

❥And on Allah put your trust if you have faith.❥ (Qur'an 5: 23)

SUMMARY

The teachings of Islam are the primary source for the Islamic perspective on Management. The planning concepts presented above were either directly learned from the teachings of Islam, derived from the way the Islamic teachings are structured and integrated together, or selected from other management sources. Based on these learning schemes we can make the following conclusions.

Mission is the general business an organization is in. Every organization shall have a very clear mission statement that will serve as its frame of reference. In case of a Muslim organization, the mission statement has to be consistent with the general mission of Islam, which is the worship of Allah and His vicegerent on earth. Organizations shall also have a well-defined objective or long-term target that they will strive for achieving. The teachings of Islam place a special emphasis on the long-term objective. Furthermore, these teachings establish a direct cause and effect relationship between every planned action and the long-term objective.

In order to achieve their objectives, organizations have to develop a plan specifying certain goals or specific targets at specific times that will be conducive to the desired objective. In case of Muslim organizations, all the actions have to be consistent with the general mission of Muslims (the worship of Allah and His vicegerence), and conducive to their objective (Paradise).

Organizations have to make sure that their sets of goals are feasible within the projected time horizon. Feasibility includes the skills and the resources required for achieving the goals. The absence of either one of these components in any task renders it unfeasible. The general objective and goals that Allah, the Almighty, assigned for Muslims are feasible, and Allah will help in achieving them provided Muslims qualify by doing the right work.

Decision making in a Muslim organization shall be done via consultation, which starts by an attempt to reach a consensus and concludes by voting if a consensus is not reached. Consultation needs to be a culture rather than a programme, yet certain programmes can always reinforce it. In their planning, managers have to use the systems approach, that is, they shall work for the benefit of the whole organization, not just for a portion of it. Managers shall also consider the behaviour of all stakeholders within their immediate and general environments. Furthermore, all the components of a plan should be supportive of one another. It is generally advised to follow a rigorous gradual procedure in pursuing any goal. However, in case some actions are badly needed and people are ready to take them, there is no point in gradualism. Muslims shall also have a good deal of flexibility in their plans and if they have detailed plans they should consider them as contingency.

Once organizations decide to pursue a certain plan and start implementing it, they have to show enough patience in incurring any planned short-term loss. This can only be achieved if they are committed to, and confident in achieving the desired goal.

On some occasions, the plan is determined to be defective, and it is therefore best to cancel the implementation. If it is determined that a certain plan will result in some hardship that the organization is likely not to be able to endure it is not wise to adopt it because a small but continuous progress is better than a huge but short lived one.

Finally, the main characteristic of strategic planning among Muslims is *tawakkul* or trust in Allah. This concept of *tawakkul* is based on the belief that Allah is the One Who will deliver the outcomes. *Tawakkul* stems from the belief in the Mercy, Power, Knowledge, Justice, and Wisdom of Allah. It provided Muslims with a sense of optimism that can help them avoid excessive risk aversion. This trust in Allah is not an excuse for asceticism, which is totally rejected in Islam. This trust necessitates that one does his/her job to the best of his/her ability.

Exercises

1. Explain the difference between *tawakkal* and *tawakkul*.

PART — III

ORGANIZING

AUTHORITY AND RESPONSIBILITY

This chapter is composed of three sections. The first section addresses the concept of authority. The second section covers the concept of responsibility. The last section includes a discussion on delegation.

1 - Authority

Authority is the power, which is legitimized within a specific social context.[1] It is the power that allows certain people to exert influence by virtue of their position in the hierarchy of an organization.[2] Hence, the different levels of authority can be depicted in the organizational structure. Authority can be passed down from a high level in the society, such as a king, an elected president, or an owner of an organization. It can also be granted by the collective will of people in committees or organizations where members elect their leaders. In the classical view of authority, formal authority gives the right to its holder to give orders, and obliges the subordinates to obey. There is another view considering that authority lies with the subordinates and their acceptance to obey the commands. This view is called the acceptance view. Chester Bernard, who believes that authority lies with the willingness of the subordinates to comply with the

---

[1] Pfeffer, J. "*Power in Organizations*," Pittman Boston (1981) Pp. 4-6.

[2] Stoner and Freeman, "*Management*," 5th ed., Prentice Hall, N. Jersey, (1992), p. 344.

decisions, delineated the following conditions of subordinate's compliance:[3]

A person can, and will, accept a communication as authoritative only when four conditions simultaneously occur:

a) He can and does understand the communication;

b) At the time of his decision he believes that it is not inconsistent with the purpose of the organization;

c) At the time of his decision he believes it to be compatible with his personal interest as a whole; and

d) He is able mentally and physically to comply with it.

Conditions a) and d) in the above list are quiet logical and we agree with them. No one can be expected to execute a certain order when he/she does not understand it, or might not even recognize that it was an order or an assignment. Further, no one can ever perform a job that is beyond his/her mental and physical capability. But it is the managers' role to make sure that the jobs they assign are behaviourally and technically feasible. There is a famous Arab idiom that says 'If you want to be obeyed give feasible orders.' Allah, the Exalted, says:

$$\text{(٢٨٦ :٢ البقرة سورة)} \quad ﴾...وُسْعَهَا إِلَّا نَفْسًا اللَّهُ يُكَلِّفُ لَا﴿$$

﴾On no soul does Allah place a burden greater than it can bear...﴿ (Qur'an 2: 286)

If Allah, the Almighty, our creator and the One who knows us better than anyone does not place on us burdens that we may

[3] Bernard, C. "*The Functions of Executives*," Harvard University Press, Cambridge, Mass., (1983) Pp. 161-184.

not be able to carry, it follows that it would be wise for organizations who aspire for success not to authorize something that is beyond its people.

Condition b) should be satisfied in order to motivate the subordinates, for the subordinates can never be motivated to execute orders that are inconsistent with the mission of the organization. In case the order clearly contradicts the purpose of the organization, the subordinates shall immediately discuss this matter with their manager. If the manager insists on the order in spite of the fact that it is proven to contradict the purpose of the organization, then it will become a duty of the subordinates to disobey him/her.

Prophet Muhammad (Blessings and Peace be upon him) said:

> "Let not any one of you be a blind follower who says if people do good, I will do the same, and if they do wrong, I will do the same. But you should stick to righteousness."
> (Tirmidhi)

The above hadith expound the principle that we should not blindly follow our leaders or the people around us, but rather we should strive for righteousness even if it does not please our leaders.

On the other hand, if it is not clearly proven that the order contradicts the purpose of the organization, it shall not be up to the individual perception of a subordinate to either obey or disobey. Because if this were the case, we would lose any order and we would lose the unity of command which is indispensable in any organization. This condition, however, reminds us of the importance of the communication of orders and the ability to relate them to the general purpose of the organization in order to get better performance from the subordinates.

Finally, the third condition stresses the importance of compatibility between the personal interest of the subordinate and their assigned jobs. The more the worker can relate his/her task to his/her personal interest, the more motivated he/she will be. In the mean time, it should be understood that the overall job of the subordinate serves his/her interest, otherwise he/she would not take it. Therefore, the fact that a certain order is not perceived to be compatible with ones personal interest should not be an impediment for its execution. If compliance with the orders is conditional on whether the subordinate immediately feels that the order is compatible with his/her interest, the concept of organizing is put to question.

The Islamic perspective on authority encompasses both the classical view and the acceptance view. In fact, the two views can not be mutually exclusive. The term authority has not been used in Islamic materials. Abu Seen explains this by the fact that Islam wants to dissociate this concept from the concept of authoritarianism. Instead, Islam uses the term "in charge." Islam emphasized discipline and obedience. Allah, the All-High, said:

$$﴿يَٰٓأَيُّهَا ٱلَّذِينَ ءَامَنُوٓا۟ أَطِيعُوا۟ ٱللَّهَ وَأَطِيعُوا۟ ٱلرَّسُولَ وَأُو۟لِى ٱلْأَمْرِ مِنكُمْ ...﴾$$

(سورة النساء ٤ : ٥٩)

﴿O you who believe! Obey Allah and obey the Messenger, and those in charge among you...﴾ (Qur'an 4: 59)

From the above verse, we see that complying with authority is *'Ibādah* (worship). We have to give our superiors the benefit of

the doubt. Obedience is relevant when we disagree with the
superior because in case we agree with a decision, we are basically
obeying ourselves. Muslims have to voice out their disagreement
with their superiors but if they fail to change the decision they
have to comply with it. Authority in Islam is however limited
within the framework of the mission of the Muslims and the
interest of the organization. Furthermore, authority in Islam is
limited by the culture of participative decision making, which
induces better quality and better productivity. Finally, the process
of enjoining what is right and forbidding what is wrong balances
authority. It is the duty of the subordinates rather than their right
not to comply with orders that flagrantly contradicts the mission
and objectives of Islam or those of the organization. It is also to be
understood that the leader should only give feasible and beneficial
orders. Most importantly, the nature and scope of compliance
should be agreed upon in the job contract, or the job description,
and then both the manager and the subordinate have to abide by
the contract. This is because every contract would be investigated
on the day of judgment thus providing the Muslims with the
control that ensure that they fulfill the part of a contract they
entered into. The above fact is expounded in the following verse:

$$﴿ ... وَأَوْفُواْ بِالْعَهْدِ إِنَّ الْعَهْدَ كَانَ مَسْئُولًا ۝ ﴾$$

(سورة الإسراء ١٧ : ٣٤)

﴾...And fulfill [every] engagement, for every engagement
will be inquired into [On the day of Reckoning].﴿
(Qur'an 17: 34)

2 - Responsibility

Responsibility is an obligation to do something with the expectation of a certain result.[4] For example a teacher has the responsibility of teaching the assigned subject to his/her students and to test them on it. On the other hand, the students are expected to gain knowledge in their courses and to do their assignments, and are thus responsible for these duties. As such, the vicegerent of Allah is certainly a huge responsibility that men have assumed. Allah, the Exalted, said:

﴿إِنَّا عَرَضْنَا ٱلْأَمَانَةَ عَلَى ٱلسَّمَٰوَٰتِ وَٱلْأَرْضِ وَٱلْجِبَالِ فَأَبَيْنَ أَن يَحْمِلْنَهَا وَأَشْفَقْنَ مِنْهَا وَحَمَلَهَا ٱلْإِنسَٰنُ إِنَّهُ كَانَ ظَلُومًا جَهُولًا ﴾ (سورة الأحزاب

(٧٢ : ٣٣)

❁Lo! We offered the trust unto the heavens and the earth and the mountains, but they shrank from bearing it and were afraid of it. And man assumed it. Lo he has proved a tyrant and an ignorant.❁ (Qur'an 33: 72)

'Ali 'Abdul Kader[5] states that this trust was nothing more than the responsibility that man decided to undertake because of his freedom of choice and his faculty of intellect. Further, it is the responsibility of people to change their status for the better.

﴿... إِنَّ ٱللَّهَ لَا يُغَيِّرُ مَا بِقَوْمٍ حَتَّىٰ يُغَيِّرُواْ مَا بِأَنفُسِهِمْ ... ﴾

(سورة الرعد ١٣ : ١١)

---

[4] Griffin and Morehead, *"Managing People and Organizations,"* 3rd ed. Houghton Mifflin, (1992) p. 542.

[5] 'Abdul Kader, 'Ali *"Islamic Leadership and Personality From Man to Mankind,"* A; *Ittihād* Spring, (1973).

❖...Lo! Allah changes not the conditions of a folk until they change that which is in their hearts...❖ (Qur'an 13: 11)

The precondition for Allah's help to change for the better is to put in all the necessary efforts on the part of the person who wants to change. This is similar to the concept of *tawakkal* discussed before.

Unfortunately, not everybody feels the obligation to accomplish the set targets that is, not everybody possesses a sense of responsibility. Responsibility grows with us since childhood. Managers have heavier responsibilities than subordinates do. Therefore, every manager should feel deeply responsible for whatever is under his/her authority, and responsibility entails accountability (see next chapter) in this world and in the Hereafter. 'Umar (may Allah be pleased with him) once said that he was afraid that if a mule falls in the mountain roads of Iraq and breaks its legs, Allah might ask him why he did not pave the roads in that area. This demonstrated the extent to which 'Umar felt the responsibility, which in turn allowed him to reach a historically recognized managerial excellence.

Responsibility depends on the sphere of authority one has. Everyone is responsible for what is under his authority.

﴿يَٰٓأَيُّهَا ٱلَّذِينَ ءَامَنُوا۟ قُوٓا۟ أَنفُسَكُمْ وَأَهْلِيكُمْ نَارًا وَقُودُهَا ٱلنَّاسُ وَٱلْحِجَارَةُ عَلَيْهَا مَلَٰٓئِكَةٌ غِلَاظٌ شِدَادٌ لَّا يَعْصُونَ ٱللَّهَ مَآ أَمَرَهُمْ وَيَفْعَلُونَ مَا يُؤْمَرُونَ ۝﴾

(سورة التحريم ٦٦ : ٦)

❖O you who believe save yourselves and your families from a fire whose fuel is men and stones, over which are [appointed] angels stern [and] severe who flinch not [from executing] the commands they receive from Allah, but do [precisely] what they are commanded.❧ (Qur'an 66: 6)

The above verse shows how we are responsible for ourselves and also our families.

The Prophet (Blessings and Peace be upon him) said:

"Behold! each one of you is a guardian, and each one of you will be asked about his subjects. A leader is a guardian over the people and he will be asked about his subjects; a man is a guardian over the members of his household and he will be asked about his subjects; a woman is a guardian over the members of the household of the husband and of his children.... Behold! each one of you is a guardian and each one of you will be asked about his subjects." (Bukhāri)

The above hadith shows that responsibility is at every level. Every single person is responsible

Authority is necessary to accomplish any responsibility. Miner[6] stated that a manager responsible for accomplishing certain results must have the power to use resources to achieve those results. Because responsibility requires authority in order for it to be assumed, and because managers cannot get everything done by themselves, these latter have to delegate authority to their subordinates.

3 - Delegation

Delegation is the act of giving a subordinate the authority to complete a certain task or project. Authority is necessary for the

---

[6] Miner, B. J., *"Theories of Organizational Structure and Process,"* Hinsdale, Ill.: Dryden Press, (1982) p. 360.

completion of any activity, making delegation an inevitable act. Prophet Muhammad (Blessings and Peace be upon him) used to instruct his Companions to obey his delegated subordinates saying that it's just like obeying him:

> "Whoever obeyed my appointed leader has indeed obeyed me, and whoever disobeys my appointed leader did in fact disobey me." (Bukhāri)

The above hadith shows the importance of delegation and how it should be conducted. As mentioned above, the leader cannot do every thing by him or her self and unless it is made clear that the person to whom authority is delegated be obeyed, problems may arise. Indeed Islam stresses the importance of obedience at the lower level of the hierarchy and makes it equal to obeying management. Unfortunately many people are usually concerned about obeying the big boss and are not much concerned about the direct superior.

Accountability is also delegated together with authority. While the person delegated has the obligation to finish the job within the specified time, quality, and cost, that is while he/she is responsible for completing the job with certain specified standards, the manager is not spared from the responsibility. The manager cannot abdicate responsibility with the excuse of delegating authority. Moreover, the delegated subordinate will keep being accountable for his/her manager. Some managers sometimes confuse delegation of authority with abdication of responsibility. Stoner and Freeman[7] outlined some incorrect understandings of delegation as follows:

---

[7] Stoner and Freeman, "*Management*," 5th ed., Prentice Hall, N. Jersey, (1992), p. 344.

1. It is not simply a matter of giving people jobs and telling them to get them done. When this approach is taken, the results a manager wants or expects are seldom achieved. The recipients of this type of delegation are put in a position of being second guessed at the end of the job.

2. It is not abandonment of managers' responsibility.

3. It does not mean the manager loses control.

4. It does not mean that managers avoid making decisions.

The manager who delegates still makes decisions. The important point is that he or she can concentrate on those decisions and issues of most importance and allow subordinates to make decisions which are best made at the point of direct contact.

The main advantage of delegation is efficiency. Delegation saves the manager a significant amount of time in dealing with the details of an activity, and therefore, gives him/her more time to focus on the overall, planning, organizing, and controlling processes. It also allows the manager to carry more responsibilities that he/she might be assigned by higher managers. Delegation also saves time by allowing a set of decisions to be made by the subordinates without referring back to the manager. This can also improve the quality of performance because the people that are closer to the job, and thus know it better, are allowed to make decisions. Quality can also be improved because the delegated subordinate gets more autonomy, and experiences more satisfaction, which brings the quality up. Finally, delegation of authority gives the subordinate a leadership training that he/she needs. Hence, delegation contributes in making new leaders. Managers that delegate authority are usually good leaders, for a good leader is one that makes many leaders as Deming stated:

"Although, delegation is generally a necessary and effective measure, many managers tend to resent it. Managers with a technical background such as engineering, despite their managerial responsibilities, tend to continue performing their engineering functions. They sometimes have difficulties in adjusting to their new managerial roles. Managers shall understand that it is not better that they do the job themselves, and that no matter how much they delegate, they still will have too many things to do. They also should learn to trust the capabilities of their subordinates. Some managers claim that it is not efficient to delegate authority since they will end up doing the job sooner or later because their subordinates are not qualified. They also might claim that delegation will lead them to spend a long time explaining to their subordinates how the job is to be done, and that they could spend less time doing the work themselves. While this argument is sometimes valid, it overlooks the fact that their subordinates would only need a lot of explanation time when they are delegated the job for the first time, and that delegation will be very efficient in the long term. If the subordinates have always been incapable of getting the work done, then these subordinates should not have been hired in the first place. In some cases, people are not hired according to their qualification, but rather according to whom they know, or according to their relationship with top management. In most cases, however, the problem of delegation lies with the managers who are too disorganized to appropriately delegate authority. Some managers are too much in love with their skills that they would not let anybody do a job that they feel is within their area of expertise. Sometimes, managers feel threatened if a delegated subordinate does a good job. Therefore, they tend to deprive their subordinates from such opportunities. These kind of paranoid managers are usually mediocre managers who lack professional strength and skills. The weaker a manager, the more vulnerable he/she feels. Most alarmingly, these kinds of managers have serious ethical problems that are likely to jeopardize the interest of the organization."

A good manager is the one who is willing to delegate authority and who knows how to do it. He/she should know what tasks and activities should be delegated and who should be responsible for completing these tasks. The delegated person should possess the necessary technical and behavioural skills to perform his/her duty. Then, the manager should delegate the person responsible for the task the necessary authority to complete it. 'Ali (may Allah be pleased with him), the fourth successor of the Prophet (Blessings and Peace be upon him), said, "He has no say who is not obeyed." Moreover, the manager should provide his subordinate with the necessary resources to accomplish responsibility. Finally he/she should stay informed about the development of the delegated task, without having to interfere with decisions that are within the prerogative of the delegated person so long as the desired results will not be jeopardized. 'Umar (may Allah be pleased with him), once received a complaint about one of the subordinates of Abu 'Ubaydah. He replied, this is within the prerogative of Abu 'Ubaydah.

Exercise

1. Define authority from an Islamic point of view.

2. What are the conditions for subordinate compliance?

3. What should subordinates do if the authority given to them contradicts the purpose of the organization?

4. Define responsibility and give two examples.

5. Responsibility depends on the sphere of control that one has. Explain!

6. What is delegation and what are its' advantages?

7. In the context of authority, responsibility and delegation, what should a good manager do in order to have an effective and efficient organization?

8. On Monday morning, your head of department asked you to finish a task by Wednesday morning. The task takes you about one day and you can only start it tomorrow morning because you have other things to finish. So you tell your head of department that he can expect the task finished by 10.00 a.m on Wednesday. Tuesday morning, the general manager sends you a note asking you to do something else that he needs in the afternoon, both assignments are urgent. What do you do and why?

ACCOUNTABILITY

Because every person is responsible and because he or she is favoured with the faculty of intellect, it is only normal that he or she be accountable for his or hers deeds. Moreover, while Muslims are commanded to work in groups, they are held accountable individually for every single deed. Allah, the Exalted, said:

﴿كُلُّ نَفْسٍ بِمَا كَسَبَتْ رَهِينَةٌ ۝ إِلَّا أَصْحَابَ ٱلْيَمِينِ ۝﴾

(سورة المدثر ٧٤ : ٣٨-٣٩)

﴿Every soul is a pledge for its own deeds; Save those who will stand on the right hand.﴾ (Qur'an 74: 38-39)

The above *āyāt* (verses) show that every one will be solely accountable for his or her actions.

﴿أَلَّا تَزِرُ وَازِرَةٌ وِزْرَ أُخْرَىٰ ۝ وَأَن لَّيْسَ لِلْإِنسَانِ إِلَّا مَا سَعَىٰ ۝﴾

(سورة النجم ٥٣ : ٣٨-٣٩)

﴿That no laden one shall bear another's load, and that man has only for which he makes effort.﴾ (Qur'an 53: 38-39)

The above *āyāt* show that no one will be accountable for the deeds of another except his or her own deeds.

﴿فَمَن يَعْمَلْ مِثْقَالَ ذَرَّةٍ خَيْرًا يَرَهُ ۝ وَمَن يَعْمَلْ مِثْقَالَ ذَرَّةٍ شَرًّا يَرَهُ ۝﴾ (سورة الزلزلة ٩٩ : ٧-٨)

❨Then shall anyone who has done an atoms weight of good, shall see good. And anyone who has done an atoms weight of evil, shall see evil.❩ (Qur'an 99: 7-8)

The above *āyāt* show that a person is accountable for every single atom of his or her deeds.

The feeling of accountability in the Hereafter has played a great role in the success of Muslim leaders throughout history. When 'Umar ibn 'Abdul 'Aziz became the caliph of the Muslims, he followed the Prophet's guidance saying:

"It is a responsibility, and it is a source of ignominy and regret in the Hereafter."

This feeling of accountability was the major characteristic of the leadership of 'Umar ibn 'Abdul 'Aziz who is considered to be the fifth righteous Muslim caliph. 'Umar (may Allah be pleased with him), the second caliph also instructed Muslims to exercise self-control:

"Judge yourselves before you will be judged and weigh your deeds before you will be weighed."

Since each person is accountable for every single deed he or she does, there has to be a process of accountability. This process can be called the control process and is explained in the following section.

1 - The Basic Control Process

In order to be able to hold people accountable, the latter must know what they are supposed to do and they have to know their mission, objective, and goals. Islam clearly defines the mission, objective, and goals of Muslims and teaches them how to achieve them. Allah, the Almighty, enabled us to distinguish right from wrong and held us accountable for choosing either one.

$$﴿وَنَفْسٍ وَمَا سَوَّاهَا ۝ فَأَلْهَمَهَا فُجُورَهَا وَتَقْوَاهَا ۝ قَدْ أَفْلَحَ مَن زَكَّاهَا ۝$$
$$وَقَدْ خَابَ مَن دَسَّاهَا ۝﴾ (سورة الشمس ٩١ : ٧-١٠)$$

﴿By the souls and the proportion and order given to it. And its enlightenment as to its wrong and its right. Truly he succeeds that he purifies it. And he fails that corrupts it.﴾ (Qur'an 91: 7-10)

Organizations should guide their people as to what is expected from them before they are made responsible for choosing either one. As evident in the above verse, Allah, the All-High, guides people as to what is right and wrong before holding them responsible for their deeds.

Allah, the All-Glorious, would not punish us had we not known what we are supposed to do:

$$﴿... وَمَا كُنَّا مُعَذِّبِينَ حَتَّى نَبْعَثَ رَسُولًا ۝﴾ (سورة الإسراء ١٧ : ١٥)$$

﴿Nor would We punish until We had sent a messenger.﴾ (Qur'an 17: 15)

Accountability comes after guidance. Therefore, managers should be sure that the functions and roles of their subordinates are very well defined, and that the subordinates are qualified and capable of assuming those functions, before they can hold them accountable. Further, accountability can only be achieved through the control process by which the manager checks if his or hers subordinates are doing the job as specified. 'Umar (may Allah be pleased with him), the second caliph once asked his Companions what would they think if he appointed one whom he believed to be the best man among them and ordered him to do justice, would 'Umar have assumed his responsibility? The Companions replied saying, "Yes." 'Umar retorted, "No, not unless he ensured that the appointee did what he was ordered to do."

After knowing that the work is not proceeding as planned, corrective actions must then be taken. 'Umar, understood and practiced the control process fourteen centuries ago. In fact, 'Umar is considered by many scholars as the founding father of modern administration. The above control process is a basic one. The complete control model practiced by 'Umar will be presented in the sixth part. The next chapter will cover the concept of organizational structure.

Exercise

1. While Muslims are commanded to work in groups, they are held accountable individually for every single deed. Does this mean that there is no group accountability in Islam? Comment.

ORGANIZATIONAL STRUCTURE

Organizational structure is the formal arrangement of tasks, responsibilities, and authority. It provides the configuration of the patterns of jobs and groups of jobs. Organizational structure is the way the organization is fashioned to achieve its objectives and goals. As such the organizational structure is a variable dependent on the mission and scope of the organization. Since any organization functions within a certain environment that affects it, the organization structure will also be influenced by environmental factors. Islam does not prescribe a certain way of organizing. It is our own job to find out the right organization perspective depending on our changing needs. Islam however, gives general guidelines as with regards to authority, responsibility and accountability as prescribed earlier. It also stresses the ability to voice differences and complaints. A structure is considered as a contract that must be respected until it is changed. In the first section of this chapter, we will briefly outline the most common structures. The second section will delineate the major dimension of an organizational structure. This section will be concluded by a comparison between mechanistic and organic structure and brief guidelines for organizational design.

1 - Basic Organization's Structures

Organizational structure presents a configuration of the division of the total task of an organization into smaller groups of jobs. These groups of jobs need to be coordinated to guarantee the functioning of the organization. The purpose behind dividing the total task to smaller groups of jobs is to facilitate managing them and to improve effectiveness. The grouping of jobs results in the formation of departments. Departmentalization is not static, rather it keeps changing according to the needs and challenges faced by the organization. Moreover, organizations do not have to have a single departmentalization form, but can simultaneously have mixture of various forms depending on their needs. The departmentalization process of an organization often takes one of the following forms:

1) Geographic departmentalization

Geographic or territorial departmentalization refers to the establishment of decentralized divisions along geographic lines. A manager is assigned to be in charge of a division of a company in a certain area. A self-contained territorial division eliminates the cost of coordinating activities and transporting materials between remote areas.

2) Functional departmentalization

Functional departmentalization is the process of dividing the total task of an organization according to its different functions. The functions of an organization are the necessary activities that the organization performs to assume its mission. The major functions of any business are finance, operation (production for manufacturing companies), and marketing. These three functions are absolutely essential for any business. Figure-10 shows the structure of an organization consisting solely of the three functions mentioned above. As organizations expand, the need for new functions usually arises. Some businesses may include the functions of personnel, accounting, purchasing, and public relations. The operations of an organization can be divided into a number of functions. For example, a hospital might include many functions such as pediatric, gynecology, internal medicine, neurology, psychiatry, and surgery.

Functional departmentalization is probably the most basic organization design. Its major advantage is certainly efficiency. Putting people with similar expertise in the same department will allow them to be highly skilled in their specialized areas. This specialization also enhances economies of scale. The major disadvantage with functional departmentalization is that the groups of people working on the same area usually develop an identity of their own that can transcend the feeling of belonging to the whole organization.

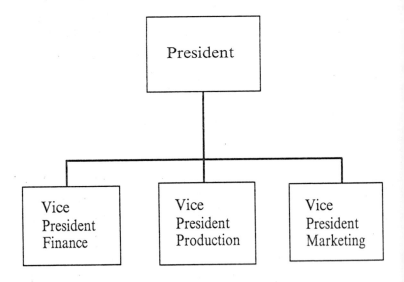

Figure 10. Basic Functional structure

This may make it difficult to achieve inter-departmental coordination.[8]

Furthermore, the routine of functional activities generally leads to low involvement and low level of innovation.[9]

3) Product departmentalization

Product departmentalization, which is similar to customer departmentalization, is probably the second most widely used structure. As the number of products produced by a firm increases, it becomes difficult for it to manage them along functional departments. Production of diverse products in a functionally structured organization is not very efficient. Marketing and promoting different products also become very complicated. To solve these problems, new units or divisions in charge of products or groups of products are created. These units shall have all the resources necessary to perform all the activities related to the products. If a company is involved in projects rather than products, a project structure emerges. Product structure allows the personnel to acquire high expertise in researching, manufacturing, and distributing a product line. The major disadvantage of this structure is, that unlike the functional one, it does not allow for economies of scale and can thus be somewhat costly. Product division is only useful when the firm is very large with huge sales volume. The organizational chart for product structure is illustrated in Figure-11.

---

[8] Daft, R., L., *"Organizational Theory and design,"* 2nd Ed., West, St. Paul, M. N., (1986).

[9] Baron, R. A., Greenberg J., *"Behavior in Organizations,"* Allyn and Bacon, Boston, (1989). p. 521

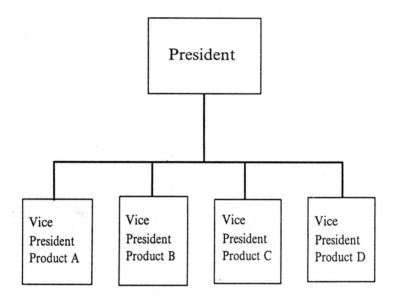

Figure 11. Product Organization

4) Matrix structure

Functional structure becomes inefficient when the number of products manufactured or projects undertaken by a company increases. Since product/project design does not allow for economies of scale and can therefore be very costly, matrix design becomes a better alternative. Matrix design is a design that combines both functional and product/project designs in order to achieve maximum effectiveness. In a matrix design, there are both functional managers and project/product managers. Product/ project managers do not have to report to the functional managers.

Instead they have authority over the resources, in the functional departments, needed for their product/project. This means that there will be people reporting to two bosses, namely, the product/ project manger and the functional manager. The people reporting to two bosses are, however, few, and they are usually located at higher levels in the organizational chain of command. At lower levels, employees usually have one supervisor only. The major advantage of this structure is that it allows for economies of scale that cannot be applied to product/project organizations with medium sales volume. It also permits effective product/project management than the functional organization. Matrix structure is very much suited for medium size firms because it allows flexible use of human and technical resources. The major disadvantage of this structure is the fact that it requires certain people to work under two bosses. This may cause employee frustration and stress that will have negative consequences on the effectiveness of the organization.

The basic dimensions that identify the differences in organizational structure are presented in the following section.

2 - Dimensions of a Structure

The basic dimensions that measure the differences in organizational structure include specialization, span of control, formalization, centralization, and complexity.

1) Specialization

Specialization refers to the extent the total task is divided into small specific jobs. High specialization in an organization means that every person has a very narrow set of activities to perform. In organizations with low specialization, employees perform a wide range of activities. High specialization leads to higher efficiency, however, this is likely to be at the expense of other measures of effectiveness such as satisfaction, and adaptiveness. In a dynamic and volatile economy such as the one we are living in, adaptiveness has very high importance. The changes in economy also made high specialization less attractive than before.

2) Span of control

Span of control refers to the number of people reporting to a single supervisor. The span of control is said to be wide if the number of people reporting to one supervisor is high, otherwise the span of control is said to be narrow. Wide spans of control result in flat organization structures while narrow spans of control result in tall organization structures. The span of control depends on the need for direct contact between the manager and the subordinates. In research and development and job of manufacturing direct contact is essential, therefore, the span of control has to be small. In simpler operations, such as assembly, the spans of control need not to be narrow because there is no high need for direct contact. Specialization is also an important variable in determining the optimum span of control. More specialization allows wider span of control. Finally, the span of control depends on the ability of managers to communicate. Good communicators are usually able to supervise more people than managers with limited communication skills.

3) Formalization

Formalization in an organization is its degree of reliance on written rules and regulations. An organization in which the expectations of individual and group behaviour are specified to a large extent by written documentation is a highly formalized organization. Organizations with low formalization have very limited written rules, procedures, and policies. These organizations rely heavily on verbal communication.

High formalization can be very useful in improving the efficiency of an organization. It is very convenient for highly specialized jobs, and for functional departments. Highly formalized companies are usually companies of mass production where the major functions are repetitive, and where efficiency is considered to be the major component of effectiveness. In these organizations, the span of control is very wide making it very difficult for a manager to directly communicate with and supervise his subordinates.

On the other hand, low formalization is conducive to better satisfaction and more involvement of the members of the organization. As such, organizations with low formalization tend to be more adaptive and more innovative. Organizations with low formalization include research companies and companies with batch or job of shop manufacturing operations. In these organizations, specialization is low, and the span of control is usually narrow.

4) Centralization

The degree of centralization in an organization refers to the extent decision making authority is confined to top management. Centralization also refers to the authority to lead and control. Organizations that adapt a participative management approach are said to be decentralized organizations. These companies show greater effectiveness in terms of members' satisfaction and involvement, and in terms of adaptiveness. Centralized organizations are usually focused on efficiency rather than on adaptiveness and involvement. Centralized organizations are usually highly formalized, and thus, they share a lot of characteristics of the highly formalized organizations. The only major difference is that highly formalized organizations are likely to have more delegation of authority.

5) Complexity

Complexity is sometimes called differentiation. It is the expansion of the organizational structure by dividing major functions or tasks and creating new departments. Organizations with more departments and groups are said to be more complex than those with fewer departments and groups. This stems from the understanding that it is generally easier and less complicated to manage organizations with fewer departments and groups. Improving the coordination and communication processes can however, solve the problems associated with complexity. There are two types of differentiation, namely vertical and horizontal. Vertical differentiation refers to the number of levels in the hierarchy of the chain of command. Organizations with many such levels are said to be vertically complex. Horizontal differentiation refers to the number of units and departments at the same vertical level. Organizations with many units and departments at the same level are said to be horizontally complex. The size and scope of an organization is the major determinant of its complexity. Smaller organizations are usually less complex than bigger ones. A small manufacturing firm, for example, will only have three major functional departments, namely finance, production, and marketing. The organization chart for such a firm is represented in Figure-9. As the firm grows somewhat larger, it might need to have a personnel department. Further growth in the scope and size of the organization will entail further complexity.

The organizational structure during the time of the Prophet (Blessings and Peace be upon him) was very simple. There was one leader who exercised the unity of command, and communication was open in every direction. There were no communication barriers whatsoever. Participative management was the dominant culture. There was no need for complex departmentalization. Prophet Muhammad (bpuh) was also the supreme judge of the state. There was not even a treasury. The money collected used to be distributed immediately. As such, the administration was very efficient, and there was no need for bureaucracy and its associated costs. The country was, however, divided geographically into a number of provinces to facilitate the services. During the time of Abu Bakr (may Allah be pleased with him), the first successor of the Prophet (bpuh), there was a need for a treasury. There was also a need to separate the position of the leader of the state from that of a supreme judge. So, another function was created. Later, in the time of 'Umar (may Allah be pleased with him), the country grew much bigger and its resources as well as its needs increased dramatically. As a result, new provinces were created, and new departments such as the departments of military and that of documentation were established. This can show that complexity is a response to new needs. In fact, the design of an organizational structure itself is a response to some needs, and thus it is means not an end in itself.

3 - Mechanistic versus Organic Structures

A mechanistic structure is a structure that emphasizes a high level of efficiency. Consequently a mechanistic structure is one that has high formalization. Written rules and regulations are extensively used. High specialization, a centralized authority, and a high complexity also characterize mechanistic structures. Communication strictly follows the organization structure. In order for an employee to communicate with top management, his message must pass through a series of superiors in the chain of command. Meanwhile, communication from top management must pass through each subordinate before it can reach the designated level. Henri Fayol is considered to be one of the first proponents of this model.[10] Max Weber provided a description of the functioning of this model and termed it "Bureaucracy."[11]

Organic structure is almost totally opposite to the mechanistic one. Organic design emphasizes involvement and adaptiveness rather than efficiency. As a result, a decentralized authority, a low formalization, a low specialization, and a low complexity characterize the organic structure. This kind of structure induces higher satisfaction and more innovation. It is

---

[10] Henri Fayol, *"General and Industrial Management,"* trans. J. A. Conbrough International Institute of Management, Geneva, (1929).

[11] Max Weber, *"The Theory of Social and Economic Organization,"* trans. Henderson and Parsons Oxford University Press, New York. (1974).

generally a very simple structure that allows communication to take place in every direction.

The structure of the Muslim State during the time of the Prophet (Blessings and Peace be upon him) was closer to an organic one. It was not formalized at all. Communication was open among all the members of the society. Participation was a duty rather than a right. This structure has led to high effectiveness in terms of satisfaction and adaptiveness. Simultaneously, the organization comprising Prophet Muhammad (Blessings and Peace be upon him) and his Companions achieved a very high level of efficiency. The high level of discipline that existed among them and the spiritual momentum that they had may explain this.

Currently, it is generally agreed upon that organizations should be designed according to the demands of the situation.[12] The design of the structure is dependent primarily upon the type of its operations and on its environment. If the operation is a repetitive task such as assembly where efficiency is the most important measure of effectiveness, a mechanistic model is preferred. On the other hand, if the operation process is seldom repetitive such as in the case of a job of manufacturing where more communication is needed and specialization is low, the organic design is preferred. Meanwhile, if the environment of the organization is stable and simple, mechanist design can be appropriate but if the environment is complex and unstable then, an organic design becomes essential. The author has a tendency to prefer an organic design as long as a high level of discipline

---

[12] Randolph, W. A., and Dess, G. G., *"The Congruence Perspective of Organization Design: A Conceptual Model and Multivariate Research Approach,"* Academy of Management review, January, (1984). Pp. 114-127

accompanies it and compliance with managers' order after a decision is reached collectively. However, realistically, this is not always possible. Strict compliance usually needs a certain culture and structure that are conducive to it. Mechanist structure is often more conducive to compliance. At the time of the Prophet (Blessings and Peace be upon him), the state structure was very much organic, yet efficiency was never forsaken. Unfortunately, this level of organizational effectiveness was not maintained for a very long time. It only outlasted the Prophet (bpuh) by a few decades.

HUMAN RESOURCE MANAGEMENT

Effective human resource development and management can on its own ensure economic development. Countries like Japan, Germany, Taiwan and Singapore are the role models for effective human resource management. Despite the worst upshot of the Second World War that led Japan and Germany in almost total destruction of their industrial and manufacturing sectors, these countries were able to emerge as competitors of their erstwhile occupiers with no resource but effective management of their people, within thirty years. Singapore and Taiwan are among the poorest countries in terms of natural resources yet they currently enjoy some the highest per capita income.

The Mirage resorts, a Las Vegas - based firm, spent approximately $ 3.5 million on pre-opening training of its people. These examples show how important people are in the development of a nation and the success of a firm.

This chapter presents human resource management from an Islamic perspective with a focus on the human resource management, processes of recruitment, selection, training and development and compensation.

1 - Introduction

Human resource management can be seen as the effective management of people at work. It examines what can or should be done to make working people more productive and satisfied. It deals with recruitment and selection, training and development.

The above definition of human resource management shows that the process of human resource management begins with the planning process. It is at that time the management knows what types of skills are needed to achieve the set goals and targeted objectives.

In Islam, work is considered as a noble endeavour. Any one capable of working is required to work and not to ask for charity from others or to depend on social security. The Holy Prophet (Blessings and Peace be upon him) said:

> "It is better for one to take his rope to get woods for fuel than to ask people for charity, whether they give him or not." (Bukhāri)

Work in the Islamic system of administration symbolizes man's commitment and servitude to Allah, the Exalted.

The Qur'an states:

$$\text{﴿إِنَّ ٱلَّذِينَ ءَامَنُوا۟ وَعَمِلُوا۟ ٱلصَّٰلِحَٰتِ إِنَّا لَا نُضِيعُ أَجْرَ مَنْ أَحْسَنَ عَمَلًا}$$
$$\text{أُو۟لَٰٓئِكَ لَهُمْ جَنَّٰتُ... ﴾ (سورة الكهف ١٨ : ٣٠-٣١)}$$

❝As to those who believe and work righteousness, Verily We shall not suffer to perish the reward of any who do a righteous deed. For them will be Gardens of Eternity.❞ (Qur'an 18: 30-31)

The principles of work in Islam include a clear definition of the requirements of a job so as to avoid any misunderstanding when the employee accepts the job. The terms and conditions of the job should also be outlined so that there would be no dissatisfaction on the part of the employer. Employers should not force employees to do work against their will by threatening to dismiss them or by other means especially if such works are against the teachings of Islam. An employee under such circumstances has the right to refuse to perform such works and the employer cannot dismiss him for disobeying such orders.

Islam encourages brotherly work environment, which is conducive for production, work and perfection of ones' job. The Holy Prophet (Blessings and Peace be upon him) said:

> "Your slaves are your brothers whom God has given into your protection." (Bukhāri)

The Prophet (bpuh) further said:

> "Do not ask them to do such things (and jobs) which are beyond their strength and endurance and if you do ask them to do such things (and jobs), then help them." (Bukhāri)

From the above hadith, we can deduce that an employee should not be burdened with excessive work load and long wearing hours because this might result in experiencing a lot of stress that may eventually lead to impairment of health or even worse, burnout. Moreover, an employee should not be given a job that does not commensurate with his qualifications, training, skills and abilities. This will cause hardship to the employee. However, if the employee is given a difficult and grueling task, then he should be given assistance whether in physical or monetary form so as to minimize the hardship he is to encounter.

Lastly, the employer should ensure the fixation of maximum working hours, the existence of a conducive working environment and the installation of safety measures in the organization since all of these are in line with the teachings of Islam.

2 - Human Resource Management Activities

1) Recruitment and selection

Recruitment is the process of getting applicants for a vacant position in an organization. Recruitment can be either internal or external. Internal recruitment aims at getting people already within the organization to apply for vacant positions. External recruitment on the other hand focuses on people outside the organization. The methods of recruitment are advertising in local newspapers, posting vacancies on company notice boards, through college internship among others. Advertising the position gives more people the opportunity of getting the job while it gives the organization a better chance of having a more qualified person.

Selection of workers with the appropriate skills, attitudes and motivation constitutes an important human resource management activity as it aims at hiring people that best fit the job in particular and the organization in general.

In the recruitment and selection of people for jobs, Islam advocates the principle of selecting the best from the available human resource. Thus in an Islamic system, a company should recruit individuals who are strong, competent and trustworthy. The Qur'an states:

$$\text{﴿... إِنَّ خَيْرَ مَنِ ٱسْتَـْٔجَرْتَ ٱلْقَوِيُّ ٱلْأَمِينُ ﴾}$$

(سورة القصص ٢٨ : ٢٦)

❖Truly the best of men for you to employ is the best man who is strong and trustworthy.❖ (Qur'an 28: 26)

In the above verse, strength corresponds to the skills and qualifications the job requires, the ability to understand Islamic principles and the power to apply them. Trustworthiness applies to the fear of God, the moral obligation and commitment to societal and organizational goals. The Holy Prophet (Blessings and Peace be upon him) has been reported to have said:

"The truthful, honest merchant will enjoy the company of the Prophets, the truthful ones and the martyrs." (Tirmidhi)

Physical and intellectual superiority as well as honesty are therefore important criteria that must be used as yardstick in the selection of employees. This is to ensure that resources are effectively and efficiently utilized in an organization. Furthermore, productivity would increase and the cost of training reduced since less time is needed to train the employees.

Because it may be difficult to evaluate the trust-worthiness of job candidates, we should focus more on their competence. In fact, there is a strong correlation between competence and ethics, the more competent a person is, the more likely it is that he is ethical. Employing someone less competent when there is a more competent one amounts to the transgression of the teachings of Islam and constitute a major treachery to the Islamic State. The Prophet (bpuh) is reported to have said:

"He whoever hires a person and knows that there is still one who is more qualified than him, has betrayed Allah and His Prophet and the Muslims."

The Qur'an further says:

﴿إِنَّ ٱللَّهَ يَأْمُرُكُمْ أَن تُؤَدُّواْ ٱلْأَمَٰنَٰتِ إِلَىٰ أَهْلِهَا وَإِذَا حَكَمْتُم بَيْنَ ٱلنَّاسِ أَن تَحْكُمُواْ بِٱلْعَدْلِ ...﴾ ۝ (سورة النساء ٤ : ٥٨)

❖Allah commands you to make over trust to those worthy of them and that when judge between people you judge with justice.❖ (Qur'an 4: 58)

The main conclusion to be drawn from the above mentioned hadith and verse is that in Islam, nepotism and favouritism are considered evil and strictly forbidden.

On the other hand, the employer should not overburden his employee. Allah, the Almighty, says:

﴿قَالَ إِنِّى أُرِيدُ أَنْ أُنكِحَكَ إِحْدَى ٱبْنَتَىَّ هَٰتَيْنِ عَلَىٰٓ أَن تَأْجُرَنِى ثَمَٰنِىَ حِجَجٍ فَإِنْ أَتْمَمْتَ عَشْرًا فَمِنْ عِندِكَ وَمَآ أُرِيدُ أَنْ أَشُقَّ عَلَيْكَ سَتَجِدُنِىٓ إِن شَآءَ ٱللَّهُ مِنَ ٱلصَّٰلِحِينَ ٢٧﴾ (سورة القصص ٢٨ : ٢٧)

❖He said: "I intend to wed one of these my daughters to you, on condition that you serve me for eight years; but if you complete ten years, it will be [grace] from you. But I intend not to place you under a difficulty: you will find me indeed, if God wills, one of the righteous."❖ (Qur'an 28: 27)

The above verse shows that the person who hired Mūsa (Peace be upon him) told him before taking the job that he would not put him under a difficulty.

2) Training and development

Training is a process, through which experiences are deliberately offered to trainees to enable them to absorb some new perspective, understanding, value, attitude, technique and skill.

Development on the other hand, is seen to prepare people to perform work beyond that which currently engages them and to accept responsibilities greater than they now have.

As can be seen the conventional definition of training and development is restricted to the physical working environment.

The goal of training and development in Islam is to make man be aware of his status as a vicegerent and the servant of Allah, the All-High, All-Glorious. On this assumption, Islam is aiming towards developing man both spiritually as well as physically.

Allah created us all not knowing anything but He equipped us with the necessary tools of learning and training. The Qur'an states:

$$\text{﴿وَٱللَّهُ أَخْرَجَكُم مِّنۢ بُطُونِ أُمَّهَٰتِكُمْ لَا تَعْلَمُونَ شَيْـًٔا وَجَعَلَ لَكُمُ ٱلسَّمْعَ وَٱلْأَبْصَٰرَ وَٱلْأَفْـِٔدَةَ لَعَلَّكُمْ تَشْكُرُونَ ﴾ (سورة النحل ١٦: ٧٨)}$$

❝It is He who brought you forth from the wombs of your mothers when you knew nothing; and He gave you hearing and sight and intelligence and affections: that you may give thanks [to God].❞ (Qur'an 16: 78)

Training is not only about skills. It is also about developing the right attitude. Creating the right attitude was what Prophet Muhammad (Blessings and Peace be upon him) did. He built a strong *aqīdah* (belief in the Almighty) and dismantled forms of worship to beings or systems other than Allah, the Exalted. This training resulted, among the *ṣaḥābah*, in such commendable values as honesty, trustworthiness, steadfastness and patience.

3) Compensation

One's wages is a reward for work done. A fair wage will encourage workers to put in their best efforts, whereas an unfair wages may lower workers morale and ultimately lead to strikes. Moreover, wages are an important source of livelihood. Islam dictates that the basis for wage fixation should take into consideration job requirements and the varying productivity of workers. This is evident in the following verse of the Holy Qur'an:

$$﴿وَلَا تَتَمَنَّوْا مَا فَضَّلَ اللَّهُ بِهِ بَعْضَكُمْ عَلَىٰ بَعْضٍ لِّلرِّجَالِ نَصِيبٌ مِّمَّا اكْتَسَبُوا وَلِلنِّسَاءِ نَصِيبٌ مِّمَّا اكْتَسَبْنَ وَسْئَلُوا اللَّهَ مِن فَضْلِهِ إِنَّ اللَّهَ كَانَ بِكُلِّ شَيْءٍ عَلِيمًا ۝﴾ (سورة النساء ٤ : ٣٢)$$

❴Covet not that wherein Allah has made some of you excel others. Men shall have a share of that which they earn and women shall have a share of what they earn. Ask Allah alone of His bounty surely Allah has perfect knowledge of all things.❵ (Qur'an 4: 32)

The above verse states the basic principle of wage setting. Men and women are to be paid according to their productivity. Wages are independent of the workers gender, race, religion or any other characteristic.

'Umar ibn al-Khaṭṭāb (may Allah be pleased with him) used to give his employees high wages in order to help them stay away from corruption. 'Umar also said that people should be paid based on their contribution and also their needs.

Another important Islamic principle regarding compensation is that it should be timely.

The Prophet (Blessings and Peace be upon him) said reward/compensate people before their sweat dries.

"Give a contacting man his wage before his sweat is dried." (Ibn Mājah)

The above hadith might have significant implications on the motivation of workers. It might indicate that workers who receive daily wages are more motivated than those who receive monthly salaries. We might want to study the effect of the frequency of payment on the performance of workers.

The wage must be agreed upon before hand. This principle is elaborated in *Sūrah al-Qaṣaṣ* verse 27. It reads:

قَالَ إِنِّيٓ أُرِيدُ أَنْ أُنكِحَكَ إِحْدَى ٱبْنَتَيَّ هَٰتَيْنِ عَلَىٰٓ أَن تَأْجُرَنِي ثَمَٰنِيَ حِجَجٍ فَإِنْ أَتْمَمْتَ عَشْرًا فَمِنْ عِندِكَ وَمَآ أُرِيدُ أَنْ أَشُقَّ عَلَيْكَ سَتَجِدُنِيٓ إِن شَآءَ ٱللَّهُ مِنَ ٱلصَّٰلِحِينَ ﴿٢٧﴾ (سورة القصص ٢٨ : ٢٧)

He said: "I intend to wed one of these my daughters to you, on condition that you serve me for eight years; but if you complete ten years, it will be [grace] from you. But I intend not to place you under a difficulty: you will find me indeed, if God wills, one of the righteous. (Qur'an 28: 27)

Exercises

1. On what basis should we hire people?

2. On what basis should we compensate people?

SUMMARY

Authority is the legitimate right to use resources to accomplish a certain task. Authority is indispensable in any collective work. Compliance with the orders of manager is, therefore, critical to the success of an organization. Compliance with orders that are consistent with the mission of the organization is mandatory. Blind compliance could, however, be detrimental. Subordinates should question things and the culture of the organization should be one of participation, which can lead to better quality and productivity.

Responsibility is the obligation to get a certain task done. It is relative to the amount of authority one has. In general, everyone is responsible for whatever is under his or her influence. Delegation is necessary for organizational success. Delegation is restricted to authority and accountability, for responsibility cannot be abdicated. Many managers find it hard to delegate authority because they usually incorrectly think that it is better that they do the job themselves. Training the managers on how to delegate and train the subordinate on how to handle the responsibility can solve this problem. Generally, delegation becomes very efficient after the first few experiences. Other managers are sometimes afraid that their subordinates would excel them in the assigned task, and, therefore, feel threatened to lose their positions. These managers are usually mediocre ones. They also have an ethical deficiency that is likely to jeopardize the interest of their organizations.

Authority and responsibility entail accountability in this world and in the Hereafter. Every person is fully accountable for what he or she does. However, people can only be held accountable if their responsibility is clearly defined. Holding people accountable also requires controlling their work.

Organizational structure is the formal arrangement of jobs, groups of jobs, authority, and responsibility. Structures depend on the strategies and the culture of the organization. Structure should adhere to the Islamic guidance on authority, responsibility and accountability. Structure should allow subordinates to voice their differences and complaints. Once a structure is in place, it should be respected until it is changed. The most common structures are territorial, functional, project/product structures, in addition to matrix structure, which is a combination of the functional, and the product/project structures. The major dimensions of an organization structure are specialization, span of control, formalization, centralization and complexity. Organizations with high specialization, high formalization, centralized authority, and high complexity are said to have a mechanistic or bureaucratic structure. The others are said to have an organic structure. Mechanistic structures are more suitable for organizations that emphasize efficiency. When adaptiveness, satisfaction, and participation are emphasized, an organic structure becomes necessary.

Recruitment should be based on skills and trust. The compensation should be fixed in advance. The needs of the employees need to be considered in addition to their skills and contributions. Training is a necessity in order to avoid obsolescence and improve quality and productivity.

Exercises

1. Define organization structure.

2. Briefly describe the basic organizational structures that firms can use.

3. What are the advantages and disadvantages of the basic structures given in answer to question two?

4. What are the basic dimensions that measure the differences in organization structure? Briefly describe each.

5. What similarities between mechanistic and organistic structures?

6. Briefly describe the organization structure of the Islamic State during the time of the Prophet (bpuh). Why did it last only for few years after the demise of the Prophet (bpuh)?

7. On Monday morning, your head of department asked you to finish a task by Wednesday morning. The task takes you about one day and you can only start it tomorrow morning because you have other things to finish. So you tell your head of department that he can expect the task finished by 10.00 a.m. on Wednesday. Tuesday morning, the General Manager sends you a note asking you to do something else that he needs in the afternoon, Both assignments are urgent. What do you do and why?

8. Describe HRM from and Islamic perspective.

PART — IV

LEADERSHIP AND MOTIVATION

LEADERSHIP

Leadership is about giving without expecting to take. It is about caring without caring to be cared about. It is about supporting without expecting to be supported. It is about being just with those who are not fair to you.

Leadership is about giving followers the missing dimensions. It is about spreading order out of chaos, creating confidence out of despair, trust out of suspicion and courage out of fear. Leadership is about making change. Leaders do not necessarily hold positions of authority. They neither derive their influence from wealth nor power.

Abu Jā'far al-Manṣoor, the founder of the *Abbasid* dynasty, once posed a question to some of his confidants, he asked:

"Who is the hawk of Quraysh?' They replied: 'The Commander of the Faithful (*Amīrul Mu'minīn*) who established the reign, quieted upheavals, and extinguished ordeals.' He said: 'You have not answered my question.' They said: 'Is it Mu'āwiyah?' He said: 'Neither he.' They said: 'Is it Abdul Malik ibn Marwān?' He said: 'No.' They said: 'Who else O the Commander of the Faithful?' He said: 'Abdur-Raḥmān ibn Mu'āwiyah, who escaped by his cunning the spearheads of the lances and the blades of the swords, traveling the desert, and sailing the seas, until he entered an alien territory. (There,) he organized cities, mobilized armies, and re-established his reign after it was completely lost, by good management and strong resolve. For Mu'āwiyah rose to his stature through the support of 'Umar and 'Uthmān, whose backing allowed him to overcome difficulties; 'Abdul Malik because of previous appointment; and the Commander of the Faithful through the struggle of his kin, and the solidarity of his partisans. But 'Abdur-Raḥmān did it alone, with the support of none other than his own judgment, depending on no one but his own resolve."' (Ibn al-Athir, 5:182)

Allah, the Almighty, created human beings, equipped them with the faculty of intellect, and made this whole universe subservient to them. This means that Allah provided humans with both skills and resources. Some people and nations had more success than others did in using what Allah has given them. The degree of success of nations depends largely on their leadership and their motivation. Muslims have achieved a historically unique success. Michael Hart considered Prophet Muhammad (Blessings and Peace be upon him) as the most influential man in human history. Currently, the countries that are showing rapid growth are the ones that are privileged with better leadership. In this chapter, we will address the concept of leadership from an Islamic perspective. We will start by defining leadership, then we will proceed by our learning the qualities of a good leader.

The performance of an organization is very much influenced by the quality of its leadership. The leader should assume the overall responsibility of the organization. Further, leadership should be understood more as a service to the organization and its members. The saying of Prophet Muhammad (Blessings and Peace be upon him) supports this understanding which is compatible with TQM concepts. The Prophet (bpuh) said:

"The leader of people is their servant." (Ṭabarāni)

Leadership is necessary for the success of any collective work as is evident in the saying of the Prophet (Blessings and Peace be upon him) quoted below:

"If there were three in a trip, they shall appoint a leader from among them." (Abu Dawūd)

Islam thus approves the utility of leadership.

The fact that different leaders were appointed by the Prophet (bpuh) in different situations support the notion that leadership effectiveness depends on the fit between the leader, the followers, and the situation.[1] This suggests that leaders that were successful at one situation with a certain group might not be successful at another situation or with another group. Imam 'Ali ibn Abu Ṭālib (may Allah be pleased with him) was once asked about the reason why his era was worse than the eras of Abu Bakr and 'Umar (may Allah be pleased with them). He indicated that the reason was that they had better followers than he did.

1 - Leadership Qualities

The required leadership skills are not only technical. As a matter of fact, the behavioural skills are the critical ones. Hibban succinctly described the character of 'Abdur-Raḥmān. He wrote, "Abdur-Raḥmān was overtly forbearing, vastly knowledgeable, and sharply insightful, with swift decisiveness and strong resolve. (He, further, was) far from inaction, expeditious and hardworking person, who neither enjoyed tranquility nor got satisfaction in indolence. (Hence,) he would not leave the (handling of) affairs to

---

[1] Gibson et al., *"Organizations"* 5th. Ed., Business Publication Inc. Texas, (1985) p. 361.

others, yet he would not single-handedly dispose of them on the basis of his individual opinion. (He was) courageous and brave, with depth and breadth. (He had moments) of fury, and very few (moments) of serenity. (He was) articulate and eloquent; poetic, perfectionist, and easygoing; generous and outspoken. He used to attend funerals and pray for the deceased; as he used to lead congregations whenever he was present at Friday and *'eid* prayers, and to deliver the *khuṭbah* at the *minbar*. (He used) to visit the sick, and come out to meet (ordinary) peoples and walk in public."

The above statement includes the leadership qualities of knowledge, forbearance, resolve, eloquence, generosity, hard work, participation, and courage. In the following, we list in details the main Islamic leadership features.

1) Strength and trust

Leaders must both be skillful and trustworthy, that is, they must be strong and faithful. The absence of one of these two pillars in a leader can seriously undermine organizations. These two pillars are expressed in the following verses of the Qur'an:

$$﴿... إِنَّ خَيْرَ مَنِ ٱسْتَـٔجَرْتَ ٱلْقَوِيُّ ٱلْأَمِينُ ۝﴾$$

(سورة القصص ٢٨ : ٢٦)

﴾Truly the best of men for you to employ is the [man] who is strong and trustworthy.﴿ (Qur'an 28: 26)

$$﴿... وَإِنِّي عَلَيْهِ لَقَوِيٌّ أَمِينٌ ۝﴾ (سورة النمل ٢٧ : ٣٩)$$

❨I have full strength for the purpose, and may be trusted.❩
(Qur'an 27: 39)

❨قَالَ اجْعَلْنِي عَلَى خَزَآئِنِ ٱلْأَرْضِ إِنِّي حَفِيظٌ عَلِيمٌ ٥٥❩

(سورة يوسف ١٢ : ٥٥)

❨[Yousuf] said: set me over the treasury of the Land: I am indeed [trustworthy] skilled custodian and knowledgeable.❩
(Qur'an 12: 55)

All the above verses are a testimony to the fact that a leader must be skillful and trustworthy. Yousuf (Joseph) (Peace be upon him) had the skills and knowledge necessary to oversee the treasury of the land and therefore offered his services to look after it.

It is certainly not a very easy task to find someone who is highly skilled (full of strength) and highly faithful. On many occasions, we find people who can score very high at one quality but who score moderately on the other. Often, one needs to make a choice on which quality will supersede. Following the tradition of the Prophet (Blessings and Peace be upon him), we can easily conclude that the needed skills come first, while faith remains to be required. For example, 'Amr ibn al-'Āṣ was appointed by the Prophet (bpuh) to lead the Muslims, including the great Companions of the Prophet, in the battle of *"Thatu Salasil,"* just four months after he embraced Islam. This was because 'Amr possessed better military skills than the rest of his army. The Caliphs also used the same criterion. This issue was well explained by Ibn Taymiya in his book *"As-Siyasah ash-Sharī'ah."* Jawdat Sa'īd[2] explained in his book, *"Work, a Skill*

---

[2] Jawdat Sa'īd, *"Work, a Skill and a Will,"* Damascus, (1983). p. 29

and a Will," that a weak leader will be very detrimental to an organization while a skillful leader can be very beneficial even if he was not faithful enough because his shortcomings can be made up for by controlling him. In fact, the leader will not have absolute power because Islam necessitates participative management and checks and balances.

2) Making many leaders, listening and forgiving

One of the better definitions of a good leader is given by Deming who said: "A good leader is one that makes many leaders, listens to people and forgives a mistake."

Prophet Muhammad (Blessings and Peace be upon him) made a whole generation of leaders. He was successful through listening to his Companions, consulting them. They were able to spread the message of Islam after him. The leaders you develop further improve your leadership by correcting your mistakes. 'Umar (may Allah be pleased with him) acted as leader among leaders. He never sent the senior Companions as his governors instead he kept them around him to make sure he can be corrected if he makes any mistake.

3) Kindness and trust in Allah

Prophet Muhammad (Blessings and Peace be upon him) was also lenient and forgiving. Leaders create willing commitment of their subordinates. Leadership does not have to do with coercion and fear. It has to do with respect and as such a leader should be kind and forgiving.

﴿فَبِمَا رَحْمَةٍ مِّنَ ٱللَّهِ لِنتَ لَهُمْ وَلَوْ كُنتَ فَظًّا غَلِيظَ ٱلْقَلْبِ لَٱنفَضُّوا۟ مِنْ حَوْلِكَ فَٱعْفُ عَنْهُمْ وَٱسْتَغْفِرْ لَهُمْ وَشَاوِرْهُمْ فِى ٱلْأَمْرِ فَإِذَا عَزَمْتَ فَتَوَكَّلْ عَلَى ٱللَّهِ إِنَّ ٱللَّهَ يُحِبُّ ٱلْمُتَوَكِّلِينَ ۝﴾ (سورة آل عمران ٣: ١٥٩)

❝It was by the mercy of Allah that you were lenient with them [O Muhammad], for if you had been stern and fierce of heart they would have dispersed from round about you. So pardon them and ask forgiveness for them and consult with them upon the conduct of affairs. And when you are resolved, then put your trust in Allah. Lo! Allah loves those who put their trust [in Him].❞ (Qur'an 3: 159)

The above verse clearly teaches us that a good leader shall be kind with his followers, that he shall not overburden them, that he shall pardon them, and ask Allah to forgive them.

4) Consultation

The above verse further teaches us about the necessity of consultation. A leader should consult his followers when taking important decisions that may affect them. This would lead to better-informed and well-accepted decisions. See the chapter on participative management.

5) Resolve

The above verse also highlights resolve as one of the characteristics of a leader. In another verse Allah, the Exalted, said:

$$﴿وَيَحْيَىٰ خُذِ الْكِتَٰبَ بِقُوَّةٍ وَءَاتَيْنَٰهُ الْحُكْمَ صَبِيًّا ۝﴾$$

(سورة مريم ١٩: ١٢)

﴾O Yaḥyā [John]! Take hold of the book with might: and We gave him wisdom even as a youth.﴿ (Qur'an 19: 12)

$$﴿ ... ۞ وَإِن تَصْبِرُوا وَتَتَّقُوا فَإِنَّ ذَٰلِكَ مِنْ عَزْمِ الْأُمُورِ ۝﴾$$

(سورة آل عمران ٣: ١٨٦)

﴾...But if you persevere patiently, and guard against evil then that will be a determining factor in all affairs.﴿ (Qur'an 3: 186)

If the leader shows perseverance at a time when his problems are of human origin of a higher power, he is said to have resolve. An example of resolve can be seen in the case of the Prophets such as Prophet Muhammad (Blessings and Peace be upon him) who was persecuted in the early stages of his mission by the leaders of Quraysh but who strongly persevered. Allah, the Almighty, said:

$$﴿فَٱصْبِرْ كَمَا صَبَرَ أُولُوا ٱلْعَزْمِ مِنَ ٱلرُّسُلِ ... ۝﴾$$

(سورة الأحقاف ٤٦: ٣٥)

﴾Therefore patiently persevere, as did the messengers of inflexible will...﴿ (Qur'an 46: 35)

6) Knowledge and wisdom

A leader must also have knowledge and wisdom. This is evident in the following verse on Yaḥyā (John) and Mūsā

(Moses) (May Allah's Peace be upon them) who were Prophets of Allah.

﴿وَلَمَّا بَلَغَ أَشُدَّهُ وَٱسْتَوَىٰٓ ءَاتَيۡنَٰهُ حُكۡمًا وَعِلۡمًا وَكَذَٰلِكَ نَجۡزِى ٱلۡمُحۡسِنِينَ﴾

(سورة القصص ٢٨ : ١٤)

❝When he [Mūsa] reached full age, and was firmly established [in life], We bestowed on him wisdom and knowledge: for thus do We reward those who do good.❞ (Qur'an 28: 14)

Leaders need to have knowledge and wisdom in their area of leadership so that they can make initiatives that can add value to the organizations. Moreover, with the specialized knowledge the leadership of a particular area requires, he is able to make informed judgment as well as command the respect of his subordinates.

7) Tawakkul

Verse 159 of *Sūrah Āl-'Imrān* also highlights the importance of *tawakkul* after a decision is made. *Tawakkul* is relying on Allah after doing one's best. The concept of *tawakkul* was discussed extensively in chapter fourteen. Abu Bakr aṣ-Ṣiddiq (may Allah be pleased with him) demonstrated *tawakkul* in its purist forms. He was described as being too faithful to leave any room for planning and too tactful and vigorous in his planning to leave any room for faith.

8) Role model

Leaders must be role models. They must let their actions speak louder than their words. Leaders have a responsibility to create and maintain the culture of the organization. If the leader is hard working, his followers are more likely to work hard. On the other hand, if a leader is not committed to the objective of the organization, he will not be able to motivate others towards it. If a leader's speech contradicts his deeds, then, he will sooner or later lose the ability to influence his followers. Islam strongly deplores those who do not practice what they say. Allah, the All-High, All-Glorious, said:

﴿يَـٰٓأَيُّهَا ٱلَّذِينَ ءَامَنُوا۟ لِمَ تَقُولُونَ مَا لَا تَفْعَلُونَ ۝ كَبُرَ مَقْتًا عِندَ ٱللَّهِ أَن تَقُولُوا۟ مَا لَا تَفْعَلُونَ ۝﴾ (سورة الصف ٦١ : ٢-٣)

﴿O you who believe! Why say you that which you do not? Grievously odious is it in the sight of Allah that you say that which you do not.﴾ (Qur'an 61: 2-3)

﴿أَتَأْمُرُونَ ٱلنَّاسَ بِٱلْبِرِّ وَتَنسَوْنَ أَنفُسَكُمْ... ۝﴾ (سورة البقرة ٢ : ٤٤)

﴿Do you enjoin right conduct on people and forget (to practice it) yourselves...﴾ (Qur'an 2: 44)

The model of this kind of leadership is best manifested in Prophet Muhammad (Blessings and Peace be upon him) about whom Allah, the Almighty, said:

﴿لَّقَدْ كَانَ لَكُمْ فِى رَسُولِ ٱللَّهِ أُسْوَةٌ حَسَنَةٌ لِّمَن كَانَ يَرْجُوا۟ ٱللَّهَ وَٱلْيَوْمَ ٱلْءَاخِرَ وَذَكَرَ ٱللَّهَ كَثِيرًا ۝﴾ (سورة الأحزاب ٣٣ : ٢١)

❖Verily in the Messenger of Allah you have a good example for him who looks unto Allah and the Last Day, and remembers Allah much.❖ (Qur'an 33: 21)

Leaders should always be aware that they are role models. Their personality usually translates to the culture of the organization. Leaders are culture makers and they would better be so by design not by default.

9) Responsibility and empathy

Leaders shall possess a greater sense of responsibility than others. A leader shall feel deeply responsible for whatever is under his or her authority, and responsibility entails accountability in this world and in the Hereafter. 'Umar (may Allah be pleased with him), the second successor of the Prophet (bpuh), once said that he was afraid that a mule might fall in the mountain roads of Iraq and break its legs, and God might ask him why he had not paved the roads in that area. This demonstrated the extent to which 'Umar felt the responsibility, which in turn allowed him to reach a historically recognized managerial excellence. 'Umar ibn 'Abdul Aziz was so careful about the use of every thing under his control believing that his responsibility is a source of ignominy and regret in the Hereafter. This attitude of 'Umar ibn 'Abdul 'Aziz resulted in an optimum use of the resources of the nation.

Leaders should not only be responsible, rather they should be empathetic towards others. Because empathetic managers put themselves in the shoes of others, they are more capable of checking the appropriateness of their decisions. Furthermore, empathy promotes trust among subordinates who are likely to reciprocate the empathy of leaders by giving more. Empathy was one of the main characteristics of Prophet Muhammad (Blessings and Peace be upon him). Allah, the Exalted, said:

$$﴿لَقَدْ جَآءَكُمْ رَسُولٌ مِّنْ أَنفُسِكُمْ عَزِيزٌ عَلَيْهِ مَا عَنِتُّمْ حَرِيصٌ عَلَيْكُم بِالْمُؤْمِنِينَ رَءُوفٌ رَّحِيمٌ ۱۲۸﴾$$

(سورة التوبة ۹: ۱۲۸)

﴿Now has come to you a messenger from amongst yourselves: It grieves him that you should perish: Ardently anxious is he over you: To the believers is he most kind and merciful.﴾ (Qur'an 9: 128)

10) Forbearance

A leader must also be forbearing this is evident in the following verse of the Qur'an. Allah, the Almighty, said:

$$﴿إِنَّ إِبْرَاهِيمَ لَحَلِيمٌ أَوَّاهٌ مُّنِيبٌ ۷۵﴾ (سورة هود ۱۱: ۷۵)$$

﴿For Abraham was, without doubt, forbearing, compassionate and given to look to Allah.﴾ (Qur'an 11: 75)

The Prophet (Blessings and Peace be upon him) is reported to have said:

"The strong among you is not the one who can overpower others, but the one who can control himself in the moment of anger." (Muslim)

$$﴿وَجَعَلْنَا مِنْهُمْ أَئِمَّةً يَهْدُونَ بِأَمْرِنَا لَمَّا صَبَرُوا ۖ وَكَانُوا بِآيَاتِنَا يُوقِنُونَ ۲۴﴾$$

(سورة السجدة ۳۲: ۲۴)

❧And we made, from among them, leaders [*a'immah*], giving guidance under our command, so long as they display patience [*ṣabr*], and continue to have firm faith [*yaqīn*] in our signs.❧ (Qur'an 32: 24)

Leaders' anger and haste could lead to disastrous outcomes. Leaders should not take things personally and react out of anger or in response to provocation. They should always keep a big heart that transcends egos. They shall keep their composure, their rationality and justice and their wisdom.

Allah, the All-High, All-Glorious, said:

$$﴿وَلَنَبْلُوَنَّكُم بِشَيْءٍ مِّنَ ٱلْخَوْفِ وَٱلْجُوعِ وَنَقْصٍ مِّنَ ٱلْأَمْوَٰلِ وَٱلْأَنفُسِ وَٱلثَّمَرَٰتِ وَبَشِّرِ ٱلصَّٰبِرِينَ ۝﴾ (سورة البقرة ٢: ١٥٥)$$

❧Be sure we shall test you with something of fear and hunger, some loss in goods and lives or the fruits [of your toil], but give tidings to those who patiently persevere.❧ (Qur'an 2: 155)

11) Vision

Leaders should also have a vision or long-term target and should be focused on achieving it gradually. Dr. Mahathir Muhammad, the Prime Minister of Malaysia,[3] said that a good leader should be a long-term planner:

---

[3] Mahathir Muhammad, Prime Minister of Malaysia, Speech given on 24th August 1993, at 11 A. M.

"I believe that leaders should look far ahead and not look for immediate gains."

Vision is what distinguishes a leader from a simple manager. In fact, Prophet Muhammad (Blessings and Peace be upon him) and his Companions were capable of enduring great hardships and losses in order to achieve a long-term success. What characterized the late American civil rights leader Dr. Martin Luther King is his vision of a racially tolerant America. This vision was expressed in Dr. Kings' saying, "I have a dream." Dr. Mahathir sharply criticized leaders that are concerned about immediate gains.

The following hadith presents a vision of the Prophet (bpuh):

> "After many vain attempts to split or dislodge a rock, 'Umar (may Allah be pleased with him) went to the Prophet (bpuh) who took the pickaxe from him and gave the rock a blow at which a flare as of lightning flashed back over the city and towards the South. He gave it another blow and again there was a flash but in the direction of Uḥud and beyond it towards the North. A third blow split the rock into fragments and this time the light flashed eastwards. Salman saw the three flashes and understood that they must have some significance. So he asked for the interpretation from the Prophet (bpuh) who said: 'Did you see them Salman? By the light of the first, I saw the castles of Yemen; by the light of the second, I saw the castles of Syria; by the third I saw the white palace of Kisra (Khusroes') at Mada'in. Through the first God opened up to me the Yemen; through the second He opened to me Syria and the West; and through the third, the East.'"

12) Communication

It is not enough for leaders to be very committed to their long-term objective and full of ideas if they don't know how to communicate. Communication skills are necessary for any leadership role. This is why when Mūsa (Moses) (Peace be upon him) was appointed as the messenger of Allah he requested to be accompanied by Hārūn (Aaron) (Peace be upon him) his brother who was eloquent in speech. This is seen in the following verse.

﴿وَأَخِي هَـٰرُونُ هُوَ أَفۡصَحُ مِنِّي لِسَانًا فَأَرۡسِلۡهُ مَعِيَ رِدۡءًا يُصَدِّقُنِيٓ إِنِّيٓ أَخَافُ أَن يُكَذِّبُونِ ۩﴾ (سورة القصص ٢٨ : ٣٤)

﴿My brother Hārūn [Aaron] is more eloquent in speech than I: so send him with me as a helper, to confirm [and strengthen] me: For I fear that they may accuse me of falsehood.﴾ (Qur'an 28: 34)

13) Eagerness to learn: Adaptiveness

According to the leadership contingency theory,[4] it is difficult to train leaders for different leadership situations; however, both leaders and followers shall always seek to increase their knowledge and improve their skills to be able to adapt to new changes in the ever-evolving world.

﴿... وَقُل رَّبِّ زِدۡنِي عِلۡمًا ۩﴾ (سورة طه ٢٠ : ١١٤)

---

[4] Fiedler, F. E., *"Contingency Model and The Leadership Process,"* In Gerkowitz (ed.), Advances in Experimental Social Psychology, Vol. 11, Academic Press, N.Y., (1978).

﴾...And say: "O' my Lord! Increase me in knowledge."﴿
(Qur'an 20: 114)

14) Fairness and clear sense of loyalty

Leadership requires fairness and a clear sense of loyalty. This is expounded in the following verse:

﴿يَٰٓأَيُّهَا ٱلَّذِينَ ءَامَنُوا۟ كُونُوا۟ قَوَّٰمِينَ لِلَّهِ شُهَدَآءَ بِٱلْقِسْطِ وَلَا يَجْرِمَنَّكُمْ شَنَآنُ قَوْمٍ عَلَىٰٓ أَلَّا تَعْدِلُوا۟ ٱعْدِلُوا۟ هُوَ أَقْرَبُ لِلتَّقْوَىٰ ...﴾

(سورة المائدة ٥ : ٨)

﴾O you who believe! Stand out firmly for Allah, as witnesses to fair dealings and let not hatred of others to you make you swerve to wrong and depart from justice. Be just that is next to piety...﴿ (Qur'an 5: 8)

Human beings have the tendency of letting their feelings cloud their judgment. This could lead to injustice. A leader must avoid this if he is to obtain and maintain the respect of his followers thereby getting the best performance from them. It is certainly not easy to apply justice if it conflicts with ones' interest. We however can only evaluate someone's justice in this case.

In another verse Allah, the Exalted, says:

﴿قُلْ إِن كَانَ ءَابَآؤُكُمْ وَأَبْنَآؤُكُمْ وَإِخْوَٰنُكُمْ وَأَزْوَٰجُكُمْ وَعَشِيرَتُكُمْ وَأَمْوَٰلٌ ٱقْتَرَفْتُمُوهَا وَتِجَٰرَةٌ تَخْشَوْنَ كَسَادَهَا وَمَسَٰكِنُ تَرْضَوْنَهَآ أَحَبَّ إِلَيْكُم مِّنَ ٱللَّهِ وَرَسُولِهِ وَجِهَادٍ فِى سَبِيلِهِ فَتَرَبَّصُوا۟ حَتَّىٰ يَأْتِىَ ٱللَّهُ بِأَمْرِهِ وَٱللَّهُ لَا يَهْدِى ٱلْقَوْمَ ٱلْفَٰسِقِينَ﴾ (سورة التوبة ٩ : ٢٤)

❖Say: If it be that your fathers, Your sons, Your brothers, Your mates or Your Kindred: The wealth that you have gained; the commerce in which you fear to decline: or the dwellings in which you delight are dearer to you than Allah or His Messenger, or the striving in His cause; then wait until Allah brings about His decision: and Allah guides not the rebellious.❖ (Qur'an 9: 24)

From the above verse, it can be deduced that under no circumstances should a leader be swayed from being loyal to Allah, the Almighty, His Messenger (bpuh) and striving for His sake. So if there is conflict between one's family interest and justice, he should go for justice.

15) Awareness of followers' potentials and limitations

A leader must be aware of his followers' potentials. He should never underestimate his subordinates. Neither should he lose hope about them. Prophet Muhammad (bpuh) said:

"Whosoever said, people are in loss is either the most lost among them or one who caused them to be in loss." (Muslim)

Leaders should also be aware of the limitations of their subordinates so that he does not place on them a burden that they cannot carry.

﴿لَا يُكَلِّفُ اللَّهُ نَفْسًا إِلَّا وُسْعَهَا لَهَا...﴾ (سورة البقرة ٢ : ٢٨٦)

❖On no soul does Allah place a burden greater than it can bear.❖ (Qur'an 2: 286)

﴿۞ وَمَا أَعْجَلَكَ عَن قَوْمِكَ يَمُوسَىٰ ۝ قَالَ هُمْ أُوْلَاءِ عَلَىٰ أَثَرِى
وَعَجِلْتُ إِلَيْكَ رَبِّ لِتَرْضَىٰ ۝ قَالَ فَإِنَّا قَدْ فَتَنَّا قَوْمَكَ مِنْ بَعْدِكَ وَأَضَلَّهُمُ
ٱلسَّامِرِىُّ ۝ ﴾ (سورة طه ٢٠ : ٨٣-٨٥)

﴿"What made you hasten in advance of your people, O'
Moses! He replied, "Behold, they are close on my footsteps:
I hastened to you, O' my Lord, to please You." We have
tested them in your absence. The Samiri has led them
Astray."﴾ (Qur'an 20: 83-85)

The above verses show that Mūsa (Moses) (Peace be upon
him) was hasty for a good cause and he thought that his people
were following him well. Unfortunately they were left behind and
they ended up worshipping the bull.

16) Awareness of his own limitations

A leader must be aware of his limitations so that he can get
the necessary help to strengthen him. Hence, enabling him to
carry out his mission efficiently and effectively and thus acquire
success. This is shown in the following verse:

﴿وَأَخِى هَـٰرُونُ هُوَ أَفْصَحُ مِنِّى لِسَانًا فَأَرْسِلْهُ مَعِىَ رِدْءًا يُصَدِّقُنِىٓ إِنِّىٓ
أَخَافُ أَن يُكَذِّبُونِ ۝﴾ (سورة القصص ٢٨ : ٣٤)

﴿My brother Hārūn [Aaron] is more eloquent in speech
than I: so send him with me as a helper, to confirm [and
strengthen] me: For I fear that they may accuse me of
falsehood.﴾ (Qur'an 28: 34)

In the above verse, Mūsa (Moses) by admitting his weakness asked for support to compensate for it. By doing he served his cause better.

2 - Leadership Development

The fact that many great leaders possessed greater abilities than most other people did suggests that leaders must have some traits that set them apart from most human beings.[5] This theory seems to be called the trait theory. This theory is supported by the teaching of Prophet Muhammad (Blessings and Peace be upon him) who was praying to Allah to guide one of two strong men of his tribe to Islam because of the traits of their personality. Prophet Muhammad (bpuh) said:

"O Allah! Strengthen Islam by the more lovable to you: Abu Jahl ('Umar ibn al-Ḥakam) or 'Umar ibn al-Khaṭṭāb."
(Tirmidhi)

Prophet Muhammad (bpuh) also said:

"People are like mines, the best among them in Jahiliyyah (before Islam) are the best after Islam if they learned."
(Bukhāri and Muslim)

The above saying of the Prophet (bpuh) suggests that the traits of leaders are very important but their effectiveness will depend on learning or acquiring the necessary knowledge. This notion can also imply that once the necessary knowledge is acquired, leaders can better adjust to different situations. Whether

---

[5] Baron R. A., Greenberg, J. *"Behavior in Organizations,"* Allyn and Bacon. Boston (1989). p. 376

the leadership traits are acquired or gifted is a philosophical issue. The author believes that they are both acquired and gifted.

The acquirements of these traits are, however, a long process that should take place at an early age. The major attribute of a leader is the sense of responsibility or empathy. Some people confine their responsibilities to themselves only. Others have a much larger sphere of responsibility. The leader should be a person with empathy for the others. Another important aspect of leadership is decisions. People should be entrusted with the authority to make decision from a young age. Managers can contribute to developing leaders by delegating authority to their subordinates. The major task in leadership development is the identification of potential leaders. These potential leaders should then be taught various leadership lessons. They also should be trained to lead and make decisions through delegation of authority.

Hosner[6] stated that the major functions of a leader is to create a sense of commitment among his followers and to induce them to contribute something extra, or some additional efforts for the benefit of the organization. This implies that the major roles of a leader are the motivation of his or her followers. The concept of motivation in Islam will be presented in the next chapter. The next chapter will also address the major factor in workers, satisfaction.

---

[6] Hosner, L., T., "*A strategic View of Leadership,*" in strategic Planning and Management handbook," edited by King and Cleland (1987). p. 47

CASE STUDY

The Leadership of Abu Bakr

Abu Bakr (may Allah be pleased with him), the first man to enter Islam, was the closest Companion and father-in-law of the Prophet (Blessings and Peace be upon him). He was distinguished for his strong belief and merciful heart. When the Prophet (bpuh) passed away, his Companions were all choked. 'Umar (may Allah be pleased with him) went to the point of denying the death. Faced with this situation, Abu Bakr said: "Whoever worshipped Muhammad, then Muhammad is dead, but whoever worshipped Allah, then Allah is alive and shall never die. Allah, the Almighty, said:

$$\text{﴿وَمَا مُحَمَّدٌ إِلَّا رَسُولٌ قَدْ خَلَتْ مِن قَبْلِهِ الرُّسُلُ أَفَإِيْن مَّاتَ أَوْ قُتِـلَ}$$
$$\text{انقَلَبْتُمْ عَلَىٰ أَعْقَـٰبِكُمْ وَمَن يَنقَلِبْ عَلَىٰ عَقِبَيْهِ فَلَن يَضُرَّ اللَّهَ شَيْـًٔا}$$
$$\text{وَسَيَجْزِى اللَّهُ الشَّـٰكِرِينَ ﴾ (سورة آل عمران ٣: ١٤٤)}$$

◆Muhammad is no more than a messenger: many were the messengers that passed away before him. If he died or were slain, will you turn back on your heels? If any did turn back on his heels, not the least harm will he do to Allah, but Allah will swiftly reward those who serve him with gratitude.◆ (Qur'an 3: 144)

People fell silent and 'Umar fell to the ground for his legs would not bear him. It was as if that *āyah* (verse) was never heard before that moment.

The statement of Abu Bakr regarding the death of the Prophet (Blessings and Peace be upon him) provided an immediate relief and calm among Companions, however, this tragedy had sparked dissension and apostasy throughout the Arab peninsula. Many of the Arab tribes refused to pay *zakāh* and some people claimed prophethood. Apostasy was the major challenge facing Abu Bakr as the first *Khalīfah* (caliph). In these circumstances, Abu Bakr had to decide whether or not to send the army of the eighteen years old Usāma ibn Zayd to fight the Romans as planned by the Prophet (bpuh). Many Companions including Usāma suggested that this operation be cancelled and that the army be kept in Madīnah to protect it from any possible attack from the apostates. Abu Bakr insisted on sending the army in spite of the risks associated with this decision. He said, "By Allah I will not open a knot knit by the Messenger of Allah. If the birds snatch us up and wild animals surround Madīnah, and if dogs ran with the feet of the mothers of the believers, I will definitely equip the army of Usāma."

Abu Bakr also decided to fight the apostates who controlled the whole Arab peninsula with the exception of Madīnah, Makkah, and Ṭaif. 'Umar objected to this decision at first. He thought it was not right to fight people just for not paying *zakāh*. He also considered that it were not a good idea to fight them while the army of Usāma was still out. Yet Abu Bakr insisted on his opinion declaring that he would fight them for abstaining from giving anything they used to give to the Prophet (bpuh). He further said: "Revelation finished and religion was completed. Would it decrease while I am alive?" When 'Umar saw the strong conviction and firmness of Abu Bakr he immediately changed his position.

Three of the apostate tribes wanted to take advantage of the absence of the army of Usāma from Madīnah in order to attack it. So, they moved to the outskirts of the city and sent their envoys to Abu Bakr in order to force him to compromise with them and accept their refusal to pay *zakāh*. Abu Bakr refused their demands and attacked them by surprise at that same night. This marked the first defeat of the apostates. Later, the army of Usāma arrived back to Madīnah and Abu Bakr started sending his armies to fight the various apostate tribes.

Abu Bakr was known for his strong will and faith in the cause of Allah as well as for his cleverness and tactics. He was described as being too faithful to leave any room for planning and too tactful and vigorous in his planning to leave any room for faith. When Abu Bakr sent an army led by Khāled to fight the self acclaimed prophet Ṭulayḥa ibn Khuwaylid he did not mention that in public. Instead he said, "O' people go in the name of Allah and His *barakah*. Your leader is Khāled until I meet you. I am going in the direction of Khaybar (Jewish tribe in the Arab peninsula) until I meet you," but Abu Bakr did not go to Khaybar. He just said that in order to take the enemy by surprise and to force Khaybar to stay in their village and not to go to help the apostates. This is but one of many events that show the cleverness and tactfulness of Abu Bakr. After finishing with the apostates Abu Bakr started sending his armies to secure the borders of the Muslims with the Persian and Romans.

Because Abu Bakr ruled only for two years and because he was mostly preoccupied with the wars of apostasy, his leadership did not witness many administrative innovations. He, however, created the treasury, appointed a supreme judge, and divided the Muslim State into different administrative regions. He also delegated authority to his commanders. These administrative achievements were very critical because they paved the way for the post revelation developments undertaken by 'Umar.

Questions

1. Leadership requires one to be empathetic and merciful with his followers, but Abu Bakr said he would fight even if the dogs ran with the feet of the mothers of the believers.

(i) How do you explain this statement?

(ii) Why did Abu Bakr's followers accept this statement?

2. 'Umar was known for his resolve and radical ideas, yet he was against the opinion of Abu Bakr who decided to fight the apostates given that the latter was known for his mercy and softness.

(i) How do you relate the positions of Abu Bakr and 'Umar with their respective personality traits?

(ii) 'Umar quickly changed his opinion on fighting the apostates. Why did he do so?

3. It was clear that the Islamic state was at the verge of collapse after the death of the Prophet (bpuh) and that the leadership of Abu Bakr turned it to a force capable of defeating the Roman and Persian empires.

(i) What are the qualities that allowed Abu Bakr to have such a success?

(ii) Relate a modern case where a leader had led an

organization from the brink of failure to a great success and compare his leadership with that of Abu Bakr.

(iii) Do you believe that the qualities of Abu Bakr can render today's businesses successful? Discuss.

Exercises

1. Some people and nations were more successful than others in using the skills and resources that Allah has given them. Discuss.

2. What are the factors on which effective leadership depends?

3. Leadership requires technical skills only. Do you agree or disagree. State the reasons for your answer.

4. List the two pillars of leadership as mentioned in the Qur'an in order of importance and explain why one is more important than the other.

5. What are the qualities of a good leader as mentioned in the Qur'an?

6. What is the distinction between a leader and a simple manager?

7. What are the major functions of a leader?

MOTIVATION

No one knows better about a machine than the one who designed and fabricated it. Similarly, no one knows more about man and his nature than his creator does.

$$﴿أَلَمْ نَجْعَل لَّهُ عَيْنَيْنِ ۝ وَلِسَانًا وَشَفَتَيْنِ ۝ وَهَدَيْنَاهُ ٱلنَّجْدَيْنِ ۝﴾$$

(سورة البلد ٩٠ : ٨-١٠)

﴾Did We not assign unto him two eyes and a tongue and two lips and guide him to the two highways [good and bad].﴿ (Qur'an 90: 8-10)

$$﴿إِنَّا هَدَيْنَاهُ ٱلسَّبِيلَ إِمَّا شَاكِرًا وَإِمَّا كَفُورًا ۝﴾$$

(سورة الإنسان ٧٦ : ٣)

﴾Lo! We have shown him the way whether he be grateful or disbelieving.﴿ (Qur'an 76: 3)

$$﴿إِذْ قَالَ رَبُّكَ لِلْمَلَٰئِكَةِ إِنِّي خَٰلِقٌ بَشَرًا مِّن طِينٍ ۝﴾$$

(سورة ص ٣٨ : ٧١)

﴾When the Lord said unto the angels: Lo! I am about to create a mortal out of mire.﴿ (Qur'an 38: 71)

Because Allah created us, He is the One who knows us the best, and therefore, we can gain an understanding of ourselves from the Qur'an. There can be many aspects of self-understanding that can be sought in the Qur'an, but at the moment we want to address the issue of motivation. We will start by presenting how to plan for motivation. Then, we will discuss reward and punishment. The third section will cover spiritual motivation and finally we will highlight justice as a hygiene factor.

1 - Planning for Motivation

The first step in motivation takes place in the planning process. It is always better that the goals be chosen and defined through a participative process. Further, the nature of the goals, how challenging they are, and whether they fall within the strength of the organization are very critical in determining the level of motivation.

A more rewarding objective inspires greater dedication and effort. Further, people need to know how the achievement of the goals will help them personally in their lives. They need to know what it is in the goals for them. In case the organizational culture includes a sense of belonging and commitment between all the members of the organization, it will not be very difficult for anybody to identify what is for him or her in the accomplishment of the goals. This means that the organizational culture affects motivation. On the other hand, the kind of motivation and the kind of reward system that it includes also affect the organizational culture. For example group rewards can foster the sense of community better than individual rewards. Further, any type of injustice will dismiss the claim of a culture of collectiveness.

The goals that fall within the strength of the organization are goals that fit well with the skills and resources of the organization. This means that it is not just feasible for the organization to achieve these goals, rather it is likely for the organization to excel in achieving them. In case the organization does not possess the necessary skills and resources to achieve its objectives, it has to plan for acquiring more resources and skills through training and or recruiting.

Management could install appropriate technical and behaviour training programmes. The training programmes are indispensable when the workers lack the necessary skills to perform their tasks, as people are enemies to what they ignore. The training programmes are also becoming more critical as the business environment is rapidly changing.

Further, the fact that the plan fits the strength of the organization should be emphasized, because people should believe that they could achieve the desired objective. This guarantees a high level of effort-performance expectancy. Without self-confidence, workers are likely to be frustrated. To address the issue of confidence, managers should try to make some statement showing their confidence in their subordinates.

In long-term planning, it is not enough that the long-term objective be very appealing and fall within the strength of the organization. It is equally important that the intermediate goals be, as appealing otherwise the accomplishment of the long-term objective will be put to question. It is also very important that a direct relationship between any action along the road leading to the long-term objective and the long-term objective itself be established. We have seen that every action, no matter how small it is, has a corresponding value (reward or punishment) in the long-term objective of Islam. This way, people will be focused on the long-term objective and will realize that mediocre or bad performance at any moment will haunt them for a long time. We have tried to use this approach in motivating two classes of business students, who share the same professor, to study for a common mid-term. Subsequently, we explained to the students of one of the classes that the mid-terms would not just affect their grade in their courses, but rather it would affect their cumulative grade point average, as the course grade will always show in their transcript. Further, we told them, that this is going to affect the kind of job they will have and whether or not they will go to graduate school. Moreover, if they can be accepted in graduate school, this mid-term will contribute to determining which school they will go to. Basically we showed the students that the mid-term would haunt them all their lives. Then, these students were asked whether understanding the importance of the mid-term in such a manner motivated them, and they all responded positively. Indeed the mean of the class that was exposed to such motivation was 117.8% that of the other class.

The example of the three construction workers discussed in the section *"Objective"* (Part II *Planning*) is relevant in this context. One of these workers was asked what he was doing, he said, he was laying bricks. This corresponds to the lowest level of action in the figure. When the second worker was asked what he was doing, he replied that he was building a wall. This corresponds to the intermediate level goals in the figure. Finally, when the third worker was asked the same question, he replied that he was building a house. This corresponds to the highest-level objective, in the figure. It is clear that the third worker was more motivated because he saw more meaning in what he was doing than the other two workers were. Managers should convince workers that they are all building a house or contributing to the end goal rather than making them feel that they are just laying bricks or performing some hardly significant task.

Muslims should focus on the long term objective of *Jannah* (Paradise). We should not be too attached to the intermediate goals in this life. We rewarded for well-intended efforts even if we fail perform well let alone to achieve the result. Unlike what is suggested by Vroom,[7] Our motivation is not dependent on the expectancies of performance and outcome.

Prophet Muhammad (Blessings and Peace be upon him) said:

"If the hour comes and one of you has a seedling, if he can plant it be he gets up, then he should plant it." (Bukhārī)

The Companions of the Prophet excelled in the pursuit of the opening of Makkah. Indeed many of them became martyrs and never witnessed Makkah becoming Muslim. The main reason behind the excellent performance of the Companions of the Prophet was that they believed in reward in *Jannah* (Paradise) for their struggle or efforts regardless of whether or not they achieved the next goal, which was the opening of Makkah.

Once the planning is completed and the direct relationships between the various required actions and the long-term objective have been established managers have to clearly divide the responsibilities among their subordinates. Then managers shall clearly explain the plan to their subordinates who have not been part of the planning process because people cannot be motivated to achieve that which they do not know. The objective and the way to achieve it have to be crystal clear for everybody.

Allah, the All-High, All-Glorious, said:

---

[7] Vroom, V. H. *"Work Motivation,"* N. Y., John Wiley, 1964.

﴿قُلْ هَٰذِهِۦ سَبِيلِيٓ أَدْعُوٓاْ إِلَى ٱللَّهِ عَلَىٰ بَصِيرَةٍ أَنَا۠ وَمَنِ ٱتَّبَعَنِيۖ ...﴾ ۞

(سورة يوسف ١٢ : ١٠٨)

﴾Say! [O Muhammad]: This is my way; I call to Allah with sure knowledge and understanding, I and whosoever follows me...﴿ (Qur'an 12: 108)

The above verse shows that both the Prophet (bpuh) and his followers clearly understood their way.

2 - Reward and Punishment

After the above issues have been addressed, comes the role of reward and punishment. Reward is a desirable outcome that results from a desirable behaviour while punishment is the undesirable outcome that follows an unwanted behaviour. Many management scholars argued that punishment should never be used as means of motivation. The arguments cited against the use of punishment include the fear that it might lead to the suppression of socially desirable behaviour. This can happen when the punishment is very severe. Further, it is argued that punishment can result in negative side effects such as anxiety, aggression, and withdrawal. In reality, punishment is commonly used in organizations in one way or another.[8] Islam uses both the appeal of reward and the fear of punishment. Indeed not every human being is a high achiever, and many people at different stages of their lives tend to be satisfied with their status and do not even consider improving it no matter how much reward they could get.

---

[8] Katz, D., and Khan, R., L., *"The Social Psychology of Organizations,"* 2nd ed. N. Y., John Wiley and Son, (1979).

These people might, however, be better motivated through the fear of punishment. People usually act out of hope or out of fear. They sometimes act due to other factors such as love and hate, but these latter can always be translated into hope and fear. Bosnia was devastated in a prolonged genocide that resulted in the death of hundreds of thousands of people and in the rape of tens of thousands of women and children.

On July 29, 1993, The foreign Minister of Bosnia, Haris Silajic who failed to persuade the international community to lift the unfair arms embargo imposed on his people, said, "There are no human norms except if you are rich or dangerous." This was an unfortunate testimony that the international community could only be motivated through fear or hope. In Islam, one is to either go backward or to go forward. Allah, the Exalted, said:

$$﴿إِنَّهَا لَإِحْدَى ٱلْكُبَرِ ۝ نَذِيرًا لِّلْبَشَرِ ۝ لِمَن شَآءَ مِنكُمْ أَن يَتَقَدَّمَ أَوْ يَتَأَخَّرَ ۝﴾$$

(سورة المدثر ٧٤ : ٣٥-٣٧)

❝This is but one of the mighty [portents]. A warning to mankind. To any of you that chooses to press forward or to follow behind.❞ (Qur'an 74: 35-37)

In Islam, there are both reward and punishment; both in this world and in the Hereafter, for men act out of fear and/or out of hope. Prophet Muhammad (Blessings and Peace be upon him) as well as the other messengers of Allah (Peace be upon them all) were sent with both glad tidings and warnings:

$$﴿إِنَّآ أَرْسَلْنَٰكَ بِٱلْحَقِّ بَشِيرًا وَنَذِيرًا ... ۝﴾$$

(سورة البقرة ٢ : ١١٩)

❝Verily, We have sent you in truth as a bearer of glad

tidings and a warner.﴾ (Qur'an 2: 119)

﴿ ۩ ... فَبَعَثَ ٱللَّهُ ٱلنَّبِيِّـۧنَ مُبَشِّرِينَ وَمُنذِرِينَ ... ﴾

(سورة البقرة ٢ : ٢١٣)

﴿...And Allah Sent messengers with glad tiding and warnings...﴾ (Qur'an 2: 213)

﴿رُّسُلًا مُّبَشِّرِينَ وَمُنذِرِينَ لِئَلَّا يَكُونَ لِلنَّاسِ عَلَى ٱللَّهِ حُجَّةٌۢ بَعْدَ ٱلرُّسُلِ وَكَانَ ٱللَّهُ عَزِيزًا حَكِيمًا ۩﴾ (سورة النساء ٤ : ١٦٥)

﴿Messengers who gave good news as well as warning, that mankind after [the coming] of the messengers, should have no plea against Allah: For Allah is Exalted in Power, Wise.﴾ (Qur'an 4: 165)

﴿وَمَا نُرْسِلُ ٱلْمُرْسَلِينَ إِلَّا مُبَشِّرِينَ وَمُنذِرِينَ ۩﴾ ...

(سورة الأنعام ٦ : ٤٨)

﴿We Send the messengers only to give good news and to warn...﴾ (Qur'an 6: 48)

In all the above cited verses, it is seen that Allah, the Almighty has sent messengers to inform mankind about the reward in the Hereafter as well as warn them about the punishment in the Hereafter.

It is only just to punish for the wrong and to reward for the good.

﴿قَالَ أَمَّا مَن ظَلَمَ فَسَوْفَ نُعَذِّبُهُۥ ثُمَّ يُرَدُّ إِلَىٰ رَبِّهِۦ فَيُعَذِّبُهُۥ عَذَابًا نُّكْرًا ۩ وَأَمَّا مَنْ ءَامَنَ وَعَمِلَ صَٰلِحًا فَلَهُۥ جَزَآءً ٱلْحُسْنَىٰ وَسَنَقُولُ لَهُۥ مِنْ أَمْرِنَا يُسْرًا ۩﴾

(سورة الكهف ١٨ : ٨٧-٨٨)

❋[Dhu al-Qarnayn] said: whoever does wrong, him shall we punish; then shall he be sent back to his Lord; and He will punish him with a punishment unheard-of. But whoever believes and works righteousness-he shall have a goodly reward; and easy shall be our speech to him [as instructions].❋ (Qur'an 18: 87-88)

In fact both reward and punishment are necessary even for minute performances.

$$﴿فَمَن يَعْمَلْ مِثْقَالَ ذَرَّةٍ خَيْرًا يَرَهُ ۝ وَمَن يَعْمَلْ مِثْقَالَ ذَرَّةٍ شَرًّا يَرَهُ ۝﴾ (سورة الزلزلة ٩٩ : ٧-٨)$$

❋Then shall anyone who has done an atom weight of good, shall see good. And anyone who has done an atoms weight of evil, shall see it.❋ (Qur'an 99: 7-8)

'Ali (may Allah be pleased with him), the fourth successor of the Prophet (Blessings and Peace be upon him) said:[9]

"Make sure that the good doer and the bad doer are not equal in status before you, for doing so is belittling good and its doers, and encouraging bad and its doers."

The most important thing is to reward or at least to recognize good performance because not doing so will discourage hard workers and encourage low performers. Allah, the Almighty, All-High, said:

$$﴿... إِنَّا لَا نُضِيعُ أَجْرَ مَنْ أَحْسَنَ عَمَلًا ۝﴾ (سورة الكهف ١٨ : ٣٠)$$

---

[9] Abusin, A., I., *"Al-Idara fil Islam,"* 3rd ed. *Al-Matba'a al-'Asriyyah*, UAE, (1987). p. 93.

❲...We never waste the reward of anyone who did good.❳
(Qur'an 18: 30)

In order to encourage process improvement rather than quick fixes, it is necessary that people be rewarded for the efforts not just for the achievements. Prophet Muhammad (bpuh) said:

"Whoever puts an effort and succeeds gets two new lands and whoever puts an effort and does not succeed gets one reward." (Abu Dawūd)

Islam rewards thus efforts not just the outcome.

"If the hour comes and one of you has a seedling, if he can plant it be he gets up, then he should plant it." (Bukhāri)

Further, the fact that Islam applies both reward and punishment is not an excuse for managers to embark in punishing their subordinates for any mistake. The tendency to punish shall be balanced by forgiveness, for a good leader is one who forgives (look at the previous section). In addition, good deeds cancel bad deeds as stated in the Qur'an:

﴾... إِنَّ ٱلْحَسَنَٰتِ يُذْهِبْنَ ٱلسَّيِّئَاتِ ذَٰلِكَ ...﴿ ⑯ (سورة هود ١١: ١١٤)

❲...For those deeds that are good remove those deeds that are evil...❳ (Qur'an 11: 114)

Moreover, being very picky on rare mistakes and imperfections of workers can lead to their embarrassment, alienation and anger, reducing thereby, their effectiveness. Anas (may Allah be pleased with him), a Companion of the Prophet (bpuh) said that he worked for the Prophet (bpuh) for twenty years and that the Prophet (bpuh) never asked him why he did and what he did nor did he ask him to do things that he did not do. However, the behaviour of the Prophet (bpuh) with Anas is not an absolute

Leadership and Motivation

rule because not every worker is as qualified and committed as Anas.

It is necessary to realize that punishment itself is not a motivator, rather, it is the fear of punishment that motivates people. Punishment is only a reinforcer that could become counter-productive if it is used excessively. Islamic teachings give warning from punishment but not punishment itself. It is argued that the punished person might get used to punishment and stop trying to avoid it. Punishment is rather a disciplinary measure.

Managers should be generally careful about using disciplinary measures. While it is good and recommended to praise good actions in front of others, it is discouraged to even take verbal disciplinary measures openly. Such measures are more effective when they are taken privately, for even advice in front of people can turn out to be an embarrassment for the person being advised. This is especially true if the one advised is the superior (in rank and position) of the people present during the advice. Hersey and Blanchard[10] stated:

"The last thing to remember is to keep disciplinary interventions private. As a guideline, it is a good idea to praise people in public and problems solve in private. If you address followers about problems when others are around, you run the risk of having them more concerned about being seen Catching Hell than on solving the problem. Discussing the problems in private tend to make it easier to get your points across and keep other persons focused on problem solving process."

---

[10] Hersey, P., and Blanchard, K., H. *"Management of Organizational Behavior,"* 6th ed., Prentice Hall, New Jersey, (1993).

Meanwhile, in order for punishment to be effective, the offender should be made aware of it very clearly, and it should be justly executed for all the responsible employees. It also has to be applied in a fashion, which is both proportional to the unwanted behaviour, and moderate. Punishment should not be so severe that it creates negative side effects, and it should not be so lenient as to not achieve its desired purpose. It is also generally better to use punishment immediately after the occurrence of the punishable response. This way, punishment can be directly related to the response. Moreover, managers have to be sure that they are punishing for the unwanted behaviour and not for any personal reasons. That is, they should punish on the act and not on the person. They also have to communicate clearly the reasons for punishments. When managers punish somebody, they should not dilute that by giving him or her a non-contingent reward. Most importantly, punishment has to be used only as a last resort. It should be preceded with training, advice, and verbal disciplinary measures.

3 - Spiritual Motivation

Motivation in Islam is not restricted to monetary and material incentives but includes spiritual incentives, which have proven their effectiveness throughout history.[11]

Actually the most important motivation we have is the belief that our work is *'ibādah* (prayer) that we will be rewarded for. Such a belief is a competitive advantage. Good words and

---

[11] (16). Al-Buraey, M. *"Management and Administrative Development in Islam,"* (1990).

good statement of recognition and praise are also important. Allah, the All-High, All-Glorious, said:

﴿... وَقُولُوا لِلنَّاسِ حُسْنًا ...﴾ ﴿٨٣﴾ (سورة البقرة ٢ : ٨٣)

❴...And speak to people Good...❵ (Qur'an 2: 83)

﴿أَلَمْ تَرَ كَيْفَ ضَرَبَ ٱللَّهُ مَثَلًا كَلِمَةً طَيِّبَةً كَشَجَرَةٍ طَيِّبَةٍ أَصْلُهَا ثَابِتٌ وَفَرْعُهَا فِي ٱلسَّمَاءِ ﴿٢٤﴾ تُؤْتِي أُكُلَهَا كُلَّ حِينٍ بِإِذْنِ رَبِّهَا ۗ وَيَضْرِبُ ٱللَّهُ ٱلْأَمْثَالَ لِلنَّاسِ لَعَلَّهُمْ يَتَذَكَّرُونَ ﴿٢٥﴾ وَمَثَلُ كَلِمَةٍ خَبِيثَةٍ كَشَجَرَةٍ خَبِيثَةٍ ٱجْتُثَّتْ مِن فَوْقِ ٱلْأَرْضِ مَا لَهَا مِن قَرَارٍ ﴿٢٦﴾﴾

(سورة إبراهيم ١٤ : ٢٤-٢٦)

❴See you not how Allah sets forth a parable? A goodly word like a goodly tree whose root is firmly fixed, and its branches reach the heavens. It brings forth its fruits at all times by the leave of its Lord. So Allah sets forth parables for people in order that they may receive admonition. And the parable of an evil word is that of any evil tree: it is torn up by the root from the surface of the earth. It has no stability.❵ (Qur'an 14: 24-26)

The above verses motivate people to do good deeds for the benefits from such a deed are never ending. As for bad deeds, nobody benefits from them and should thus be avoided.

Stressing the importance of recognizing and thanking people for their efforts, Prophet Muhammad (Blessings and Peace be upon him) said: "He who does not thank people does not thank Allah." (Abu Dawūd)

Iacoca found encouragement to be vital for maintaining the involvement of his subordinates

In corporate life, you have to encourage all your people to make a contribution to the common good and to come up with better ways of doing things. You do not have to accept every single suggestion, but if you do not get back to the guy and say hey, that idea was terrific, and pat him in the back, he will never give you another one. That kind of communication lets people know they really count.[12]

Religious teaching can play a great spiritual motivation role. There are ample Islamic teaching that encourage Muslims to be productive:

﴿وَمِنْهُم مَّن يَقُولُ رَبَّنَآ ءَاتِنَا فِى ٱلدُّنْيَا حَسَنَةً وَفِى ٱلْآخِرَةِ حَسَنَةً وَقِنَا عَذَابَ ٱلنَّارِ ۝﴾ (سورة البقرة ٢: ٢٠١)

﴿And of them [also] is he who says: Our Lord! Give us in the world that which is good and in the Hereafter that which is good, and Guard us from the doom of fire.﴾ (Qur'an 2: 201)

﴿وَٱبْتَغِ فِيمَآ ءَاتَىٰكَ ٱللَّهُ ٱلدَّارَ ٱلْآخِرَةَ وَلَا تَنسَ نَصِيبَكَ مِنَ ٱلدُّنْيَا ... ۝﴾ (سورة القصص ٢٨: ٧٧)

﴿But seek the abode of the Hereafter in that which Allah has given you and neglect not your portion of the world...﴾ (Qur'an 28: 77)

﴿فَإِذَا قُضِيَتِ ٱلصَّلَوٰةُ فَٱنتَشِرُوا۟ فِى ٱلْأَرْضِ وَٱبْتَغُوا۟ مِن فَضْلِ ٱللَّهِ وَٱذْكُرُوا۟ ٱللَّهَ كَثِيرًا لَّعَلَّكُمْ تُفْلِحُونَ ۝﴾ (سورة الجمعة ٦٢: ١٠)

---

[12] Iacoca, L., "*Iacoca: An Autobiography*," Batman books, NY, 1984 p. 52.

❧And when the prayer is finished, then may you disperse through the land and seek of the bounty of Allah: and celebrate the praises of Allah often that you may prosper.❧ (Qur'an 62: 10)

﴿وَقُلِ ٱعْمَلُواْ فَسَيَرَى ٱللَّهُ عَمَلَكُمْ وَرَسُولُهُ وَٱلْمُؤْمِنُونَ ... ﴿١٠٥﴾﴾

(سورة التوبة ٩ : ١٠٥)

❧And say: Work, soon will Allah observe your work, and His Messenger and the believers...❧ (Qur'an 9: 105)

When Allah, the All-Merciful, abrogated the late night prayers (*Qiyām*) for the Companions, He mentioned, as one of the reasons of the abrogation, the hardship that was faced by the merchants in their business trips.

﴿ ﴿ وَءَاخَرُونَ يَضْرِبُونَ فِي ٱلْأَرْضِ يَبْتَغُونَ مِن فَضْلِ ٱللَّهِ وَءَاخَرُونَ يُقَٰتِلُونَ فِي سَبِيلِ ٱللَّهِ ... ﴿٢٠﴾﴾ (سورة المزمل ٧٣ : ٢٠)

❧...Others traveling through the land seeking of Allah's bounty and others fighting in Allah's cause...❧ (Qur'an 73: 20)

Prophet Muhammad (Blessings and Peace be upon him) said:

"He whose two days are equal (in accomplishments) is a loser." (Daiylamy)

"The most lawful food of a servant is the earning of the hand of a producer if he did it to his best abilities (with sincerity)." (Bukhāri)

"The truthful and trusty merchant is with (at the level of) the apostles, the men of truth, and martyrs." (Tirmidhi)

"The upper hand is better than the lower hand." (Bukhāri and Muslim)

"The creatures are the dependents of Allah and the most loved by Allah among them is the most beneficial for them." (Aṭ-Ṭabarāni)

"It is better for one to take his rope to get woods for fuel than to ask people for charity, whether they give him or not." (Bukhāri)

All of the Qur'anic verses and the hadiths mentioned above points to the importance of work in Islam and the reward expected from it. There is therefore no excuse for being unproductive. We are created to worship Allah and a great part of this worship is working hard in His way.

Further, most of the Prophets had done some manual work including Prophet Muhammad (Blessings and Peace be upon him) who was a shepherd in his childhood and then became a merchant. This fact can provide some intrinsic motivation by restoring the value of such professions. Prophet Muhammad (Blessings and Peace be upon him) said:

"David was fabricating shields, Ādam was a farmer, Noah was a carpenter, Idrīs was a tailor, and Moses was a shepherd." (Al-Ḥākim)

The teachings of Islam also stressed quality and excellence in performing any job.

"Allah, the Almighty, wants that when one of you does a job, he/she does it well." (Al-Bayhaqi)

"Allah has decreed excellence for everything. When you kill, do it in the best way; and when you slaughter (an animal for sacrifice), do it in the best way. So every one of you should sharpen his knife, and let the slaughtered animal die comfortably." (Muslim)

Motivation can be hindered by any unfair treatment workers might receive or perceive. On the other hand, if workers feel that they are treated with equity, they would even be able to cope with some possible economic and physical stress. The following section outlines the value of justice in the work place.

4 - Hygiene Factor; Justice

The most critical point in workers satisfaction is justice, for injustice befalls civilization as Ibn Khaldoun correctly stated in his *Muqaddimah*. The worker has to be sure that his work is rewarded, or at least he or she should be recognized for the good work, otherwise he/she might lose any incentive to keep up the same productivity and quality. The worker has to feel treated fairly and has to be granted his rights as he has to assume his duties. Prophet Muhammad (Blessings and Peace be upon him) is reported to have said: "Injustice is darkness in the Hereafter." (Bukhāri and Muslim)

> "I will be against three persons on the Day of Resurrection: One who makes a covenant in my name but he proves treacherous, One who sells a free person as a slave and eats his price, and one who employs a labourer and gets the full work done by him, but does not pay him his wages." (Bukhāri)

> "Beware, if anyone wrongs a contracting man, or diminishes his right, or forces him to work beyond his capacity, or takes from him anything without his consent, I shall plead for him on the Day of Judgment." (Abu Dawūd)

Employers should not treat their employees with injustice nor place on them jobs that are beyond their capacity. Islam is against injustice.

"Give a contacting man his wage before his sweat is dried." (Ibn Mājah)

The above hadiths implies that people should be paid the wages due them immediately they finished their work.

"Whoever wishes to be delivered from Hell-Fire and enter the Garden (Paradise) should treat the people the way he wishes to be treated." (Muslim)

Nobody wants to be treated unjustly. Therefore people should treat one another the way they like to be treated. This is a call for empathy.

Justice is one of the major goals of Islam. Allah, the All-High, said:

﴿۞ إِنَّ ٱللَّهَ يَأْمُرُ بِٱلْعَدْلِ وَٱلْإِحْسَٰنِ وَإِيتَآئِ ذِى ٱلْقُرْبَىٰ وَيَنْهَىٰ عَنِ ٱلْفَحْشَآءِ وَٱلْمُنكَرِ وَٱلْبَغْىِ يَعِظُكُمْ لَعَلَّكُمْ تَذَكَّرُونَ ۝﴾

(سورة النحل ١٦ : ٩٠)

﴿Allah commands justice, the doing of good, and liberality to kith and kin and He forbids all shameful deeds, injustice and rebellion: He instructs you, that you may receive admonition.﴾ (Qur'an 16: 90)

In other verses Allah, the Almighty, said:

﴿يَٰٓأَيُّهَا ٱلَّذِينَ ءَامَنُوا۟ كُونُوا۟ قَوَّٰمِينَ لِلَّهِ شُهَدَآءَ بِٱلْقِسْطِ وَلَا يَجْرِمَنَّكُمْ شَنَـَٔانُ قَوْمٍ عَلَىٰٓ أَلَّا تَعْدِلُوا۟ ٱعْدِلُوا۟ هُوَ أَقْرَبُ لِلتَّقْوَىٰ ...۝﴾

(سورة المائدة ٥ : ٨)

❦O you who believe! Stand out firmly for Allah, as witnesses to fair dealing, and let not the hatred of others to you make you swerve to wrong and depart from justice. Be just, that is next to piety...❦ (Qur'an 5: 8)

People should not witness unfair dealings but should rather eliminate them by all means. Further, personal emotions must not stand in the way of justice.

﴿... وَأُمِرْتُ لِأَعْدِلَ بَيْنَكُمُ ...﴾ ﴿١٥﴾ (سورة الشورى ٤٢ : ١٥)

❦...And I am commanded to judge justly between you...❦ (Qur'an 42: 15)

When judging between people, judge fairly and give to people what they deserve.

﴿ ... وَلَا تَبْخَسُوا ٱلنَّاسَ أَشْيَاءَهُمْ ...﴾ ﴿٨٥﴾ (سورة الأعراف ٧ : ٨٥)

❦...Do not discredit people from what they deserve...❦[13] (Qur'an 7: 85)

The concept of justice is more encompassing than the concept of equity introduced by Stacy Ādams, for the former is not restricted to the comparison of one's perceived ratio of inputs and outcomes with others. To investigate the scope and importance of justice in the workplace, we conducted a survey of the academic staff of the International Islamic University. 83.87 percent of the people surveyed believed that justice is a hygiene

---

[13] N.B.: ❦...Withhold not from the people the things that are their due...❦ ['Abdullah Yusuf 'Ali]

❦Give full measure and full weight and wrong not mankind in their goods...❦ [Pickthall]

factor whose absence results in dissatisfaction. 16.3 percent considered it a motivator. Some of the people surveyed explained that their performance would not decrease if they feel treated unjustly because of the great satisfaction they are getting from their jobs and because of their moral responsibility towards it. Others mentioned that justice assures them that they would be rewarded for their efforts and thus, contributes to their motivation. This is equivalent to saying that justice increases the performance outcome expectancy. Only 6.45 percent of those surveyed confined their perception of injustice to the comparison of their input output ratios with others. The rest of those surveyed also included value judgment based on justice in its absolute terms and on comparisons with others in similar organizations.

It is not enough for managers to be just. They also have to make sure that their subordinates perceive them so. The decisions that managers make should be thoroughly explained, so that the workers do not feel any injustice. 'Umar (may Allah be pleased with him) used to clearly explain the reasons behind his decisions to change his governors.

On the other hand, justice will not prevail by only emphasizing that it is mandatory. Many managers get away with some grave injustices towards their subordinates, and it is not uncommon for managers to cover up for each other's injustices. To claim that justice is part of the culture of an organization is not enough. Justice should be looked after by some programmes that includes the enforcement of justice. There should be a section of complaints within or without the personnel department. Even though justice was the cornerstone of the culture of the Companions of the Prophet, and even though it is one of the general goals of Islam, 'Umar created an agency of complaints that had the authority to restore justice.

SUMMARY

Leadership is a necessary service in any organization. Leadership effectiveness is dependent on the leader, the followers, and the situation. Leaders shall respect and consult their followers. Once a decision is made, they shall have the resolve to implement it, while putting their trust in Allah. Vision is what distinguishes a leader from a simple manager. While both strength (skills) and faith or sincerity are required in a leader, the skills should always have the priority. Leaders should have a great sense of responsibility. They also should possess a high level of empathy of their followers. They are role models that deeply influence the culture of the organizations. The major task in leadership development is the identification of potential leaders who possess a high sense of responsibility.

Motivation starts at the planning stage. Organizations should make sure that their members can relate and be committed to their goals. Further, establishing a direct cause and effect relationship between the various actions to be undertaken, and the long-term objective of the organization is likely to increase the level of motivation.

Motivation includes both the appeal of reward and the fear of punishment, for people act out of fear and/or out of hope. Reward should be used more than punishment because the tendency to punish should be balanced by forgiveness. Further, it is the fear of punishment not punishment itself that increase motivation. Punishment is rather a disciplinary measure. Spiritual methods are also very effective motivators and justice is the cornerstone of workers satisfaction.

Next part will deal with competition and conflicts. In the next chapter, two classes of competition will be presented. Islam encourages the first class while the second is prohibited.

Exercises

1. What are the critical factors in determining the level of motivation?

2. Give an example of how the organizational culture and motivation mutually affect each other.

3. Define reward and punishment.

4. In what ways Islam uses both the appeal of reward and the fear of punishment in the context of motivation?

5. Should punishment be used as a means of motivation? Why and why not?

6. Should rewards focus only on achievement or should efforts be rewarded as well?

7. Is punishment a motivator?

8. Outline the principle of punishment.

9. State some Qur'anic verses and hadiths that encourage people to be productive.

10. What is the most critical factor in workers satisfaction?

11. How can justice be enforced in an organization?

PART – V

COMPETITION AND CONFLICTS

COMPETITION

There are two ethically different types of competition. One of which is positive competition, which is praised and encouraged by Islam. The other one is a negative competition that Islam rejects. This chapter will present these two types of competition.

1 - Positive Competition

Allah has asked Muslims to compete in doing good deeds, and in helping others. The objective of this competition is none but the ultimate reward of entering the Gardens of Paradise. Allah, the Exalted, said:

﴿سَابِقُوٓاْ إِلَىٰ مَغْفِرَةٍ مِّن رَّبِّكُمْ وَجَنَّةٍ عَرْضُهَا كَعَرْضِ ٱلسَّمَآءِ وَٱلْأَرْضِ أُعِدَّتْ لِلَّذِينَ ءَامَنُواْ بِٱللَّهِ وَرُسُلِهِۦۚ ذَٰلِكَ فَضْلُ ٱللَّهِ يُؤْتِيهِ مَن يَشَآءُۚ وَٱللَّهُ ذُو ٱلْفَضْلِ ٱلْعَظِيمِ ﴾ ۝ (سورة الحديد ٥٧ : ٢١)

﴿Race one with another for forgiveness from your Lord and a Garden [Paradise] whereof the breadth is the breadth of the heavens and the earth, which is in store for those who believe in Allah and His messengers. Such is a bounty of Allah, which He bestows upon whom He will, and Allah is of infinite bounty.﴾ (Qur'an 57: 21)

﴿وَسَارِعُوٓاْ إِلَىٰ مَغْفِرَةٍ مِّن رَّبِّكُمْ وَجَنَّةٍ عَرْضُهَا ٱلسَّمَٰوَٰتُ وَٱلْأَرْضُ أُعِدَّتْ لِلْمُتَّقِينَ ۝ ٱلَّذِينَ يُنفِقُونَ فِى ٱلسَّرَّآءِ وَٱلضَّرَّآءِ وَٱلْكَٰظِمِينَ ٱلْغَيْظَ

وَٱلْعَافِينَ عَنِ ٱلنَّاسِ ۗ وَٱللَّهُ يُحِبُّ ٱلْمُحْسِنِينَ ﴿١٣٤﴾

(سورة آل عمران ٣: ١٣٣-١٣٤)

❊And vie one with another for forgiveness from Your Lord, a Paradise as wide as are the heavens and the earth, prepared for those who ward off [evil]; Those who spend [of that which Allah has given them] in ease and in adversity, those who control their wrath and are forgiving toward mankind; Allah loves the good.❊ (Qur'an 3: 133-134)

﴿خِتَـٰمُهُۥ مِسْكٌ ۚ وَفِى ذَٰلِكَ فَلْيَتَنَافَسِ ٱلْمُتَنَـٰفِسُونَ ﴿٢٦﴾

(سورة المطففين ٨٣: ٢٦)

❊The seal thereof will be Musk: and for this let the competitors compete.❊ (Qur'an 83: 26)

This competition also includes organizational excellence and business success. This is because an effective business is one that better allocates the intellectual and material resources that Allah, the Almighty, has given it. This effectiveness reflects a high level of responsibility and a deep commitment to assuming the vicegerence of Allah. Striving to have a successful business is a kind of worship of Allah. This kind of worship is very much needed nowadays because it serves as a catalyst for better allocation of our scarce resources. Through competition humanity can enjoy better quality of products and services at lower costs. International competition could induce companies and nations to do what they do best. As such, competition would further improve quality and productivity and, hence, improve the standards of living. The problem is that a free and fair competition hardly exists in today's world. In fact, the forces of protectionism are stronger today than they ever were in the last few decades.

Competition cannot be considered as the only force of improving achievements. In fact, Islam stresses that Muslims shall be in a race against the clock while they improve and increase their accomplishments because people have a limited time to live and they would better do their homework before death. Every Muslim will be accountable before Allah for whatever, intellect, health, wealth, and power Allah gave him.

2 - Negative Competition

The competition that Islam prohibits is the one that involves envy and hatred. It is the competition in which a Muslim does not wish for his brother that which he wishes for himself. It is the competition aimed at self aggrandizement and satisfying one's ego. People involved in such competition could resort to unethical and unfair practices. Prophet Muhammad (Blessings and Peace be upon him) was asked by his Companions whether the efforts of a very enduring and hyperactive man is for the sake of Allah, and he replied:

> "If he left seeking to support young children, then it is for the sake of Allah. If he left seeking to support his elderly parents, then it is for the sake of Allah. If he left seeking to provide for himself and have a decent life, then it is in the sake of Allah. If he left seeking to show off and boast about himself, then it is for the sake of Satan." (At-Tabarāni)

Prophet Muhammad (Blessings and Peace be upon him) also said:

> "Beware of suspicion. Suspicion is the untrue speech. Do not spy and do not eavesdrop. Do not compete with each other and do not envy each other and do not hate each other

and do not shun each other. Be slaves of Allah, brothers."
(Al-Muwaṭṭa)

Al-Buraey stated[1]:

"Islam invites man to harness all material and human resources for the promotion of virtue, justice, and peace, which make his function easier. Material progress, yes-but not for its own sake."

Competition can turn to be very dangerous and can include hate when it is not in accordance with the Muslim mission, objective, and goals. Competition is accompanied by envy when people consider wealth and power as pure rewards that do not entail responsibility and accountability. Islam teaches us that we are only the vicegerents and not the real owners of whatever is within our sphere of influence. Money and power belong to Allah who allocates them to whomever He pleases as is evident in the following verses:

$$\text{﴿...وَءَاتُوهُم مِّن مَّالِ ٱللَّهِ ٱلَّذِىٓ ءَاتَىٰكُمْ ۚ (٣٣)...﴾ (سورة النور ٢٤ : ٣٣)}$$

﴿...Give them out of the wealth that Allah has given to you...﴾ (Qur'an 24: 33)

$$\text{﴿... وَأَنفِقُوا۟ مِمَّا جَعَلَكُم مُّسْتَخْلَفِينَ فِيهِ ۖ ...﴾}$$

(سورة الحديد ٥٧ : ٧)

﴿...And spend out of the [substance] whereof He made you trustees...﴾ (Qur'an 57: 7)

---

[1] Al-Buraey, M. *"Management and Administration in Islam,"* (1990).
p. 113

From the above two verses, it is obvious that whatever wealth man has is a trust from Allah and he is to give from it to those that are needy.

$$\langle ... أَنَّ ٱلْقُوَّةَ لِلَّهِ جَمِيعًا ... ۝ \rangle \quad (سورة البقرة ٢ : ١٦٥)$$

⟨...That to Allah belongs all power...⟩ (Qur'an 2: 165)

$$\langle ... لَا قُوَّةَ إِلَّا بِٱللَّهِ ... ۝ \rangle \quad (سورة الكهف ١٨ : ٣٩)$$

⟨...There is no power but with Allah...⟩ (Qur'an 18: 39)

Having more money and more authority should be looked at as a burden because Muslims are held accountable for whatever power and money they have. 'Umar ibn 'Abdul 'Aziz (may Allah be pleased with him), a righteous Umawi Caliph, said when he was appointed to his post:

"It is a responsibility and it is a source of ignominy and regret in the Hereafter."

Moreover, competition becomes negative when people forget about the trust in Allah and the fact that Allah is the only Sustainer and that His sustenance will never be depleted. The Western concept of competition is based on the Darwinian interpretation of evolution,[2] which is disputed biologically[3] and rejected, by all major religions of the world. Islam teaches that the success of one business does not mean the bankruptcy of another. The following verse talk about sustenance:

---

[2] Spyros, M., and Heau, D., "*The evolution of Strategic Planning and Management*," in Strategic Management Handbook, edited by King and Cleland, (1987), p. 10.

[3] Grasse, P.P., "*L'evolution du Vivant*," Abrie Nichel, Paris, (1973), Ruffie, J., "*De la biologie a la culture*," Flamarion, Paris, (1974).

﴿وَمَا مِن دَآبَّةٍ فِي ٱلْأَرْضِ إِلَّا عَلَى ٱللَّهِ رِزْقُهَا...﴾ ۝

(سورة هود ١١ : ٦)

﴿There is no moving creature on earth but its sustenance is provided by Allah.﴾ (Qur'an 11: 6)

﴿إِنَّ لَكَ أَلَّا تَجُوعَ فِيهَا وَلَا تَعْرَىٰ﴾ ۝ (سورة طه ٢٠ : ١١٨)

﴿There is therein [enough provision] For you not to go hungry, nor to go naked.﴾ (Qur'an 20: 118)

﴿وَفِي ٱلسَّمَآءِ رِزْقُكُمْ وَمَا تُوعَدُونَ﴾ ۝ (سورة الذاريات ٥١ : ٢٢)

﴿And in the heaven is your sustenance and also that which you are promised.﴾ (Qur'an 51: 22)

﴿إِنَّ ٱللَّهَ هُوَ ٱلرَّزَّاقُ ذُو ٱلْقُوَّةِ ٱلْمَتِينُ﴾ ۝ (سورة الذاريات ٥١ : ٥٨)

﴿For Allah is He who gives [all] sustenance — Lord of power-steadfast [for ever].﴾ (Qur'an 51: 58)

﴿إِنَّ رَبَّكَ يَبْسُطُ ٱلرِّزْقَ لِمَن يَشَآءُ وَيَقْدِرُ إِنَّهُ كَانَ بِعِبَادِهِ خَبِيرًا بَصِيرًا﴾ ۝ (سورة الإسراء ١٧ : ٣٠)

﴿Verily your Lord does provide sustenance in abundance for whom He pleases, and He provides in a just measure, for He does know and regard all His slaves.﴾ (Qur'an 17: 30)

﴿... وَمَن يَتَّقِ ٱللَّهَ يَجْعَل لَّهُ مَخْرَجًا ۝ وَيَرْزُقْهُ مِنْ حَيْثُ لَا يَحْتَسِبُ ...﴾ ۝ (سورة الطلاق ٦٥ : ٢-٣)

﴿...And for those who fear Allah, He [ever] prepares a way out, and He provides him from [sources] he never could imagine...﴾ (Qur'an 65: 2-3)

﴿تُولِجُ ٱلَّيْلَ فِى ٱلنَّهَارِ وَتُولِجُ ٱلنَّهَارَ فِى ٱلَّيْلِ وَتُخْرِجُ ٱلْحَىَّ مِنَ ٱلْمَيِّتِ وَتُخْرِجُ ٱلْمَيِّتَ مِنَ ٱلْحَىِّ وَتَرْزُقُ مَن تَشَآءُ بِغَيْرِ حِسَابٍ ﴿٢٧﴾﴾

(سورة آل عمران ٣ : ٢٧)

﴾You cause the Night to gain on the Day, and You cause the Day to gain on the Night; You bring the living out of the dead and You bring the dead out of the living; and You give sustenance to whom You please, without measure.﴾ (Qur'an 3: 27)

﴿... وَٱللَّهُ يَرْزُقُ مَن يَشَآءُ بِغَيْرِ حِسَابٍ ﴿٢١٢﴾﴾ (سورة البقرة ٢ : ٢١٢)

﴾...For Allah bestows His abundance without measure on whom He will.﴾ (Qur'an 2: 212)

﴿ٱللَّهُ ٱلَّذِى خَلَقَكُمْ ثُمَّ رَزَقَكُمْ ... ﴿٤٠﴾﴾ (سورة الروم ٣٠ : ٤٠)

﴾It is Allah Who has created you: Further, He has provided for you sustenance...﴾ (Qur'an 30: 40)

From the above verses it can be deduced that the concept of absolute scarcity is alien to Islam for Allah has made it abundantly clear that man's sustenance is with Him and that His bounties are never ending. What can be claimed to exist is relative scarcity.

The fact that Allah is the Sustainer shall not be a cause of procrastination or asceticism, rather it should be a source of motivation, for a Muslim should work hard trusting that Allah will reward him/her for his/her work. This should also lead Muslims to avoid excessive risk aversion.

Moreover, it is dangerous for people to give in to materialism and indulge in competition over money and luxury. Doing so is an indication that they ruined their purpose of existence, which is worshipping Allah. Further, material competition is an endless process that only gives pain. Muslims should be content with their security and basic needs. They should use their extra wealth for the betterment of the Ummah and this world. Wealth beyond the necessary does not improve the quality of life because if people are not satisfied with fulfilling their necessary needs, they will never be satisfied with anything more than it.

Exercises

1. Outline the two types of competition mentioned in this chapter.

2. What are the differences between the two?

3. Is Islam against competition? Substantiate your answer with verses from the Qur'an.

4. Discuss the Islamic concept that Allah is the Sustainer.

CONFLICTS

Conflicts are very common in organizations. Different functions within an organization have different perceptions and different priorities. In a manufacturing company for example, the finance department is more concerned about the cost of operations and their expected returns. The production department wants to produce effectively by standardizing the products and increasing the production volume. The marketing department is more concerned about the diversity of the products and their outside appearance. Within the same department, we might find different groups that have different views on how the department should run.

Conflicts are almost inevitable. However, one need not to be alarmed by this reality because many conflicts are beneficial. Gibson et al.[4] classified conflicts into functional conflicts and dysfunctional conflicts. A functional conflict is one that enhances the performance of an organization. This conflict usually arises when different groups within an organization agree about achieving a certain goal but differ on the means to achieve it. This conflict can motivate the different groups to improve their methods. When the conflict is settled, the goal can be achieved in the most effective manner. A dysfunctional conflict is usually one that individuals and groups take personal.

---

[4] Gibson et al., *"Organizations,"* Business Publications Inc, Houston, (1985). p. 294

The fact that an organization can benefit from the functional conflict after it is settled demonstrates that the effect of a conflict depends primarily on the way it is managed. In case a conflict is not well managed, it automatically becomes a dysfunctional one that hinders the operations of an organization. There is usually a thin line between functional and dysfunctional conflicts. Managers shall make sure that this line is not crossed. The location of this thin line is not constant. It usually depends on the groups' culture, tolerance, and ability to take stress. Mu'awiya (may Allah be pleased with him), the fifth successor of the Prophet (Blessings and Peace be upon him) said that if there were one string of hair linking him to the people, it would not be cut. If the people relaxed it, he would pull it, and if they pull it he would relax it.

1 - Functional Conflicts

Given the fact that conflicts can turn out to be dysfunctional, shall we eliminate them even if they were at low levels? The answer to this question is certainly a NO. This is because the cost of eliminating conflicts can be very high. While the unity and coherence of a group are usually praised, they can present a serious impediment to progress, development, adaptiveness and innovation. Conflict can be positive if it takes the form of enjoining what is good and forbidding what is evil with full sincerity and without taking it personally. In some cases when conflicts do not exist, the organizational survival might be jeopardized, and sometimes everything in the sphere of influence of the organization will suffer.

Irvin Janis[5] analyzed American foreign policy decisions made by some presidential administrations. He concluded that these teams were highly cohesive and close-knit. He called their decision process 'group think' which he described as a "deterioration of mental efficiency, reality testing, and normal judgment." 'Group think' led the Kennedy administration to the disastrous attempt to invade Cuba in April 1961.

Group solidarity and cohesiveness gets dangerous when they become the end rather than the means. This is why the Islamic perspective on management stresses that one has to exercise an uninterrupted feedback process between his or her actions and the general mission, objective, and goal of Muslims. If an action is determined to be inconsistent with this framework, it is immediately rejected. Janis cited the following causes of 'group think':

(i) Illusion of invulnerability.

(ii) Tendency to moralize.

(iii) Feeling of Unanimity.

(iv) Pressure to Conform.

(i) Illusion of invulnerability: It is a situation whereby the members of a group believe that they are invincible. On the eve of the Bay of the Pigs invasion (Cuba 1961), Robert Kennedy stated that, with the talents in the group, they could overcome whatever challenged them. This belief of invincibility is totally rejected in Islam. It is called arrogance, which can only lead to disastrous outcomes in this world and in the Hereafter. This feeling is a real

---

[5] Irvin Janis, "*Victims of a Groupthink: A psychological study of foreign Policy Decisions and Fiascos,*" Houghton Mifflin, Boston, (1973). p. 9

impediment for further learning, improvement, and for seeking other learned opinions. Allah told us that we only possess a limited amount of knowledge.

$$﴿... وَمَآ أُوتِيتُم مِّنَ ٱلۡعِلۡمِ إِلَّا قَلِيلًا ۝﴾ (سورة الإسراء ١٧ : ٨٥)$$

﴿...You have only been granted a small amount of knowledge.﴾ (Qur'an 17: 85)

In the mean time, Islam requires us to seek knowledge and increase our learning. Prophet Muhammad (Blessings and Peace be upon him) said:

"Seeking knowledge is a must for every Muslim." (Ibn Mājah)

Allah, the Almighty, also said:

$$﴿... وَقُل رَّبِّ زِدۡنِي عِلۡمًا ۝﴾ (سورة طه ٢٠ : ١١٤)$$

﴿...And say! My Lord, increase me in knowledge.﴾ (Qur'an 20: 114)

From the above verses and the hadith, it is obvious that nobody knows everything and we thus must avoid arrogance, which hinders learning and improvement.

The attitude of arrogance can be contrasted with the attitude of Abu Bakr (may Allah be pleased with him), the first successor of the Prophet (bpuh), who said in his inauguration speech:

"I have been given authority over you but I am not the best of you. If I do well help me, and if I do wrong put me right."

(ii) Tendency to moralize: The groups studied by Janis had a general tendency to regard the US as the leader of the free world. Any deviation from this view was characterized as weak, evil, or unintelligent. This concept can also be called self-righteousness, which is related to arrogance. Muslims are required to be just even with their enemy. Allah, the All-High, said:

$$﴿... وَلَا يَجْرِمَنَّكُمْ شَنَآنُ قَوْمٍ عَلَىٰ أَلَّا تَعْدِلُوا ۚ اعْدِلُوا هُوَ أَقْرَبُ$$
$$لِلتَّقْوَىٰ ۚ ...﴾ (سورة المائدة ٥ : ٨)$$

﴿...Let not the hatred of other people to you swerve you to wrong and make you unjust. Be just it is closer to piety...﴾ (Qur'an 5: 8)

A bad deed is always considered a bad deed in Islam. The fact that a wrong was committed by a Muslim does not make it right.

$$﴿لَيْسَ بِأَمَانِيِّكُمْ وَلَا أَمَانِيِّ أَهْلِ الْكِتَابِ ۗ مَن يَعْمَلْ سُوءًا يُجْزَ$$
$$بِهِ ... ﴾ (سورة النساء ٤ : ١٢٣)$$

﴿It is not up to your wishes, neither is it up to the wishes of the people of the Book, whoever does wrong will be punished accordingly...﴾ (Qur'an 4: 123)

Self-righteousness begets injustice, and dismissing others' opinions is arrogance, which violates the Islamic moral conduct as well as the principle of consultation. All the righteous Muslim Caliphs encouraged Muslims to advise them and to correct them when they are wrong.

(iii) Feeling of Unanimity: Members of a group might not voice their disagreement because they believe that everyone else was in total agreement, and that they have the only differing view. In Islam, it is a religious duty rather than a right to voice ones opinion about important matters. Prophet Muhammad (Blessings and Peace be upon him) said:

"Whosoever sees wrong shall correct it with his hand, if he could not, then he should correct it with his tongue, if he could not, then he should correct it with his heart and that is the weakest of faith." (Muslim)

Correcting the wrong is mandatory in Islam and it is especially encouraged when the perpetrator of this wrong is a tyrant ruler. This is because it is more difficult and often costly to correct the tyrants. Prophet Muhammad (Blessings and Peace be upon him) said:

"The best struggle is a word of truth before a tyrant ruler." (An-Nasāi)

Tyranny is not confined to political rulers. It also can include the leaders of an organization, and sometimes even the members of an organization. Speaking up and correcting the wrong are the tools of checks and balances without which this earth will be full of mischief. Allah, the Exalted, said:

$$﴿ ... وَلَوْلَا دَفْعُ ٱللَّهِ ٱلنَّاسَ بَعْضَهُم بِبَعْضٍ لَّفَسَدَتِ ٱلْأَرْضُ ... ﴾$$

(٢٥١) ﴿ (سورة البقرة ٢ : ٢٥١)

﴿...Did not Allah check one set of people by means of another, the earth would indeed be full of mischief...﴾ (Qur'an 2: 251)

In another verse Allah, the Almighty, said:

$$﴿... وَلَوْلَا دَفْعُ ٱللَّهِ ٱلنَّاسَ بَعْضَهُم بِبَعْضٍ لَّهُدِّمَتْ صَوَٰمِعُ وَبِيَعٌ وَصَلَوَٰتٌ وَمَسَٰجِدُ يُذْكَرُ فِيهَا ٱسْمُ ٱللَّهِ كَثِيرًا ... ﴾$$

(سورة الحج ٢٢ : ٤٠)

❖...Did not Allah check one set of people by means of another there would surely have been pulled down monasteries, churches, synagogues, and mosques in which the name of Allah is commemorated in abundant manner...❖ (Qur'an 22: 40)

(iv) Pressure to conform: During the Kennedy administration, Robert Kennedy once mentioned to Arthur Schlesinger that he could see some problems with a particular decision. The president needed unanimous support on the issue. This emphasis on unanimity and solidarity is very dangerous. It almost deprives people from using their faculty of intellect. A Muslim shall not be just an extra number in a group. He shall have to make a serious contribution in the decision process. Prophet Muhammad (Blessings and Peace be upon him) said:

"Let not any one of you be a blind follower who says if people do good, I will do the same, and if they do wrong, I will do the same. But you should stick to righteousness." (At-Tirmidhi)

As a result of "group think," opposing ideas are usually dismissed and those who propose them could be questioned about their loyalty. In critical matters, it is incumbent upon those who hold opposing ideas to convey them. The only way to overcome the dismissal of opposing ideas is by forming an ad-hoc coalition to support them. It is impossible for one to be able to appropriately convey an opposing idea during a conflict without building some support for it. However, the coalition within the group should be careful not to create another dysfunctional conflict within the group. Islam encouraged correcting the wrong in a collective manner. Allah, the All-Merciful, said:

وَلْتَكُن مِّنكُمْ أُمَّةٌ يَدْعُونَ إِلَى الْخَيْرِ وَيَأْمُرُونَ بِالْمَعْرُوفِ وَيَنْهَوْنَ عَنِ الْمُنكَرِ

... ﴾(١٠٤) (سورة آل عمران ٣: ١٠٤)

❁Let there arise out of you a band of people inviting to all that is good, enjoining what is right, and forbidding what is evil...❁ (Qur'an 3: 104)

It is important to note that the extent to which one, or an ad-hoc coalition should try to change the group decision depends on the extent to which the decision seems to be wrong.

In addition to the dismissal of opposing views within the group, individuals outside the group who criticize or oppose any decision hardly receive any attention. This has to do with the illusion of invulnerability and self-righteousness. Muslims are asked to seek wisdom from any source even from the their enemies. In order to get different views, 'Umar (may Allah be pleased with him), the second Muslim Caliph used to ask juveniles for their opinions about critical matters.[6] Prophet Muhammad (Blessings and Peace be upon him) said:

"Wisdom shall be sought by Muslims, wherever they find it, they are the ones most deserving it." (Ibn Mājah)

The organization that emphasizes cohesiveness tends to have an autocratic leadership and a hierarchical organizational structure. These organizations have shown little adaptiveness with the environment and they are achieving mediocre results.

---

[6] Tamawi, M. S., *"Umar and the Fundamentals of Modern Politics and Administration,"* 2nd ed., Cairo, (1976). p. 138

2 - Dysfunctional Conflicts

In the above discussion, we have concluded that the absence of conflicts can be very dangerous. On the other hand, when the conflict level is very high, the very survival of an organization is threatened. This conflict can lead to the division that Allah, the Exalted, has prohibited.

$$\text{...﴿وَٱعۡتَصِمُواْ بِحَبۡلِ ٱللَّهِ جَمِيعٗا وَلَا تَفَرَّقُواْ﴾}$$

(سورة آل عمران ٣ : ١٠٣)

﴿And hold fast all together, to the rope of Allah and do not be divided...﴾ (Qur'an 3: 103).

Even if the organization does not fall apart, the conflict can seriously hinder its operations because without a certain level of cooperation between all its groups, an organization loses its synergy.

Conflicts usually become dysfunctional when they turn personal. We shall make sure to focus on the issue of the conflict and not get personal or draw the conflict to other issues. Getting outside the conflict issue is considered as *"Fujūr"* which is one of the signs of *"Nifāq"* or hypocrisy.

Thomas[7] developed a model that considered conflict as an ongoing relationship between two or more parties. According to this model conflicts only occur when the parties involved recognize that they have opposing interests. This recognition of

---

[7] Thomas, K. W. *"Conflict and Negotiation Process in Organizations,"* in M. D. Dunnette (ED.), Handbook of Industrial/Organizational Psychology, 2nd ed., Palo Alto, CA: Consulting Psychology Press, (1989).

opposing interests will generate certain emotions that will instigate a group to take some actions affecting the other group(s). The actions will generate reactions and further stimulate the conflict. This model gives a very encompassing understanding of conflicts. In the rest of this chapter, we will present the causes, consequences, and management of dysfunctional conflicts in some details.

1) Causes of conflicts

Interpersonal conflicts, interdependence, difference in goals, and difference in perception usually causes group conflicts in an organization. Conflicts stemming from interpersonal conflicts are always covered by some causes that are common to the whole group.

a) Interpersonal conflicts

Baron and Greenberg[8] cited four major factors behind interpersonal conflicts, namely, lasting grudges, faulty attribution, faulty communication, and destructive criticism. Lasting grudges could be due to deep anger with a person or group of persons that have or are perceived of having badly hurt the subject. Islam dealt with this factor by stressing the value of justice, which is considered by the scholars of field, the goals of Islam, among the major goals of Islam. Allah, the All-High, said:

---

[8] Baron, R. A., Greenberg J., "*Behavior in Organizations*," Allyn and Bacon, Boston, (1989). p. 376

$$﴿إِنَّ ٱللَّهَ يَأْمُرُ بِٱلْعَدْلِ وَٱلْإِحْسَٰنِ وَإِيتَآئِ ذِى ٱلْقُرْبَىٰ وَيَنْهَىٰ عَنِ ٱلْفَحْشَآءِ وَٱلْمُنكَرِ وَٱلْبَغْىِ يَعِظُكُمْ لَعَلَّكُمْ تَذَكَّرُونَ ٩٠﴾$$

(سورة النحل ١٦: ٩٠)

﴿Allah commands justice, the doing of good deeds, and liberality to kith and kin, and He forbids, all shameful deeds, and injustice, and transgression: He instructs you that you may receive admonition.﴾ (Qur'an 16: 90)

Furthermore, Islam commanded forgiveness and linked it to the forgiveness of Allah:

$$﴿... وَلْيَعْفُوا۟ وَلْيَصْفَحُوٓا۟ أَلَا تُحِبُّونَ أَن يَغْفِرَ ٱللَّهُ لَكُمْ وَٱللَّهُ غَفُورٌ رَّحِيمٌ ٢٢﴾$$

(سورة النور ٢٤: ٢٢)

﴿...Let them forgive and overlook, do you not wish that Allah should forgive you, for Allah is Oft forgiving, Most Merciful.﴾ (Qur'an 24: 22)

In another verse Allah, the Almighty, called upon His Messenger (bpuh) to forgive his followers.

$$﴿... فَٱعْفُ عَنْهُمْ وَٱسْتَغْفِرْ لَهُمْ... ١٥٩﴾$$ (سورة آل عمران ٣: ١٥٩)

﴿...So forgive them and ask for [Allah's] forgiveness for them...﴾ (Qur'an 3: 159)

Allah considered forgiveness as an attribute of the believers who will be greatly rewarded in the Hereafter.

$$﴿وَٱلَّذِينَ يَجْتَنِبُونَ كَبَٰٓئِرَ ٱلْإِثْمِ وَٱلْفَوَٰحِشَ وَإِذَا مَا غَضِبُوا۟ هُمْ يَغْفِرُونَ ٣٧﴾$$

(سورة الشورى ٤٢: ٣٧)

❖Those who avoid the major sins and shameful deeds, and when they are angry even then forgive.❖ (Qur'an 42: 37)

Forgiveness is not always easy and not everybody is expected to forgive, however, everybody shall be just and is not accepted to transgress. Allah, the Exalted, said:

﴿... وَلَا يَجْرِمَنَّكُمْ شَنَآنُ قَوْمٍ عَلَىٰ أَلَّا تَعْدِلُوٓا۟ ٱعْدِلُوا۟ هُوَ أَقْرَبُ لِلتَّقْوَىٰ ...﴿٨﴾﴾ (سورة المائدة ٥ : ٨)

❖...Let not the hatred of other people to you swerve you to wrong and make you unjust. Be just it is closer to piety...❖ (Qur'an 5: 8)

Faulty attribution: Interpersonal conflicts can be due to faulty attribution which is the negative interpretation of others' behaviour. It is a sort of suspicion and conjecture that is rejected in Islam.

﴿يَٰٓأَيُّهَا ٱلَّذِينَ ءَامَنُوا۟ ٱجْتَنِبُوا۟ كَثِيرًا مِّنَ ٱلظَّنِّ إِنَّ بَعْضَ ٱلظَّنِّ إِثْمٌ ...﴿١٢﴾﴾ (سورة الحجرات ٤٩ : ١٢)

❖O you who believe avoid suspicion as much [as possible]: for suspicion is in some cases a sin...❖ (Qur'an 49: 12)

Islam prohibits passing judgment based on suspicions and conjecture.

﴿وَلَا تَقْفُ مَا لَيْسَ لَكَ بِهِۦ عِلْمٌ إِنَّ ٱلسَّمْعَ وَٱلْبَصَرَ وَٱلْفُؤَادَ كُلُّ أُو۟لَٰٓئِكَ كَانَ عَنْهُ مَسْـُٔولًا ﴿٣٦﴾﴾ (سورة الإسراء ١٧ : ٣٦)

❖And pursue not that of which you have no knowledge; for every act of hearing, or of seeing or of [feeling] of the heart will be inquired into.❖ (Qur'an 17: 36)

Faulty attribution can also be caused by some deliberate misinformation. Islam commands Muslims to verify the information they receive before passing any judgment. Hasty judgments without the verification of the information on which the judgment is made may lead to future regrets.

﴿يَٰٓأَيُّهَا ٱلَّذِينَ ءَامَنُوٓا۟ إِن جَآءَكُمْ فَاسِقٌۢ بِنَبَإٍ فَتَبَيَّنُوٓا۟ أَن تُصِيبُوا۟ قَوْمًۢا بِجَهَٰلَةٍ فَتُصْبِحُوا۟ عَلَىٰ مَا فَعَلْتُمْ نَٰدِمِينَ ٦﴾ (سورة الحجرات ٤٩ : ٦)

❖O you who believe! If a wicked person comes to you with any news, ascertain the truth, lest you harm people unwittingly, and after that become full of regret for what you have done.❖ (Qur'an 49: 6)

Faulty communication: Faulty communication is another major cause of interpersonal conflicts. It happens when individuals, willingly or unwillingly, communicate with others in a way that disturbs or angers them. The Qur'an warned against this problem and praised the good mannered communication indicating that it is always fruitful:

﴿وَقُل لِّعِبَادِى يَقُولُوا۟ ٱلَّتِى هِىَ أَحْسَنُ إِنَّ ٱلشَّيْطَٰنَ يَنزَغُ بَيْنَهُمْ ... ٥٣﴾ (سورة الإسراء ١٧ : ٥٣)

❖Say to My slaves to say those things that are best, for Satan sows dissensions among them.❖ (Qur'an 17: 53)

﴿أَلَمْ تَرَ كَيْفَ ضَرَبَ ٱللَّهُ مَثَلًا كَلِمَةً طَيِّبَةً كَشَجَرَةٍ طَيِّبَةٍ أَصْلُهَا ثَابِتٌ وَفَرْعُهَا فِى ٱلسَّمَآءِ ٢٤ تُؤْتِىٓ أُكُلَهَا كُلَّ حِينٍۭ بِإِذْنِ رَبِّهَا وَيَضْرِبُ ٱللَّهُ ٱلْأَمْثَالَ لِلنَّاسِ لَعَلَّهُمْ يَتَذَكَّرُونَ ٢٥ وَمَثَلُ كَلِمَةٍ خَبِيثَةٍ كَشَجَرَةٍ خَبِيثَةٍ

اَجۡتُثَّتۡ مِن فَوۡقِ ٱلۡأَرۡضِ مَا لَهَا مِن قَرَارٍ ﴿۞﴾

(سورة إبراهيم ١٤ : ٢٤-٢٦)

◆See you not how Allah sets forth a parable? A goodly word like a goodly tree whose root is firmly fixed, and its branches reach the heavens. It brings for its fruits at all times by the leave of its Lord. So Allah sets forth parables for people in order that they may receive admonition. And the parable of an evil word is that of any evil tree: It is torn up by the root from the surface of the earth: It has no stability.◆ (Qur'an 14: 24-26)

Destructive criticism: Destructive criticism is a feedback delivered in a manner that angers the recipients rather than helps them. Islam discouraged advices that can hurt or embarrass the recipient and encouraged people to first advise one another in a more private fashion.

b) Interdependence

Interdependence can be pooled where the outcome of the performance of groups working separately determines the effectiveness of the whole organization. Different branches of a retail store can be an example of this pooled interdependence. Conflicts in this situation are rare and occur only when the organization is in a deep crisis.

Sequential interdependence occurs when the output of a group serves as input for another. The work of an engineering design group, for example, serves as input for the production group. In order to avoid such a conflict, this interdependence should be coordinated in the planning stage. Recently many companies have adopted the concept of simultaneous engineering where all the functions of an organization work together in the development of a product.

Reciprocal interdependence is similar to sequential interdependence except that it is a two-way interdependence. This means that the output of every group is the input of another. This kind of interdependence exists between anesthesiologists, nurses, technicians, and surgeons in an operating room. This kind of conflict is usually handled by the use of formal authority, and by a carefully coordinated planning.

c) Differences in goals

In the beginning of this chapter, the likelihood of conflicts between different functions of an organization was presented. The reason behind these conflicts is the difference in goals. The production department has efficiency as its goal. This department would like to produce large quantities of standardized products. On the other hand, the marketing department would like to have more variety of products and to emphasize the outside appearance of the products. In case the reward system is based on group performance rather than on the overall organizational performance, the level of this kind of conflict is likely to be higher. This reward system would be adding fuel to fire. Further, every group needs a certain amount of resources to perform its function. Since resources are usually limited, the allocation of these resources is likely to cause more conflicts.

d) Difference in perceptions

Differences in goals are usually accompanied by different perceptions of what constitutes reality. Different time horizons can also result in different perceptions. Groups performing activities with very long time scope would pay little attention to short term developments. An example of this can be found in a research and development group that has a much longer time scope than a production department. Differences in perception are also caused by status incongruence. Many departments might think that they have higher status than others. This usually has to do with ego and with stereotypes. Stereotypes also usually exist between the generalists and the specialists, and as the need for specialization increases, these stereotypes are reinforced.

2) The Consequences of conflicts

The behaviour of people during conflicts depends on their culture and values. Conflicts affect the behaviour of the group internally as well as its relationship with the other conflicting group.

a) Consequences within the group

We would like to reiterate that the behaviour of groups during conflicts depends largely on their values. However, there are some behaviours that are common for every people, and are linked to human nature. The values of people can be used to check these behaviours and to avoid them. The tendency towards these behaviours will always exist. These conflict consequences include:

(i) Increased group cohesiveness: In conflicts, members of a group usually put aside their differences and emphasize group solidarity and cohesiveness. This attitude can be very dangerous as explained in the "group think" concept. As Muslims we should always remember that our ultimate loyalty is to Allah and that unity is means rather than an end. We shall never commit to unity at the expense of our principles and values.

(ii) Rise of autocratic leadership: Participative management is usually ignored during conflicts, instead, members of a group would be welcoming autocratic leadership. From an Islamic perspective, there is no excuse whatsoever for forsaking participative management, or consultation.[9] Indeed, it is in critical situations, such as conflicts, that participative management becomes more important.

(iii) Emphasis on Loyalty: There is little tolerance for different opinions during conflicts. Non-conforming members are accused of disloyalty to the group. Islam prohibits any kind of loyalty except if it were for what is right. If a group adopts a wrong decision, it is mandatory on every member to try to correct it.

(iv) Focus on activity: Finally the group will put more efforts in performing its functions and workers satisfaction will not remain to be important. In other words, workers will have more patience and perseverance in doing what they used to do. This kind of patience can be good if it contributes to the benefit of the overall organization, otherwise it is a detrimental one.

---

[9] Awwa, M. S., "*On the Political System of an Islamic State,*" Cairo, (1980). Pp. 335-336

b) Consequences between groups

The major consequences of conflicts are the distortion of perception about the other party, the decrease in communication, and the reservations about third parties or even their mistrust.

(i) Distorted perceptions: During conflicts, members of a group tend to give more value and importance to what they are doing. On the other hand, they tend to belittle what the other groups are doing. Gossiping becomes more frequent and negative stereotypes that might have always existed are reinforced. This kind of behaviour is totally unaccepted in Islam under any circumstances. Allah, the Almighty, said:

﴿يَٰٓأَيُّهَا ٱلَّذِينَ ءَامَنُوا۟ لَا يَسْخَرْ قَوْمٌ مِّن قَوْمٍ عَسَىٰٓ أَن يَكُونُوا۟ خَيْرًا مِّنْهُمْ وَلَا نِسَآءٌ مِّن نِّسَآءٍ عَسَىٰٓ أَن يَكُنَّ خَيْرًا مِّنْهُنَّ وَلَا تَلْمِزُوٓا۟ أَنفُسَكُمْ وَلَا تَنَابَزُوا۟ بِٱلْأَلْقَٰبِ بِئْسَ ٱلِٱسْمُ ٱلْفُسُوقُ بَعْدَ ٱلْإِيمَٰنِ وَمَن لَّمْ يَتُبْ فَأُو۟لَٰٓئِكَ هُمُ ٱلظَّٰلِمُونَ ۝ يَٰٓأَيُّهَا ٱلَّذِينَ ءَامَنُوا۟ ٱجْتَنِبُوا۟ كَثِيرًا مِّنَ ٱلظَّنِّ إِنَّ بَعْضَ ٱلظَّنِّ إِثْمٌ وَلَا تَجَسَّسُوا۟ وَلَا يَغْتَب بَّعْضُكُم بَعْضًا أَيُحِبُّ أَحَدُكُمْ أَن يَأْكُلَ لَحْمَ أَخِيهِ مَيْتًا فَكَرِهْتُمُوهُ وَٱتَّقُوا۟ ٱللَّهَ إِنَّ ٱللَّهَ تَوَّابٌ رَّحِيمٌ ۝﴾

(سورة الحجرات ٤٩ : ١١-١٢)

﴾O you who believe! Let not some of men among you deride others: It might be that they [the latter] are better than them [the former]: Nor let some women deride other women: It may be that the latter are better than the [former]: Nor defame nor be sarcastic to each other nor call each other by [offensive] nicknames: Ill-seeming is a name connoting wickedness, [to be used by one] after he has believed; And those who do not desist are [indeed] doing wrong. O you who believe avoid suspicion as much [as possible]: for suspicion is in some cases a sin: And spy not on one another, nor speak ill of one another behind their backs. Would anyone of you like to eat the flesh of his dead brother? Nay, you would abhor it... But fear Allah: For Allah is Oft-Returning, Most Merciful.⟩ (Qur'an 49: 11-12)

The individuals and groups should confine the conflict to the relevant issues and should not try to magnify it by including other matters, perceptions and personalities. Taking the conflict beyond the issue is considered *"fujūr,"* one of the attributes of *munāfiqs* or hypocrites.

(ii) Decreased Communication: Communication between conflicting groups decreases dramatically and at times it disappears completely. In this case, the cooperation between the groups will suffer and the organization loses its synergy. This is especially dangerous when there is a sequential interdependence between the two groups. Communication in Islam is very important. Never was there a Prophet who refused to speak to his foes, let alone his friends, whether he was at war with them or at peace. Communication always lessens the degree of conflict and provides opportunities for settling them. A Muslim cannot abstain from talking to a fellow Muslim beyond a period of three days. A breakdown of communication is a crime because it causes a lot of losses for the organization that the groups have a responsibility to serve. Muslim Groups in conflict shall check their behaviours against the general mission and objective of Muslims (worship and vicegerence of Allah, and entering Paradise). They also shall remember their responsibility, and the fact that they are accountable for it, in this world and in the Hereafter.

(iii) Reservations about Third Parties: Because a group in conflict stresses loyalty and can hold a grudge to the other groups, third parties are sometimes suspected of favouring the opposite group. This stems from a feeling that if one is not the enemy of my enemy, he must be my enemy.

3) Conflict management

There are various methods of solving conflicts. The selection of the appropriate method depends on the situation. These methods are:

(i) Confrontation: The decrease of communication between conflicting groups can only deepen the conflict. Management can bring the conflicting groups in a face to face meeting. In this meeting, the groups are supposed to identify the problem, and then solve it. This method has proven to be very effective when the conflict stems from misunderstanding. In more complex problems, this method was not as effective.

(ii) Expansion of resources: Increasing the resources can certainly solve conflicts that are caused by the limitation of resources. The problem with this method is that resources are usually scarce, and it is not very easy to expand them. Nevertheless, the feasibility of this method shall always be considered.

(iii) Providing an expert opinion: Conflicts between groups can be caused by different perception of the reality or by different understanding of some matters. On many occasions, the groups involved in the conflict do not have enough knowledge to judge with authority, which view is right or which view is best. Jawdat Saʿīd[10] said, "The judge of a conflict is only knowledge." To support his opinion, Saʿīd quoted the following Qur'anic verse:

$$﴿... قُلْ هَلْ عِندَكُم مِّنْ عِلْمٍ فَتُخْرِجُوهُ لَنَآ إِن تَتَّبِعُونَ إِلَّا ٱلظَّنَّ وَإِنْ أَنتُمْ إِلَّا تَخْرُصُونَ ﴾ (سورة الأنعام ٦ : ١٤٨)$$

﴿...Say: Have you any [certain] knowledge? If so, produce it for us. You follow nothing but conjecture: you do nothing but lie.﴾ (Qur'an 6: 148)

In this situation, it is best to bring an outside expert that will be able to make a judgment on the issue. This outside expert should be able to win the trust of the conflicting groups, and should possess the necessary professional credibility. The expert shall make a professional judgment and shall be able to convince both parties that he/she did so. Convincing both parties about the experts' judgment is instrumental in the settlement of the conflict.

(iv) Negotiation: Negotiation is the bargaining between the two parties that have recognized their conflict. Representatives of the conflicting groups can handle it. This negotiation process is very efficient when there is a tendency for reconciliation or agreement. It is not as effective when the settlement will require judging in favour of one side. Allah, the All-High, said regarding marriage conflicts:

$$﴿وَإِنْ خِفْتُمْ شِقَاقَ بَيْنِهِمَا فَٱبْعَثُوا۟ حَكَمًا مِّنْ أَهْلِهِۦ وَحَكَمًا مِّنْ أَهْلِهَآ إِن يُرِيدَآ إِصْلَٰحًا يُوَفِّقِ ٱللَّهُ بَيْنَهُمَآ إِنَّ ٱللَّهَ كَانَ عَلِيمًا خَبِيرًا ﴾ (سورة النساء ٤ : ٣٥)$$

---

[10] Saʿīd Jawdat, *"Work is a skill and a Will,"* Damascus, (1983). p. 45

❈If you fear a breach between them twain, appoint two arbiters, one from his family and the other from hers; if they wish for reconciliation, Allah will cause their reconciliation: For Allah has full knowledge, and is acquainted with all things.❈ (Qur'an 4: 35)

McKersie[11] stated that negotiators could view negotiation as a win-lose situation where gains by one party mean losses by the other. Negotiations can also be viewed as a win-win situation where the interest of both parties can be maintained. This situation appears to be unrealistic, however, there is usually an innovative potential solution that offers greater joint benefits than compromise. These solutions are termed integrative agreements.

(v) Arbitration: As the degree of communication between conflicting groups decreases, the need for arbitration becomes urgent. Delays in arbitration can worsen the conflict. Arbitration can take various forms. An accepted neutral person or committee, or an official authority can handle it. In all cases, the arbitrators have to show knowledge of the issue, understanding of the overall interest of the organization, and especially impartiality and justice. Allah, the All-High, All-Glorious, said:

﴿ ۞ إِنَّ ٱللَّهَ يَأْمُرُكُمْ أَن تُؤَدُّوا۟ ٱلْأَمَٰنَٰتِ إِلَىٰٓ أَهْلِهَا وَإِذَا حَكَمْتُم بَيْنَ ٱلنَّاسِ أَن تَحْكُمُوا۟ بِٱلْعَدْلِ إِنَّ ٱللَّهَ نِعِمَّا يَعِظُكُم بِهِۦٓ إِنَّ ٱللَّهَ كَانَ سَمِيعًۢا بَصِيرًا ۝ ﴾

(سورة النساء ٤ : ٥٨)

❈Allah does command you to render back your trusts to

---

[11] Pruit, D. G et al., "*Incentives for cooperation in Integrative Bargaining*," in R. Tiez, Aspiration in Bargaining and Economic Decision Making, Berlin: Spring-Verlag.

those to whom they are due; and when you judge between people, that you judge with justice: verily how excellent is the teaching which He gives you! For Allah is He Who hears and sees all things.❯ (Qur'an 4: 58)

In another verse Allah, the Exalted, ordained His messenger (Blessings and Peace be upon him) to judge with equity.

﴾... وَإِنْ حَكَمْتَ فَٱحْكُم بَيْنَهُم بِٱلْقِسْطِ إِنَّ ٱللَّهَ يُحِبُّ ٱلْمُقْسِطِينَ ﴿٤٢﴾﴾ (سورة المائدة ٥ : ٤٢)

❮...If you judge, judge in equity between them, for Allah loves those who judge in equity.❯ (Qur'an 5: 42)

We should stress here that judgments rendered by the arbitrators should be with equity and justice.

Arbitration should involve conflict smoothing by emphasizing the common interests of the groups and de-emphasizing their differences. Allah has ordained Muslims to reconcile the differences between one another, emphasizing the bonds of brotherhood that exist among them. Further, because ego and grudge usually accompany conflicts, Allah, the Almighty, has coupled reconciliation with belief and awareness of Allah. Allah, the All-Merciful, said:

﴾إِنَّمَا ٱلْمُؤْمِنُونَ إِخْوَةٌ فَأَصْلِحُوا بَيْنَ أَخَوَيْكُمْ وَٱتَّقُوا ٱللَّهَ لَعَلَّكُمْ تُرْحَمُونَ ﴿١٠﴾﴾ (سورة الحجرات ٤٩ : ١٠)

❮The believers are but a single brotherhood: So reconcile between your contending brothers; and fear Allah, that you may receive mercy.❯ (Qur'an 49: 10)

Reconciling conflicting parties is something ordained by Allah.

Use of authoritative command can be very efficient in arbitration. However, if it is not coupled with justice and a clear explanation of the reasons behind the authoritative decision, it will only work in the short run. Authoritative command is needed when conflicts persist and start hurting the organization, or when one party is determined to be right while the other is at fault. In fact, if one party has transgressed upon another, Muslims are ordained to firmly stop this transgression. Once this aggression is stopped, Muslims have to reconcile between the two parties. Allah, the Exalted, said:

﴿وَإِن طَآئِفَتَانِ مِنَ ٱلْمُؤْمِنِينَ ٱقْتَتَلُوا فَأَصْلِحُوا بَيْنَهُمَا فَإِنۢ بَغَتْ إِحْدَىٰهُمَا عَلَى ٱلْأُخْرَىٰ فَقَٰتِلُوا ٱلَّتِي تَبْغِي حَتَّىٰ تَفِيٓءَ إِلَىٰٓ أَمْرِ ٱللَّهِ فَإِن فَآءَتْ فَأَصْلِحُوا بَيْنَهُمَا بِٱلْعَدْلِ وَأَقْسِطُوٓا إِنَّ ٱللَّهَ يُحِبُّ ٱلْمُقْسِطِينَ ٩﴾ (سورة الحجرات ٤٩ : ٩)

❨If two parties among the believers fall into a quarrel, make you peace between them: But if one transgresses beyond bonds against the other then fight you against the one that transgresses until it complies with the command of Allah, but if it complies, then make peace between them with justice, and be fair for Allah loves those who are fair.❩ (Qur'an 49: 9)

(vi) Super-ordinate goals and/or common enemies: The fact that a dysfunctional conflict started to have its tolls on an organization proves that the latter is failing at directing and motivating its members towards achieving a desired goal. Therefore, the organization has to develop or to redefine its objective and goals in such a way that they transcend conflicts. That is, these goals shall be appealing and should only be feasible through the cooperation of all groups. From an Islamic perspective, the feedback between the actions of a group during conflict, and the objective of entering Paradise can smooth conflicts. Further, the compatibility between the general objective of Muslims and their goals at their organization shall make the latter more appealing.

Groups tend to unite and to focus on their activities during inter-group conflicts. Similarly, organizations can also unite and overlook their internal differences when faced by a common enemy. While internal unity is needed for an organization, which is faced with a common enemy, this internal unity shall not transform into 'group think.' The organization shall try to avoid all the negative behavioural consequences of conflicts. Further, the fact that dysfunctional conflicts can close the ranks of an organization does not justify creating them. Creating an enemy can go out of control. Emphasizing a common enemy is only recommended when one really exists. Islam commanded Muslims to be united together because there was a real danger in their disunity, while the pagans were united in fighting them.

Allah, the Almighty, All-Merciful, said:

﴾... وَقَٰتِلُوا۟ ٱلۡمُشۡرِكِينَ كَآفَّةً كَمَا يُقَٰتِلُونَكُمۡ كَآفَّةً ... ﴿٣٦﴾﴾

(سورة التوبة ٩ : ٣٦)

﴾...And fight the pagans all together as they fight you all together...﴿ (Qur'an 9: 36)

The above verse shows an example where a real enemy exits and is thus emphasized and the Muslims are urged to unite against this common enemy.

This danger is not confined to Muslims rather it is threatening the whole world. Allah, the Exalted, said:

﴿وَٱلَّذِينَ كَفَرُوا۟ بَعْضُهُمْ أَوْلِيَآءُ بَعْضٍ إِلَّا تَفْعَلُوهُ تَكُن فِتْنَةٌ فِى ٱلْأَرْضِ وَفَسَادٌ كَبِيرٌ ٧٣﴾ (سورة الأنفال ٨ : ٧٣)

﴾The unbelievers are protectors one of another: Unless you do this [protect one another], there would be tumult and oppression on earth, and great mischief.﴿ (Qur'an 8: 73)

On the other hand, the unity of Muslims is a mercy for mankind. Allah, the All-High, All-Glorious, said:

﴿وَمَآ أَرْسَلْنَٰكَ إِلَّا رَحْمَةً لِّلْعَٰلَمِينَ ١٠٧﴾ (سورة الأنبياء ٢١ : ١٠٧)

﴾We sent you not, but as a mercy for all creatures.﴿ (Qur'an 21: 107)

In another verse Allah, the All-Merciful, said:

﴿وَإِنَّهُۥ لَهُدًى وَرَحْمَةٌ لِّلْمُؤْمِنِينَ ٧٧﴾ (سورة النمل ٢٧ : ٧٧)

﴾And it [the Qur'an] certainly is a Guide and a Mercy to those who believe.﴿ (Qur'an 27: 77)

Finally, emphasizing organizational super-ordinate goals and common enemies can help settle conflicts in the short term but as soon as the goals are achieved or the enemy disappears, the internal conflicts are likely to reemerge. One way of dealing with this problem could be to keep identifying new challenging goals. Creating enemies is not acceptable, for we are created to know one another and to cooperate together, rather than to become enemies.

(vii) Changing Organizational Structure: Organizational structure affects interdependence among the groups. Changing the organizational structure can include changes in communication channels, the chain of command, the work processes, product development, and job design. Changing some of these variables can solve conflicts by eliminating their possible causes. The problem with this method is that, once the organization structure has been changed, there is no guarantee that another dysfunctional conflict will not arise.

(viii) Changing the Human Variables: The behaviour of people during conflicts depends on their values and attitudes. The approach of changing the human variables does not consider conflicts to be the real problem. Instead, it considers that the real problem lies with the attitudes of the people. It is, therefore, recommended to try to change these attitudes. This approach is supported by the teachings of the Qur'an. Allah, the Exalted, said:

$$ ﴾ ۞ ... إِنَّ ٱللَّهَ لَا يُغَيِّرُ مَا بِقَوْمٍ حَتَّىٰ يُغَيِّرُوا۟ مَا بِأَنفُسِهِمْ ... ﴿ $$

(سورة الرعد ١٣ : ١١)

﴾...Lo! Allah changes not the conditions of a folk until they change that which is in their hearts...﴿ (Qur'an 13: 11)

If the cause of the conflict is behavioural, and it usually is, unless and until such behaviour is changed, conflict will continue and will stop to reemerge again.

The problem with altering the human variables is that it takes a very long time. It is therefore, needed to have another method that will smooth the conflict or solve it in a short term, in addition to the process of altering the human variables. This method of treating the conflict in a short term is analogous to a pain killer medication, while altering the human variable is the real cure. Organizations shall have an ongoing personnel development programme to keep improving the human variables. Unfortunately most companies restrict their personnel development programmes to the technical side and totally ignore the behavioural side.

SUMMARY

Competition is welcomed in Islam if it pertains to better assuming the vicegerence of Allah, and working harder to achieve the general objective and goal of Muslims. In such a case competing for business success is desirable. When competition is for self-aggrandizement and ego satisfaction, it becomes prohibited. This kind of competition usually involves envy, hatred, and not loving for fellow Muslims what one loves for him/ herself.

As for conflicts, Muslims shall neither reject them altogether, nor allow them to deepen until they become dysfunctional. Muslims have to follow the wise policy of being justly balanced:

﴿وَكَذَلِكَ جَعَلْنَٰكُمْ أُمَّةً وَسَطًا لِّتَكُونُوا شُهَدَآءَ عَلَى ٱلنَّاسِ وَيَكُونَ ٱلرَّسُولُ عَلَيْكُمْ شَهِيدًا ... ﴾ (سورة البقرة ٢: ١٤٣)

◆Thus we have made of you an ummah justly balanced, that you might be witnesses over the nations, and the Messenger be a witness over yourselves...◆ (Qur'an 2: 143)

Conflict is necessary in the form of enjoining what is good and forbidding what is evil. But such conflicts should never get personal. It is the duty of every Muslim to voice his or her opinion on matters of common interest, and to oppose what he or she perceives to be wrong. The process of correcting a decision should be free of any personal attacks, gossip, or stereotypes. In case the conflict is deep enough to be dysfunctional, the groups have to avoid its negative consequences within their own group and in relation to the other groups. Arbitration is necessary to smooth or solve conflicts. The arbitrators shall be knowledgeable, just, and aware of the overall interest of the organization. The arbitrators should also possess the necessary communication skills to convince the conflicting parties of the righteousness of their arbitration. This is because the level of suspicion among conflicting groups is usually high. Emphasizing super-ordinate goals, and/or common enemies, are very useful methods of conflict resolution, however their effect is limited to the duration of the existence of these goals and/or enemies. Changing the structural variables is a very efficient method of conflict resolution; however, this method does not prevent the inception of other dysfunctional conflicts that could be related to the new structure.

The method that can both solve dysfunctional conflicts in the long term and prevent others to happen in the future, is the changing of the human variables:

$$﴿ ... إِنَّ ٱللَّهَ لَا يُغَيِّرُ مَا بِقَوْمٍ حَتَّىٰ يُغَيِّرُوا۟ مَا بِأَنفُسِهِمْ ... ﴿١١﴾ ﴾$$

(سورة الرعد ١٣ : ١١)

﴾...Lo! Allah changes not the conditions of a folk until they change that which is in their hearts...﴿ (Qur'an 13: 11)

Since this method is designed to achieve long term purposes, it has to be accompanied by one of the above mentioned methods to treat what can be called the symptoms of the conflict. Organizations shall have ongoing personnel development programmes that can help them avoid dysfunctional conflicts.

Unfortunately, most companies ignore the behavioural side of personnel development.

Exercises

1. Outline the types of conflicts mentioned in the chapter and briefly describe each.

2. Conflict is a necessary evil. Discuss.

3. What are the causes of interpersonal and inter-group conflicts?

4. Briefly discuss the various methods of conflict management and the situation under which each should be used.

5. What is *"Fujūr"* in conflicts?

PART — VI

THE LEADERSHIP OF 'UMAR IBN AL-KHAṬṬĀB

THE LEADERSHIP OF
'UMAR IBN AL-KHAṬṬĀB

'Umar ibn al-Khaṭṭāb (May Allah be pleased with him) was the second successor of Prophet Muhammad (Blessings and Peace be upon him). He is considered by many scholars as the founding father of modern administration. He was the only Muslim besides Prophet Muhammad (bpuh) to be chosen by Michael Hart[1] among the one hundred most influential persons in history. In this chapter, we will represent an introduction of 'Umar including his background, his personality traits, and his achievement. Then, we will outline the characteristics of his leadership.

1 - Introduction of 'Umar

In this introduction, we will present a background of 'Umar before he became a Muslim followed by the general traits of his personality which can be concluded from his biography both before and after becoming a Muslim. Then, we will shed some light on his major achievements.

1) Background

'Umar was from the tribe of 'Ady ibn Ka'ab, which was one of ten noble tribes of Quraysh. This tribe was not as wealthy or as

---

[1] Micheal Hart, *"The 100 Ranking of the most Influential Persons in History,"* Golden Book Center, K L, (1979).

powerful as the tribes of Bani Hāshim [the tribe of the Prophet (Blessings and Peace be upon him)], or Bani Umayya (the tribe of Uthmān). However, 'Umar's tribe was distinguished by its knowledge, wisdom, and intellect. The knowledge and wisdom of this tribe allowed its members to hold the positions of ambassadors to other towns and arbitrators in disputes.[2] The uncle of 'Umar, Zayd ibn 'Amr, who was one of the leaders of his tribe, was so intelligent and knowledgeable that he rejected the worship of idols and embraced Islam (the religion of Abraham). Al-Khaṭṭāb, the father of 'Umar and another leader of the tribe, was also very intelligent, respectable, and courageous.

'Umar was born around 586 AD. He was one of very few people in Quraysh who learned how to read. It is reported that there were only 17 people who knew how to read when Muhammad (Blessings and Peace be upon him) received revelation.[3] 'Umar was also distinguished by his physical abilities. He was very tall and very strong. He was also a great cavalier and an unbeatable wrestler.

As an adult, 'Umar had been known for his resolve and sometimes toughness. Emotions and softness were not much noticeable in 'Umar's behaviour. He was also very knowledgeable and very educated. He memorized a lot of poetry, and read a lot of history. Like many people of Quraysh, 'Umar worked in trade. While he was generally a successful trader who made more trading trips than anybody else was, 'Umar did not make huge profits. He was more interested in acquiring knowledge than in

---

[2] Haikal, M.H.,"*Al-Farouq 'Umar*," Dār al-Ma'arif, Cairo, (1994) p. 35.

[3] Ibid. p. 42.

gaining money. The knowledge of 'Umar also allowed him to be the envoy or ambassador of Quraysh in many other parts of the region. This role helped 'Umar acquire more knowledge about various people and different cultures. The knowledge of 'Umar deepened his sense of responsibility and his concern about his people and what could help their welfare. This knowledge had also contributed to 'Umar's strong feelings about his opinions and his arguments. 'Umar was highly disciplined and committed to law and order. He was very tough on those who deviated from the norms of the society. He was very adamant on the unity and order of Quraysh. 'Umar was among the staunch opponents of the early Muslims because he felt that they were dividing and weakening his people. Prophet Muhammad (Blessings and Peace be upon him) was praying to Allah to guide 'Umar to Islam in spite of his opposition to Muslims and even their oppression. Prophet Muhammad (Blessings and Peace be upon him) used to say:

> "O Allah! Strengthen Islam by the more lovable to you: Abu Jahl ('Umar ibn al-Ḥakam) or 'Umar ibn al-Khaṭṭāb." (Tirmidhi)

The Prophet (bpuh) saw in 'Umar a strong person that can be relied on.

When 'Umar realized that the Muslims were calling to their religion with good manners, and that they were not causing any damage, but rather, they were the objects of torture and suppression. He started to have second thoughts about this new religion. He was also impressed by the strong faith of the Muslims who have endured and persevered in face of an extremely harsh suppression.

2) Personality traits

'Umar became the leader of the Muslims at about the age of fifty which is an age during which one possesses a great mental maturity while still keeping a strong physique. At the beginning of this subsection, we will concentrate on the physical traits of 'Umar, then, we will move on to his behavioural traits.

'Umar had a huge body. He was so tall that he appeared to be riding something when he walked with his companions.[4] He had a somewhat reddish and good-looking face. 'Umar had a very strong yet beautiful voice. He was also bald and the hair remaining on his head lay on the sides. He walked briskly. He had noticeable strong muscles and very rough hands and feet. He was very strong and worked with both hands. The physical strength of 'Umar allowed him to be a great cavalier, and a wrestling champion. It also allowed him to be a great fighter both before and after becoming a Muslim. As a leader, his physical abilities together with his behavioural traits gave him a lot of reverence. They also permitted him to physically help many Muslims and to put huge efforts in looking after the Muslims' interests.

On the behaviour level, 'Umar was distinguished by his sense of responsibility which will be elaborated on when we talk about the characteristics of his leadership in the next section. 'Umar was also known for being tough both before and after becoming a Muslim. He usually opted for more radical solutions than the Prophet (Blessings and Peace be upon him) and Abu Bakr (may Allah be pleased with him), the first Caliph, and this toughness led some of the Companions of the Prophet to fear his

---

[4] At-Tamawi, "*'Umar and the Fundamentals of Modern Politics and Administration,*" Dār al-Fikr, Cairo, (1976). p. 23

leadership. When Abu Bakr was contemplating nominating 'Umar for his succession, he asked 'Abdur Raḥmān ibn 'Awf for his opinion about him. The latter replied saying that he held the best opinion about 'Umar but he found him to be tough. The toughness of 'Umar stems from his commitment to discipline, law, and order. 'Umar was a man of strong will and faith. In spite of being a former heavy drinker, he was the first to advocate the prohibition of alcohol. Prophet Muhammad (Blessings and Peace be upon him) said:

"Satan had always taken a way other than 'Umar's."

Further, 'Umar was not tough in every matter. His toughness was not an end rather it was a means to serve the interest of Islam. It can better be called as strength or resolve. Prophet Muhammad (bpuh) said:

"The most graceful person for my nation is Abu Bakr and the toughest person in my nation for the sake of the religion of Allah is 'Umar."

The above saying shows that 'Umar was tough solely for the sake of the religion of Allah. Moreover 'Umar noticed some softness in his leader Abu Bakr and wanted to balance it with his toughness. In fact, Abu Bakr replied to 'Abdur Raḥmān ibn 'Awf saying, "He does that (be tough) because he sees that I am soft and if he succeeds me he will give up a lot of that (toughness)." This argument was repeated by 'Umar himself during his inauguration speech when he said that his toughness would decrease. He also said that toughness would still be maintained in dealing with the transgressors and the wicked, however he will be softer with the decent and sincere people than they are with one another. Through his leadership, 'Umar showed a lot of leniency and softness as he pledged. Indeed, he was very balanced in his dealing with people. It is reported that he said:

> "Be not soft to the point that you get squeezed and be not rigid to the point that you get broken."

'Umar was also very brave and very courageous. His courage was clearly demonstrated during the battles he participated in whether before or after becoming a Muslim. 'Umar had also declared his Islam publicly challenging thus, the tyranny of Quraysh. He was also reported to be the only Muslim who had migrated to Madīnah publicly. Nevertheless, the courage of 'Umar was accompanied by rationality. 'Umar would not put the Muslims in a losing battle. He was very cautious about the strength and the weakness of Muslims, and he was very focused on serving and maintaining the interests of the Muslims. 'Umar, for example, escaped from Syria when he learned about the spread of an epidemic there. When a Companion rebuked him saying, "Are you escaping from the destiny of Allah?," 'Umar replied, "I escape from the destiny of Allah to the destiny of Allah."

'Umar was also very smart and possessed a great deal of intuition. The background of 'Umar gave him a lot of knowledge and experience as he was from a very intelligent, wise, and educated family (see previous subsection). 'Umar once described himself saying, "I am not a sly person and the sly cannot deceive me." The intuition and cleverness of 'Umar were manifested in many occasions including the discovery of a conspiracy for killing the Prophet (bpuh), his appointment and dismissal of governors, and his advises to the Prophet (bpuh). In fact, revelation had supported his opinion many times. This included verses pertaining to the following matters:

1. The choice of Ka'bah in Makkah as the direction of prayers.

2. The treatment of the prisoners of war in the battle of *Badr*.

3. The covering of the wives of the Prophet (bpuh).

4. The prohibition of alcohol consumption.

5. The prohibition of praying for the dead hypocrites and in joining their funerals.

6. The necessity of taking permission before entering private rooms.

Prophet Muhammad (Blessings and Peace be upon him) complemented the cleverness and intuition of 'Umar by saying:

> "Allah (the Almighty) had put truth and righteousness on the tongue and heart of 'Umar."

'Umar had also accumulated a lot of knowledge by being a close advisor to the Prophet (bpuh) and by being among very few literate Companions. His strong voice and his mastery of history and poetry made him a very eloquent speaker and negotiator.

The physique, resolve, courage, knowledge, eloquence, conscience, and justice of 'Umar won him a lot of respect and reverence, and left no choice for his followers but to obey him. Indeed, 'Umar's personality was very instrumental in the unity and order of the rapidly growing Muslim state.

3) The Achievements during the leadership of 'Umar

It is difficult to enumerate the Muslims' achievements during the leadership of 'Umar. For the purpose of this book, the major accomplishments of 'Umar's era can, however, be briefly stated as follows:

❑ The conquest of Iraq and Persia.

❑ The conquest of Egypt and other parts of North Africa that were under the Romans.

❑ The conquest of the Greater Syria which included Syria, Lebanon and Palestine that were under the rules of the Romans.

❑ The buildings of new cities such as Al-Kufa and Al-Baṣra in Iraq.

❑ The organization of the country into states or provinces.

❑ The establishment of new institutions such as the police, prisons, the office of complaints where complains from the public were received and investigated, the tax collection agency which was independent from the governors, an annual conference gathering Muslims from all over the state during *Ḥajj*, a postal service, and different other administrative divisions to provide the necessary services of the nation.

❑ The adoption of a new calendar starting from the date of migration or *hijrah*.

❑ The installation of a canal linking the Nile River to the Red Sea.

Some of these accomplishment will be discussed in some details when we present the administrative innovations of 'Umar.

2 - The Characteristics of 'Umar's Leadership

In presenting the characteristics of the leadership of 'Umar, we will start by his sense of responsibility which was the real motivator behind his excellent performance. Then, we will address his participative management style. The third subsection will cover the application of total quality management in the leadership of 'Umar. In the next subsection, we will present

'Umar's full understanding of the control process. Finally, the major administrative innovations during the rule of 'Umar will be highlighted.

1) 'Umar and the feelings of responsibility

'Umar, like other successful leaders, possessed a very high sense of responsibility. He felt that he was accountable before Allah for the welfare of everything under his influence including animals. 'Umar once said that he was afraid that a mule would fall in the mountain roads of Iraq and break his legs, and Allah would ask him why he had not paved the roads in that area. 'Ali (may Allah be pleased with him), the fourth Caliph said, "I saw 'Umar rushing so I asked him where he was going." 'Umar replied, "I am catching one of the camels of charity that had run away." Then 'Ali expressed that this is too much, in that it is making the task of the followers of 'Umar very difficult. 'Umar replied saying that if a goat were lost in the rims of the Euphrates (river in Iraq), 'Umar would be accountable for it in the Day of Judgment."[5] The sense of responsibility of 'Umar made him very keen on knowing the real situation of his people by having an open door policy and inquiring about the status of his people both formally and informally. 'Umar established an annual conference during Ḥajj where Muslims from all over the world conveyed their complaints to him. He also established the agency of complaints. Further 'Umar used to change his looks and to make surprise visits to different quarters of the Madīnah in order to get first hand information on how his people were doing. 'Umar used to immediately solve any problem he encountered. Moreover, 'Umar used to make frequent visits to

---

[5] Narrated by Ibn al-Jawzy, Ibid. p. 26.

other towns to check the predicament of his followers there. He also exercised a rigorous control over his subordinates. This control process will be presented later on. The sense of responsibility of 'Umar had also led him to be a great role model whose actions spoke much louder than his words. He is reported to have said,

"I am very keen on satisfying every single need you might have as long as that is possible. If we could not (satisfy the needs of everybody), we would help one another (share what we have) until we all reach the same level of the necessary minimum... and I am only teaching you through actions."[6]

2) 'Umar and participative management

Participative management is the continuous involvement of people in decision-making. It is a culture rather than a programme. Participation is a must in Islam. It is accomplished through consultation, righting the wrong, and advice, which are all mandatory in Islam. Participation was therefore, a culture that everybody shared during the time of the Prophet (Blessings and Peace be upon him) and his four righteous successors. However, the practice of this duty varied throughout the Muslim history. 'Umar is considered to be a historical champion of participative management. Though participative management was the culture of the Companions of the Prophet who did not need to be invited or taught to apply it, 'Umar reinforced this concept by creating a number of programmes and institutions to foster it. 'Umar did not take any major decision without consulting his people. 'Umar used to consult his people in the appointments of governors and

---

[6] Op. cit p. 61.

army commanders. He had also followed the opinions of his followers and did not participate by himself in battles. Consultation was also used in the day-to-day administration of the country's expanding resources. It was by virtue of consultation that the various administrative departments *"Dawawīn"* were established. 'Umar kept the people of highest caliber among his companions with him in Madīnah so that he can benefit from their opinions. The people that he appointed as governors were not as refined as his advisors. Consultation did not stop at the level of the highly experienced and qualified Companions of the Prophet (bpuh), rather it was so wide that it included everybody in the society regardless of age, race, or gender. When the council of advisors failed to reach a decision on the issue of sharing the land of Iraq and Syria, 'Umar called for a general public meeting in Madīnah to take a decision. Moreover, 'Umar organized an annual conference for Muslims to speak up their mind about public matters and to address their complaints about the way the government is run. The most peculiar elements in the decision process during the rule of 'Umar were his consultations of the Muslim juveniles and especially the consultation of some of his enemies. 'Umar believed that juveniles had sharper minds that enabled them to give original ideas. He also understood that the best people to inform him about his enemies are none but his enemies.

3) 'Umar and total quality management

Total quality management can be defined as the strategic commitment to improving quality by combining programmes and methods with a cultural commitment to searching for incremental improvements that increase productivity and lower cost. Total

Quality Management aims at meeting or exceeding customers' expectations. Dilworth[7] stressed that total quality is a culture not a programme such as quality circles. He also stated that total quality is total in time, in that, it never ends because there is no level of quality that is "good enough." This statement of Dilworth is indicative of the important total quality cultural component of continuous improvements. The pillar of total quality management is, however, the culture, commitment, involvement, and improvement.[8] Without these cultural components it becomes unlikely to achieve a continuous improvement.

The fact that total quality management is a culture rather than a programme does not mean that programmes are no longer needed. As a matter of fact, the total quality culture shall be reinforced with certain programmes such as quality circles, regularly inviting outside consultants, training, and research and development. The culture and the programmes should complement and support each other.

Furthermore, total quality requires a high degree of discipline and a clear unity of command. Authority still remains essential for achieving any task. Dilworth[9] stated:

"When an efficient procedure that results in good quality is established, it is to be followed until a better way is tested and approved. You can see that creativity and openness to change are

---

[7] Dilworth, J. B., "*Production and Operation Management,*" 5th ed. McGraw Hill, (1993). p. 346

[8] Jabnoun, N. "*Rethinking Total Quality Management and Making it work,*" Prentice Hall, Malaysia (1999).

[9] Dilworth, J. B., "*Production and Operation Management,*" 5th ed. Mc Graw Hill, (1993). p. 346

needed, but it is creativity in conjunction with teamwork and discipline that achieves consistent good quality and leads to improvements."

Another aspect of total quality management lies in the fact that it is not free, but rather it requires a suitable allocation of resources. The phrase 'quality is free' only means that quality is profitable, that is, it is more than pays off. This does not mean that it should be neglected in the budget.

Quality is very much emphasized in the teachings of Islam. Prophet Muhammad (Blessings and Peace be upon him) said:

> "Allah the Almighty wants that when one of you does a job, he/she does it well." (Bayhaqi)

The Prophet (Blessings and Peace be upon him) also said:

> "Allah has decreed good for everything. When you kill, do it in the best way; and when you slaughter (an animal for sacrifice), do it in the best way. So every one of you should sharpen his knife, and let the slaughtered animal die comfortably." (Muslim)

'Umar's feeling of responsibility and his ever present awareness of his accountability before Allah on the Day of Judgment led him to be accurate and very rigorous in taking any action. 'Umar was especially very careful in appointing his leaders. The leaders chosen by 'Umar were highly scrutinized. Al-Buraey[10] stated that 'Umar used to test the performance of his governors by appointing them on ad-hoc basis for two to three months prior to their regular appointments. 'Umar was also very committed to high quality if not perfect performance in every act

---

[10] Al-Buraey, *"Management and Administration in Islam,"* (1990). p. 249

of life. He would not start the prayer until he makes sure that all people behind him were in perfect lines and he appointed a special person for this task. 'Umar would not be rushed to perform any task at low quality. If he noticed that a certain process was not going, as it should be, he would take immediate corrective actions. 'Umar used to clearly define what he wants from his governors or army generals, and he used to provide them with the necessary resources to achieve the soughed quality of success,[11] for quality is not free.

'Umar appointed Sharaḥbil ibn Ḥasnah (may Allah be pleased with him) as governor over Syria and then changed him with Mu'awia ibn Abi Sufiyān. The former asked 'Umar whether he was angry with him for anything. 'Umar replied saying, "No you are exactly as I like, but I want a man stronger than the other."[12] This event showed that 'Umar was satisfied with the performance of his former governor, however, the moment he found a stronger governor, he decided to replace him. 'Umar took a similar action with his governor in Bahrain 'Utba ibn Azwan who was replaced by Al-'Ala al-Haḍramy. This attitude of 'Umar is similar to the management philosophy of continuous improvement that is adopted in total quality management and in just-in-time manufacturing. The control process for such quality management is discussed in the next subsection. It is important to know that 'Umar made it very clear to the public that he was fully satisfied with his governors and that he only changed them because he found someone who could perform better. This gives the public an appreciation of improved quality while closing the door in front of possible rumors and misinterpretations of 'Umar's actions.

---

[11] Al-'Aqqad A., M. Nahdat Miṣr, "*Abquariyyatu 'Umar,*" Cairo, p. 85.

[12] At-Tamawi, "*'Umar and the Fundamentals of Modern Politics and Administration,*" Dār al-Fikr, Cairo, (1976). p. 270

4) 'Umar and the control process

Control is one of the four components of the management process. Control can be defined as the process of ensuring that actual activities conform to planned activities.[13] The fact that control is the fourth management process after planning, organizing, and leading does not mean that it is last in importance. In fact, the control process also provides some measures of the quality in the planning, organizing, and leading processes.

Basic Control Process

The basic steps in the control process include[14]:

1. Setting standards and the means of measurement of performance:

This involves clearly stating the objectives and goals of the organization in specific measurable terms. Any vagueness in the statement of the objectives and goals renders the control process impossible. Then, the performance standards for each work package leading to the goals and objectives have to be clearly established. The main components of performance are time, money, and quality or technical performance. Establishing the standards is essential to the control process especially because different people usually assume the planning and control responsibilities.[15]

---

[13] Mockler, R. J., *"The Management control process,"* Englewood Cliffs, N. J: Prentice Hall. (1984). p. 2.

[14] Ibid.

[15] Sathe, V., *"The Controller's Role in Management,"* Organization Dynamics 11, no. 3, winter (1983). Pp. 31-48

2. Measuring the performance:

This is supposed to be a frequent and regular process during which the actual performance is measured. The more frequent the measurements are, the more effective the control process is. Ideally, measurement should be continuous, however, this might not be cost effective.

3. Comparing actual performance to standards:

The purpose of measuring actual performance is certainly to find out whether or not it conforms to the predetermined standards. In case the performance matches the standards, it should continue without any modification. Otherwise, some corrective actions have to be taken.

4. Taking corrective actions:

Once it is found that performance is not conforming to standards, it becomes necessary to take corrective actions otherwise the previous steps of the control process will be in vain. Performance has to be altered to fit the standards. Sometimes the control process may reveal the standards to be too low or too high. In such a case, the corrective actions should consist of changing the standards.

The major problem with the control process discussed above is the fact that it stems from a traditional understanding of management. The role of organizational culture or the system of shared values and beliefs that produce norms of behaviour in the organization,[16] for instance, has not been evoked in the basic control process. This is somewhat strange, given the conspicuous

---

[16] Linda Smircich, "*Concepts of Culture and Organizational Analysis*," Administrative Science Quarterly, Sept. (1983). p. 342

importance recently assigned to the cultural theory of organizational effectiveness. This theory of organizational effectiveness takes as its foundation the notion that the values, beliefs and meanings that underlie a social system are the primary source of motivated and coordinated activity.[17] In the 1980s, many books on organizational studies and management, such as *"The Art of Japanese Management,"*[18] *"Corporate Cultures"* and especially "In Search of Excellence" have become bestsellers.

A major development in the field of management, which the basic control process does not take into consideration, is the concept of total quality management. This concept was explained in the last section.

Control Process Practiced By 'Umar

'Umar did not go to any management school for training, but his education, wisdom, and especially the company of the Prophet (Blessings and Peace be upon him) allowed him to master the art of management. 'Umar used to clearly define a set of criteria for appointing leaders.[19] [20] He used to extensively define the roles of his commanders and his governors, and he made sure that they followed his general direction while allowing them their

---

[17] Op. cit p. 2.

[18] Pascal, R. T., and Athos, A. G., *"The Art of Japanese Management: Applications for American Executives,"* New York: Simon and Schuster, (1981).

[19] Ash-Sharqāwi, Al-Farouq, *"'Umar ibn al-Khaṭṭāb,"* Cairo, (1979).

[20] A; 'Aqqad A. M. Nahdat Miṣr, *"The Ingeniousity of 'Umar,"* Cairo, (1979).

operational freedom.[21] He used to provide those among his appointees, who felt that their tasks were so difficult, with extra resources in order for them to be able to achieve their desired goals.[22]

'Umar once asked his companions, what they would think if he appointed one whom he believed to be the best man among them and ordered him to do justice. Would 'Umar have done his share? They replied saying, "Yes." 'Umar retorted "No," not unless he saw whether the appointee did what he ordered him to do.[23]

The above quote demonstrated that 'Umar had fully known the control process. 'Umar indicated that he would not have done his share had he not checked whether his appointee did what he ordered him to do. This signifies that 'Umar's first task is to explain to the appointee what he is expected to do. Then, he has to check whether the appointee is doing what he was ordered to do. The checking of 'Umar over the performance of his appointees was carried out through certain programmes such as the annual Ḥajj conference, 'Umar's personal visits, intelligence agents, and the agency of complaints which received the public complaints about the various rulers. It was also carried out informally through the culture of the people, which was based on forbidding what is evil and enjoining what is good. In cases where the appointees did not carry out their duties appropriately, 'Umar did not hesitate to change them. As a matter of fact, 'Umar did not take such actions just to correct some wrong rather, he was very decisive in making

---

[21] Ibid., p. 86.

[22] Ibid., p. 85.

[23] At-Tamawi, "*'Umar and the Fundamentals of Modern Politics and Administration.*" Dār al-Fikr, Cairo, (1976). p. 270

any decision that could improve an already good performance. 'Umar was committed to continuous improvement as pointed out in last section. The process of improvements was facilitated by the culture of advice as Prophet Muhammad (Blessings and Peace be upon him) said, "Religion is advice," and by the participative management programmes established by 'Umar. It was also facilitated by the cultural emphasis on quality as Prophet Muhammad (bpuh) said:

> "Allah, the Almighty, wants that when one of you does a job, he/she does it well." (Bayhaqi)

Based on the above discussion, we can summarize the control process practiced by 'Umar as follows:

1. The standards have to be well clarified.

2. The necessary input should be provided. This input should include the necessary resources and skills as well as the needed authority.

3. A continuous search for new ways of improving the performance and its standards should be established.

This search is carried out through a favourable culture and some specially designed programmes. The culture should be that of: Commitment to Quality, Participation, and Involvement. The programmes in modern organizations can include quality circles, regular invitations of outside consultants, training, research and development and customer surveys.

4. Both the performance and the output are closely checked against the standards through the existing culture of commitment and involvement, and some specially designed activities such as regular measurement, statistical quality control, and customers' surveys.

5. If the performance and/or the output do not conform with the standards then corrective actions must be taken.

6. If the performance conforms with the standards, then the possibility of improving the performance is checked.

7. If there is a way of improving the process, then the necessary corrective actions to implement it should be taken. These corrections should encompass the ongoing performance, the input, and the standards themselves.

Note that the standards are dynamic in this case because they change each time a new method of improvement is found.

The above control model is presented in figure 12 (at the end of this chapter).

In the following subsection we will cover the administrative innovations during the tenure of 'Umar as the caliph.

5) 'Umar and administrative innovations

We would like to first define administration as the task of achieving predetermined goals.[24] According to Shepard,[25] innovation occurs when an organization learns to do something it did not know how to do before, and then proceeds to do it in a sustained way or learns not to do something that it formally did and proceeds not to do it in a sustained way. Whether the new ideas come from within or out of the firm does not matter so long

---

[24] Hofer, C., W., and Schendel, "*Strategy Formulation. Analytical Concepts,*" West Publishing, St. Paul, (1978).

[25] Shepard, H. A., "*Innovation Resisting and Innovation Producing Organization Organizations,*" Journal of Business 40, (1967). Pp. 470-477

as the ideas are new to the firm.[26] While there is a tremendous amount of literature on innovation, the major factors leading to innovation can be summarized in the culture, the organizational structure, the leadership, and the environment. The culture of the Companions of the Prophet was a very fertile ground for innovations. There were no status or organizational barriers that could impede communication and the suggestion of innovative ideas. The structure of the organization was organic. Further, the commitment of the Companions of the Prophet to the welfare of the nation and their striving for it, had granted them a great success in developing new solutions to their new problems and challenges. 'Umar served as a catalyst for these innovations and developments by further expanding the sphere of participation and organizing special programmes for it as outlined in the subsection on participative management. Moreover, the cleverness, leadership, courage, and resolve of 'Umar paved the way for the development and implementation of new ideas. Another reason for the significant administrative development during the time of 'Umar was the unprecedented development in the state of affairs, as the country, its resources, and its challenges grew bigger.

The organizational structure during the time of the Prophet (Blessings and Peace be upon him) was very simple. The Prophet (bpuh) had the unity of command and used a participative approach to decision making. He had a consultation council made of fourteen members, seven of whom were from Makkah and

---

[26] Mc Ginnis, M., A., and Ackelsberg, M.R., *"Innovation of the Strategic Management Process,"* in the *Strategic Planning and Management handbook*, edited by King and Cleland, Van Nostrand Reynold Company, NY, (1987). p. 37

seven others were from Madīnah, however, the sphere of consultation encompassed all the citizens. Prophet Muhammad (bpuh) had also administratively divided the Muslim land into smaller provinces. The Prophet (bpuh) had also a number of secretaries including one responsible for stamping, and a special poet to reply to the poetic propaganda of his enemies, but these people were appointed individually and did not represent institutions or departments. Nevertheless, it was during the time of the Prophet (bpuh) that the organizational culture was created and it was during his time that the administrative development emerged.

Abu Bakr only ruled the Muslims for two years. Moreover, he was pretty much preoccupied with the wars of apostasy. His administrative contributions were limited to the appointments of a treasurer, a supreme judge, and a different geographical division from the one that existed during the time of the Prophet (bpuh). Nevertheless, the administrative achievements of Abu Bakr were very critical because they laid the ground for the post revelation development.

The first public departments in the Islamic history were established in the time of 'Umar. These departments were called *dawawīn* (plural of *Diwān*). As the resources of the Muslim nation expanded, 'Umar asked for proposals from the Companions on how to better manage and serve the needs of the people. Many alternative ways were suggested, then, it was finally agreed to create some departments such as the department of the army, the department of grants or the payroll department. The department of grants maintained a list of all the citizens, evaluated their needs, and granted them a proportional amount of money. There was also the department of documentation where the important documents were kept. These departments were also established in the various provinces. At-Tamawi stated that the departments in Damascus, Iraq, and Egypt used the native language of the people of the land (i.e. Roman, Persian, and Coptic respectively) which indicates that the people running in the provincial departments were not Arabs.[27]

'Umar had also ordered the building of new cities such as Kufa and Baṣra. The reason behind his decision was that the climate of the existing cities of Iraq did not conform with what the Arabs were used to, and was not healthy to them. He also wanted to uphold the same way of life of his soldiers. He wanted them to keep living together in austerity and in tough condition and to safeguard their courageous and sacrificing attitudes. This resembles the modern concept of army bases. 'Umar had also changed the geographical division of the country into new provinces.

Abu Bakr appointed 'Umar as the Judge of Muslims. After assuming this legal responsibility with decisiveness, 'Umar became the second successor of the Prophet (Blessings and Peace be upon him). As the executive leader, 'Umar appointed 'Ali as an independent judge. He also appointed different judges to the various provinces. These judges were totally independent from the governors. Further, 'Umar had established a constitution for judging. This constitution outlined the basic guidelines and etiquette of judging.

'Umar also established an agency for complaints that had the responsibility of investigating legal cases whose verdicts did

---

[27] At-Tamawi, *"'Umar and the Fundamentals of Modern Politics and Administration,"* Dār al-Fikr, Cairo, (1976). p. 310

not convince the parties involved. The main function of this agency was, however, to enforce the law against the people of power and authority and to investigate the complaints of the people against their governors. This agency is similar to the role played by some contemporary human rights organizations except that the latter have no enforcement authority.

'Umar's administration was also very efficient in information gathering especially about his enemies of war. 'Umar used to have excellent intelligence and he used to ask for information from any source including his enemies. His cleverness allowed him to know whether an enemy was trying to deceive him or not. 'Umar was also effective in managing information through his department of documentation.

'Umar who is known by his self-discipline was also very successful in delegating authority. He was very precise in explaining his policies and the amount of authority delegated. Most importantly, 'Umar was known for abiding by the agreements between him and his delegates. One time, 'Umar received a complaint about one of the commanders of the army, that Abu 'Ubaydah was delegated to lead. 'Umar replied, "That is within the prerogatives of Abu 'Ubaydah."[28]

'Umar was also well aware of the strength of his people, which laid predominantly in their culture of faith, justice, generosity, and courage. He also was aware of their practical limitations and weaknesses. For example, he knew that his soldiers who came from the desert had little experience with the ocean. As a result, he was against allowing them to get involved in naval battles.

---

[28] Muhammad Kurd, "*'Umar ibn al-Khaṭṭāb*," p. 96.

Finally the control process used by 'Umar, had commitment to continuous improvement of the programmes. He established to reinforce the already existing participative culture. All these have been presented in earlier sections.

Figure 12. Describing Control Process For T.Q.M. as Practiced by 'Umar can be seen in the following page.

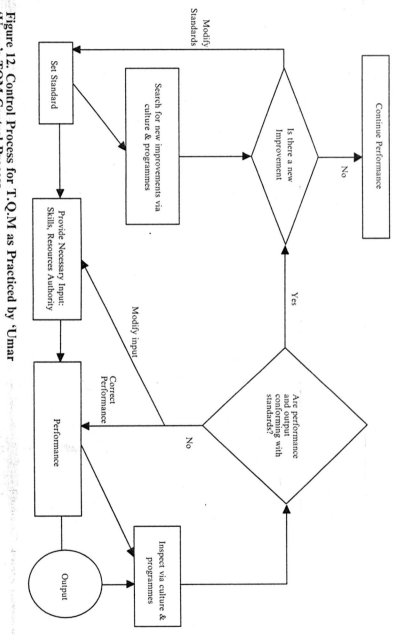

Figure 12. Control Process for T.Q.M as Practiced by 'Umar 'Umar's TQM Control Process

PART – VII

A VALUE BASED MANAGEMENT MODEL

A GUIDE TO MUSLIM MANAGERS

1. INTRODUCTION

Conventional management has undeniably valuable contributions to the efficiency and effectiveness of organizations the world over. We should, however pay attention to the danger of the cut and paste approach. We cannot just practice any management approach we learn from conventional management without asserting its validity in our environment and its consistency with our values. We have to pay attention to differences in premises of thought, cultural context of cases and empirical studies, and differences in values. Most importantly, we have to realize that conventional management ignores revelation (our supreme source of knowledge) and is, therefore, deprived from an inexhaustible source of knowledge.

The Islamic school of management has existed in practice since the beginning of Islam and it had outperformed other schools of management during the heights of the Islamic civilizations. Muslims nowadays are, however, being organizationally outperformed by most Non-Muslims. While the analysis of Muslims underperformance is beyond the scope of this document, it is undeniable that Muslims are currently not following an Islamic management model. There are certain Islamic management practices having different degrees of success here and there, but there is yet a total integrated Islamic model to be practiced anywhere. This monograph provides an Islamic management model that can be used as guide to Muslims organizations. This Model can be also used as basis for Muslim organizations to be certified with an Islamic management certificate just like many organizations being ISO certified for example. This model can also be used as basis for an Islamic Management award.

Having an Islamic management standards for the purpose of certification or an Islamic management award are highly important because they move the Islamic management efforts from theory and preaching like approaches to clear systems that need to be enacted in order to achieve certification or contend for an award. ISO certifications and quality awards have been more effective in achieving quality than did the teachings of quality gurus, similarly we expect Islamic management certification and awards to be more effective in achieving success and falāḥ.

2. Why This Islamic Management Model

The list below includes the possible benefits of proposed Islamic management model.

To seek the pleasure of Allah

To learn from the inexhaustible source of knowledge (Qur'an) and from our rich history.

To guide Muslims in their efforts to manage their companies

To have absolute ethical guidelines

To achieve unity of purpose, unifying thereby the *Dunia* purpose with the *Ā'khira* purpose and personal values with organizational values

To satisfy and motivate employees

To improve quality and productivity

To gain the trust of customers and suppliers

To enhance competitiveness

To develop our Ummah and help it play its proper civilizational role

To develop a knowledge bank that will provide many cases and many contemporary role models, something that can help Muslim researchers and mangers all over the world.

To contribute to development of management and to resurface an internationally leading school of management

3. Islamic Management Model

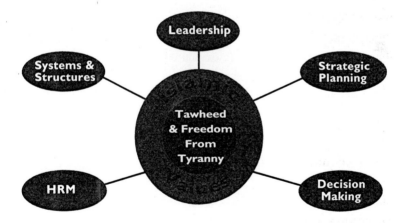

Figure 1. Islamic Management Model

The proposed Islamic management model is values centered. The values stem from *Tawḥīd* and freedom from tyranny. All the practices of strategic planning, decision-making, HRM, leadership and systems and structures are chosen based on the extent they serve the Islamic values. All management practices that support Islamic values can and should be included in this Model particularly in systems and structures. Muslims do not shy away from learning from any source.

Prophet Muhammad (bpuh) said:

> "Wisdom should be sought by every Muslim, wherever he finds, he is most deserving of it." (Ibn Mājah)

Unlike many quality models, this model is not divided into enablers and results. This is because Islam focuses on the process and not on results. Improving success does indeed guarantee improving results. This model does also include a special section on customer satisfaction because it is a value centered model and the importance of all stakeholders and particularly customers is an integral part of the Islamic values.

3.1. Measurement

The measurement of this model is based on joint system based on the experience of the author. The Islamic values that are the centre and the focus of the model are given a weight of 20%. Leadership was given a weight of 21%, Planning was allocated 18%, and Decision Making was allocated 8%. Human Resource Management (HRM) was given a weight of 12% wile systems and structures are given a weight of 21%.

One may ask why the Islamic values don't have a higher weight. The answer to this question lies in the fact that all management practices included in the other five dimensions of the model were selected because of their support of the values and their measurements do, therefore, reflect the measurement of the values.

Decision-making was only allocated 8% because of its strong relationship with planning which was allocated 18%. HRM was only given a weight of 12% because it is a separate function whose activities are not necessarily continuously involved in every aspect of the organization like leadership and systems and structures.

The specific weights and measurement of each item will be listed next sections.

4. Values (20 Points)

Values are the focus and purpose of the teachings of Islam.

The Prophet (Blessings and Peace be upon him) said:

> I have only been sent to complete good manners (*Makarim al Akhlāq*) — (Bukhāri)

The verse of the Qur'an reads:

$$﴿... إِنَّ ٱللَّهَ لَا يُغَيِّرُ مَا بِقَوْمٍ حَتَّىٰ يُغَيِّرُواْ مَا بِأَنفُسِهِمْ ...﴾$$

(سورة الرعد ١٣ : ١١)

﴿...Lo! Allah changes not the conditions of a folk until they change that which is in their hearts...﴾ (Qur'an 13: 11)

Currently the most successful companies in the world are those that adhere strongly to their values.

Muslim Organizations must have regular workshops to infuse and reinforce Islamic values. These workshops should include surfacing the existing values, determining the gap between the existing values and the Islamic ones, agreeing on a sanctioning system to close to gaps.

Points allocated to values are predominantly based on the conduct of the workshops in addition to the documentation of the values; interviews conducted with randomly selected workers in addition to minutes of meeting that will reflect such values as trust and freedom from tyranny.

Below are listed the main Islamic values upon which the model is developed.

VALUES

4.1 *Tawḥīd* and Freedom from Tyranny

At the source of all values is *tawḥīd* and freedom from tyranny be it idols, desires, people, or anything other than Allah

❀Allah! There is no god but He, the Living, the Self-Subsisting, Eternal, No slumber can seize Him, nor sleep. His are all things in the heavens and on earth. Who is there that can intercede in His presence

BENEFITS

❑ Taking initiatives

❑ Solving problems without being ordered by anyone to do so

❑ Speaking up and correcting the wrong

❑ Feeling secure in every sense including economically.

except as He permits? He knows what is before [His creatures] and what is behind them. Nor shall they compass aught of His knowledge except as He wills. His throne does extend over the heavens and the earth, and He feels no fatigue in Guarding and preserving them. For He is the Most High, The Supreme [in Glory]﴾ (Qur'an 2: 255)

﴾...Whoever rejects tyranny and believes in Allah has grasped the most trustworthy handhold, that never breaks...﴾ (Qur'an 2: 256)

4.2. Humbleness

Charity never decreases wealth and Allah only increases a forgiving person in honour and whosoever is humbled for Allah is elevated (By Allah) (Muslim)

❑ Willingness to improve

❑ Willingness to listen and be corrected

He will Not enter Paradise who has (in his heart) a weight of arrogance (Muslim)	❑ Willingness to cooperate ❑ Respecting others

4.3. *Tawakkul*

Tawakkul means doing our best and putting our trust in Allah (The Merciful, The Wise, the Knowledgeable, All Mighty) to deliver the outcome

❑ Confidence and optimism

❑ Resolve

❑ Diligence

❖And when you are resolved, then put your trust in Allah. Lo! Allah loves those who put their trust [in Him].❖ (Qur'an 3: 159)

❖But that which is with Allah is better and more lasting: [It is for those who believe and put your trust in their Lord].❖ (Qur'an 42:16)

4.4. Abstaining from *Ḥarām*

If I forbid from something then avoid it and I order you to do something then do it as much as you can (your

❑ Abstaining from evil

❑ Not hurting ourselves

utmost) - (Bukhāri)

❑ Not hurting others

❑ Serving our long term interests

4.5. Flexibility

Most of the Islamic teachings appear in terms of Noxiants. This gives us more flexibility. This is because being told not to do specific points allows doing everything else while being asked to do certain specific points prevents us from doing anything else. The figure below shows we have plenty of green space and only a few red dots that we shall avoid.

Figure 2. Noxiants Model

You are more knowledgeable about the issues of your *Dunia* — (Muslim)

❑ Satisfaction with the high degree of freedom

❑ Innovation

❑ Avoiding conflicts that can cause by lack of clarity of the prohibited

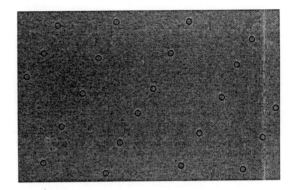

4. 7. Fairness

❨Allah commands justice, benevolence, and liberality to kith and kin, and he forbids all shameful deeds, and injustice and transgression: He instructs you, that you may receive admonition❩ (Qur'an 16: 90)

❑ Employee's satisfaction

❑ Retention of good employees and not sending them to competitors

All people are equal as the teeth of the comb. (At-Ṭabarāni)

❑ Retaining good customers, contractors, and suppliers

The only basis for preference between an Arab and a non-Arab, a white and a black, and a male and a female is piety. (Ibn Isḥāq)

❑ Saving time and money

❑ Producing good quality

⊰O you who believe! Stand out firmly for Allah, as witnesses to fair dealing, and let not the hatred of others to you make you swerve to wrong and depart from justice. Be just, that is next to piety.⊱ (Qur'an 5: 8)

4.8. Caring and sharing, *Iḥsān*

⊰Allah commands justice, benevolence, and liberality to kith and kin, and he forbids all shameful deeds, and injustice and transgression: He instructs you, that you may receive admonition⊱ (Qur'an 16: 90)

❑ Employee's delightedness and loyalty

❑ Attracting new employees and not sending them to competitors

The believers are like one man if his head is in pain his whole body suffers and if

his eye is in pain his whole body suffers. (Bukhāri)

None among you will believe until he loves for his brother what he loves for himself. (Bukhāri)

❑ Attracting new customers, contractors, and suppliers

❑ Saving time and money

❑ Producing higher quality

❑ Satisfaction of community at large

He did not believe. He did
not believe. He did not
believe, he who slept with a
full stomach knowing that
his neighbour is hungry. (Al
Ḥākim)

⁂But those before them,
had homes and had adopted
the faith show their
affection to those as came
to them for refuge, and
entertain no desire in their
hearts for things they were
given, But give preference
over themselves, even
though poverty was their
[own lot]. And those saved
from the covetousness of
their own souls-they are the
ones that achieve
prosperity.⁂ (Qur'an 59: 9)

Whoever wishes to be
delivered from hell-fire
and enter the Garden
should treat the people the
way he wishes to be treated.
(Muslim)

4. 9. Cooperation

◆Help one another unto righteousness and pious duty. Help not one another unto sin and transgression, but keep your duty to Allah. Lo! Allah is severe in punishment.◆ (Qur'an 5: 2)

❑ Customer satisfaction
❑ Employee's satisfaction
❑ Supplier's satisfaction
❑ Regulators satisfaction
❑ Cost saving
❑ Time saving

4. 10. Dignity and respect

◆We have honoured the children of Ādam, transported them in the land and in the sea, given them for sustenance things good and pure and conferred on them special favours above a great part of Our creatures.◆ (Qur'an 17: 70)

❑ Customer satisfaction

❑ Employee's empowerment and satisfaction

❑ Supplier's satisfaction

◆And speak to people Good.◆ (Qur'an 2: 83)

Whoever wishes to be delivered from hell fire and enter the Garden should treat the people the way he wishes to be treated. (Muslim)

❑ Regulators satisfaction

4.11. Trust

❖O you who believe avoid suspicion as much [as possible] for suspicion is in some cases a sin and spy not on each other.❖ (Qur'an 45: 12)

A leader who is suspicious of his people will lead them to mischief. (Abu Dawūd)

❑ Ensuring transaction take place, for no transaction can ever take place if no trust exist even if the best lawyers are hired and all efforts are put to close loopholes

❑ Reducing time and cost of transactions

❑ Eliminating spying that wastes time energy and mental focus

❑ Improving communication

❑ Improving morale

4.12. Cost Efficiency

❖Verily spendthrifts are brothers of satan and satan is to his Lord ungrateful.❖ (Qur'an 17: 27)

Do not extravagate in (using) water even if you were taking ablution on the bank of a running river (Ibn Mājah)

❑ Preserving the resources of Allah

❑ Protecting the environment

❑ Gaining market share

❑ Increasing savings

❑ Increasing profits

‹Make not your hand tied
[like a niggard's] to your
neck, nor stretch it forth to
its utmost reach, so that you
become blameworthy and
destitute.› (Qur'an 17: 29)

❏ Increasing investment
opportunities

❏ Increasing opportunities to
pay *Zakāt* and *Ṣadaqah*

4.13. Time efficiency

Man will be asked about his
life, how he spent it, his
youth, how he used it and
his money, how he earned it
and how he spent it.
(Tirmidhi)

❏ Improving productivity

❏ Decreasing cost

Take advantage of five before
five: Your youth before your
aging, your health before
your sickness, your wealth
before your poverty, your free
time before your busy time,
and your life before your
death. (Tirmidhi)

❏ Gaining market share

❏ Improving product and
service

❏ Finding time for learning
and innovation

4.14. Quality/Diligence

Prophet Muhammad (bpuh) said:

He whose two days are equal (in accomplishments) is a loser. (Daylami)

The most lawful food of a servant is the earning of the hand of a producer if he did it to his best abilities (with sincerity). (Bukhāri)

Allah Almighty wants that when one of you does a job, he/she do it well. (Reported by Al Bayhaqi)

Allah has decreed excellence for everything. When you kill, do it in the best way; and when you slaughter (an animal for sacrifice), do it in the best way. So every one of you should sharpen his knife, and let the slaughtered animal die comfortably. (Muslim)

❑ Customer Satisfaction

❑ Gaining market share

❑ Cost saving

❑ Time saving

4.15. Long-term orientation

Deeds are based on the ends. (Bukhāri)

- ❑ Becoming more ethical
- ❑ Increased diligence
- ❑ Spending wisely
- ❑ Achieving higher goals

4.16. Unity of purpose

Muslims should not be divided between their *dunia* and *Ākhira* goals anything that Muslims do is considered *'ibādah* that is rewarded for in the Hereafter provided it is *halāl* and done for the sake of Allah.

❋Allah has not made for any man two hearts in his body...❋ (Qur'an 33: 4)

- ❑ Elimination of dissonance and schizophrenia

- ❑ Increased work Motivation

- ❑ Higher efficiency

- ❑ Better enjoyment in leisure time since this enjoyment is *'ibādah*

4.17. Discipline

Obedience is an Islamic duty. It should be therefore a willing obedience not a coerced one. We are rewarded by Allah for obeying our leaders so long as the orders are not *harām*

- ❑ Better use of resources

- ❑ Higher efficiency

- ❑ Good Morale

❞Oh you who believe! obey Allah and obey the messenger, and those in charge among you.❝
(Qur'an 4: 59)

Whoever obeyed my appointed leader has indeed obeyed me, and whoever disobeys my appointed leader did in fact disobey me. (Bukhāri)

4.18. Participative management.

My nation cannot agree upon an error and if a conflict persists be with the majority. (Ibn Mājah)

❞Those who harken to their Lord and establish regular prayer; who [conduct] their affairs by mutual consultation; who spend out of what we bestow on them for sustenance.❝
(Qur'an 42: 38)

❞It was by the mercy of Allah that thou wast lenient with them [O Muhammad],

- ❏ Better Decisions

- ❏ Better implementations

- ❏ Defect prevention

- ❏ Continuous improvement

- ❏ Higher morale

for if you hadst been stern
and fierce of heart they
would have dispersed from
round about thee. So
pardon them and ask
forgiveness for them and
consult with them upon the
conduct of affairs. And
when thou art resolved then
put your trust in Allah. Lo!
Allah loves those who put
their trust [in Him].
(Qur'an 3: 159)

Religion is sincere advice.
(Muslim)
Whosoever sees wrong
should correct it. (Muslim)

4.19. Eagerness to learn and to share knowledge

Read! In the name of your
Lord and Cherisher, who
created — created man, out
of a mere clot of congealed
blood: Read! And your
Lord is Most Bountiful, —

He Who taught with the
pen — taught man that
which he knew not
(Qur'an 96: 1-5)

❑ Higher skills

❑ Higher quality

❑ Continuous improvement

Seeking knowledge is a must for every Muslim (Ibn Mājah)

≪And say! My Lord, increase me in knowledge.≫ (Qur'an 20: 114)

The best among you is he who learns Qur'an and teaches it (Bukhāri)

≪And remember Allah Took covenants from the people of the book, to make it known and clear to people and not to hide it..≫ (Qur'an 3: 187)

5. Planning (18 Points)

Item	Values it serves	Measurement
Having a vision leading to the general vision of Islam which is to enter paradise	Long term orientation Unity of purpose	documents, interviews (2 point)
Having a mission consistent with the general mission of *Ibādah*	Long term orientation Unity of purpose	documents, interviews (2 point)

Setting goals to be achieved at specific times and making sure that they are conducive to the vision of the organization as well as with the general vision of entering paradise	Long term orientation Unity of purpose Time efficiency Cost efficiency	documents, interviews (1.5 point)
Establishing links between the goals of the organization and its values	Unity of purpose Being value-centered	documents, interviews (2 point)
Linking actions to vision of the organization and the general vision of entering paradise ❨Then shall anyone who has done an atom weight of Good, Shall see Good. And anyone who has done an atoms weight of evil, shall see evil.❩ (Qur'an 99: 7-8)	Unity of purpose Diligence / quality Time efficiency Cost efficiency Long term orientation	documents, interviews (2 point)

Figure 3. Actions-objective relationships

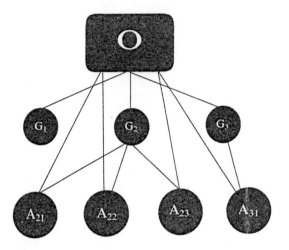

Long-term bias

Long term
orientation

documents,
interviews
minutes (2 points)

Creating synergies
among the
departments/
divisions of the
organization and
between the
organization and its
environment
❊Do they not reflect
about the Qur'an?
Had it been from
other than Allah,
they would surely
have found therein

Cooperation
Caring and sharing
Time efficiency
Cost efficiency
Unity of purpose

documents,
interviews
minutes (2 points)

much discrepancy.
(Qur'an 4: 82)

Figure 4. Goals Mutual Support

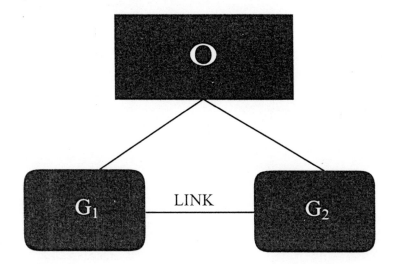

| Developing continuous improvement goals to satisfy changing customers needs. He whose two days are equal (in accomplishments) is a loser. (Daylami) | Humbleness Caring and sharing Responsibility Respect Time efficiency Cost efficiency Diligence / quality | documents, interviews minutes (1 point) |
| Planning for the whole organization | Fairness unity of purpose responsibility dignity and respect | documents, interviews, minutes (1 point) |

Planning for contingencies	tawakkul diligence responsibility long term orientation	documents, interviews, minutes (1 point)
Maintaining flexibility of plans	flexibility long term orientation trust respect	documents, interviews, minutes (1.5 points)

6. Decision Making (8 Points)

Item	**Values it serves**	**Measurement**
Encouraging mutual consultation at every level	participation humbleness quality / diligence time efficiency cost efficiency caring respect responsibility eagerness to learn cooperation trust unity of purpose	(2 points) documented work procedures, interviews, minutes
Using consensus in strategic decision	participation humbleness quality/diligence time efficiency cost efficiency	unity of purpose (2 points) documented work procedures, interviews, minutes

caring
respect
responsibility
eagerness to learn
cooperation
trust
unity of purpose

Encouraging Individual decisions at the operational level	Responsibility Participation Trust Respect caring and sharing	(2 points) documented work procedures, interviews, minutes
Taking decisions that take advantage of strength and opportunities and avoid weaknesses and threats while still putting Trust on Allah	humbleness *tawakkul* responsibility diligence cost efficiency time efficiency	(2 points) documented work procedures, interviews, minutes

7. Leadership (21 Points)

Item	Values it serves	Measurement
Championing Islamic values by acting as a role model and intervening when these values are	Values Unity of purpose Abstaining from *Ḥarām*	(2 points) documented communication, interviews, minutes

endangered or the noxiants are violated ❖Verily in the Messenger of Allah ye have a good example for him who looketh unto Allah and the Last Day, and remembers Allah much.❖ (Qur'an 33: 21)

Commitment to service The leader of people is their servant. (Aṭ-Ṭabrāni)	caring and sharing responsibility respect	(1 point) documented communication, interviews, minutes, site visits and evaluation of facilities and equipments
Supporting without expecting to be supported Clearly exemplified in the leadership Abu Bakr after the death of the Prophet, "But give preference over themselves, even though poverty was their (own lot)."	caring and sharing responsibility respect diligence	(1 point) documented decisions, employee's interviews, minutes

And those saved from the covetousness of their

Constantly communicating the vision and values of the organization with a strong sense of hope Whosoever said people are in loss is either the most lost among them or one who caused them to be in loss. (Muslim)	unity of purpose long term orientation trust caring and sharing responsibility respect diligence	(1 point) documented communication, interviews with employees, minutes
Holding regular meetings with employees and being open to their ideas and empathetic towards them	participation caring and sharing responsibility respect diligence	(1 point) documented decisions, employees interviews, minutes

❧Now hath come to you a messenger from amongst yourselves: It grieves him that you should perish: Ardently anxious is he over you: To the believers is he most kind and merciful.❧ (Qur'an 9: 128)

Holding regular meetings with customers and being responsive to their needs	caring and sharing responsibility respect diligence	documented decisions, employee's interviews, minutes (1 point)
Persistently making sure that sufficient efforts are made to implement strategy ❖O Yaḥyā! Take hold of the book with might: and We gave him wisdom even as a youth.❥ (Qur'an 19:12) ❖Therefore patiently persevere, as did the messengers of inflexible will.❥ (Qur'an 46: 35)	Discipline responsibility diligence / quality	documented decisions, employee's interviews, minutes (1 point)
Avoiding being suspicious and spying	dignity and respect trust	(1 point) documented work procedures, employees interviews, minutes
Respecting structures	responsibility/*amānah* respect discipline	(1 point) employees interviews, minutes

Being aware of potentials and weaknesses of followers	Caring and sharing	(1 point) employees interviews, minutes
❧"What made thee Hasten in advance of the people, He replied O Moses" "Behold, they are close on my footsteps: I hastened to Thee, O my Lord, to please Thee." The Samiri has led them Astray.❧ (Qur'an 20: 83-85)		
Getting involved in coaching	Caring and sharing *Ihsān* diligence	(1 point) employees interviews
Leading by example particularly in times of difficulties Case of the prophet during the treaty of Hudeibiya	responsibility Caring and sharing	employees interviews, minutes, documented decisions (1 point)
Partnering and building alliances	Humbleness Cooperation unity of purpose long term orientation	(1 point) documented decisions, minutes, interviews with partners

Commitment to social responsibility	responsibility cooperation unity of purpose	(1 point) documented decisions, minutes
Commitment to quality and productivity improvement programmes through personal involvement and providing the necessary systems of input	time efficiency cost efficiency quality	(1 point) employee's interviews, minutes, examination of systems of input such as row materials, equipment, and documented work procedure
Being rigorous and carefully examining reports and contracts	responsibility quality	(1 point) examinations of reports reviewed by the leader, minutes
Participating in learning, teaching and mentoring	Eagerness to learn & sharing knowledge	(1 point) employees interviews, minutes, certificates of attendance training programmes by leader
Having a long term bias in decision making and asking	long term orientation unity of purpose	(1 point) documented decisions, minutes

about long term consequences of actions

Being fair to those he likes and benevolent to those he dislikes	fairness *Ihsān*	(1 point) documented decisions, minutes, interviews
Using authority to stop the aggression that may be inflicted by one party on another	Discipline Fairness responsibility	documented decisions, minutes, interviews (1 point)

8. Hrm (12 Points)

Item	Values it serves	Measurement
Having transparent recruitment procedures based on qualification and trustworthiness ❀Truly the best of men for thee to employ is the best man who is strong and trustworthy.❀ (Qur'an 28: 26)	Fairness Responsibility Respect quality time efficiency cost efficiency Caring and sharing	(3 points) documented procedures, employees interviews, minutes

Not assigning people to jobs that overburden them He said: "I intend to wed one of these my daughters to thee, on condition that thou serve me for eight years; but if thou complete ten years, it will be (grace) from thee. But I intend not to place thee under a difficulty: thou will find me indeed, if God wills, one of the righteous.	Caring and Sharing Fairness Cost efficiency	(1 point) documented procedures, employee's interviews, minutes
Having fair and transparent promotion procedure ◈Allah commands you to make over trust to those worthy of them and that when judge between people you judge with justice.◈ (Qur'an 4: 58)	Fairness responsibility respect quality time efficiency Cost efficiency Caring and sharing	(2 points) documented procedures, employee's interviews, minutes

Paying competitive salaries based on qualifications and also on needs Practice of 'Umar He who does not thank people, does not thank Allah. (Reported by Abu Dawūd) ❖Do not discredit people from what they deserve.❖ (Qur'an 7: 85)	Fairness Respect Quality/diligence Time efficiency cost efficiency Caring and sharing	(1.5 points) payroll documents, employees interviews
Rewarding for the efforts not just for the results	Long term orientation Quality Fairness	(1 point) payroll documents, employees interviews, minutes
Sharing part of the revenues with the employees	Caring and sharing Long term orientation Quality Fairness	(1.5 point)
Having on the job training & providing continuous learning opportunities ❖It is He who brought you forth from the wombs of your	Humbleness Eagerness to learn Quality/diligence Time efficiency Cost efficiency	(2 points) payroll documents, employees interviews

mothers when you knew nothing; and He gave you hearing and sight and intelligence and affections: that ye may give thanks [to God]. (Qur'an 16: 78)

9. Systems and Structure

Item	Values it serves	Measurement
Building a flexible structure that recognizes the utility of leadership If there were three in a trip, they shall appoint a leader from among them. (Reported by Abu Dawūd)	Flexibility Discipline	(3 points) documents, interviews
Building teams	Humbleness Cooperation	(1 point) documents, interviews
Having a grievance committee Practice of 'Umar	Caring Fairness	(1 point) documents, interviews, minutes

Having a reward systems that distinguishes between a good doer and a bad doer while focusing on team rewards 'Ali, the fourth successor of the prophet said: Make sure that the good doer and the bad doer are not equal in status before you, for doing so is belittling good and its doers, and encouraging bad and its doers	Fairness Time efficiency Cost efficiency Quality Cooperation	(1.5 point) documents, interviews
Building control systems based on values and aggregate control as opposed to concurrent control	Respect Trust	(2.5 points) documents, interviews
Having customer satisfaction programs and measuring customer satisfaction	Respect Responsibility Caring and sharing Diligence/Quality	documents, interviews (2 points)

Having a good working environment in terms of safety, ergonomics and respect, and measuring employees satisfaction	Respect Responsibility Caring and sharing	(2.5 points) documents, assessment of facilities, interviews
Having a code of ethics	A set of noxiants flexibility Discipline Abstaining from *harām*	(1.5 points) documents, interviews
Developing a knowledge map and a knowledge bank	Eagerness to learn and sharing knowledge	(1.5 points) documents, database, interviews
Scheduling time for mutual learning	Eagerness to learn and sharing knowledge	(1 point) documents, interviews
Simplifying and reengineering processes to cut cost and decrease lead time	Time efficiency Cost efficiency Responsibility	(2 points) documents, interviews

| Keeping sufficient cash reserves and avoiding large debts | Humbleness *Tawakkul* Responsibility Caring and sharing Long term orientation | (1.5 points) documents |

10. Final Remarks

This model was based on the Islamic values that are in turn based on *tawheed*. It is certainly not a perfect one. Improvements can be made in more than one way including the items included and the weight allocated to them. This Model is more suitable for Muslim organizations than other existing Models. It is superior to other models in terms of comprehensiveness, consistency and integration. This Model can be used by any organization or certifying body, possibly after making some changes that suit their environment. At later stages, and subject to experiences, different versions of this model can be developed as it was done for ISO certification, which has been revised in 1994 and in 2000.

GLOSSARY

Ākhirah	آخرة	:	Hereafter.
Āyāt	آيات	:	(Sing: *Āyah*) Verses, Signs etc.
Aḥkāmāt	أحكامات	:	Ordainments.
Akhlāq	أخلاق	:	Behaviour.
'Aqīdah	عقيدة	:	Belief, Faith, Creed.
Awqāf	أوقاف	:	(Sing: *Waqf*), Trust, Endowment.
Barakah	بركة	:	Mercy of Allah, Blessings.
Dawāwīn	دواوين	:	(Sing: *Diwān*) Administrative units.
Dunia	دنيا	:	World.
Ibāḥah	اباحه	:	Liberality.
Fujūr	فجور	:	Sins, transgressions, tyranny.
Hadith	حديث	:	The sayings and the actions of the Prophet (Blessings and Peace be upon him).
Ḥalāl	حلال	:	Legal, Permitted in Islamic *Sharī'ah*.
Ḥarām	حرام	:	Forbidden according to Islamic *Sharī'ah*.
Hijrah	هجرة	:	Migration, it connotes to the

migration of the Muslims from Makkah to Madīnah; Islamic Calendar is called Hijri era.

'Ibādah	عبادة	:	Worship.
Jannah	جنة	:	Paradise, Garden.
Jihād	جهاد	:	Struggle, Striving for Islamic order, Warfare.
Khalīfah	خليفة	:	Caliph, ruler.
Khuṭbah	خطبة	:	Sermon, Speech, Lecture.
Minbar	منبر	:	Stage, the place from where a Sermon is delivered.
Munāfiq	منافق	:	Hypocrite.
Nifāq	نفاق	:	Hypocricy.
Qiyām	قيام	:	(Lit. to stand) Night prayers.
Ṣadaqah	صدقة	:	Charity, also used for *Zakāh*.
Ṣaḥāba	صحابة	:	Companions of the Prophet (Blessings and Peace be upon him).
Ṣalāh	صلاة	:	Prayer, obligatory or optional.
Sh'ā'er	شعائر	:	Motto, watchword.
Sharī'ah	شريعة	:	Islamic Laws.
Shirk	شرك	:	Associating partners with Allah.
Shūra	شورى	:	Consultation, Consultation Council.

Tābi'yīn	تابعين	:	The immediate Followers of the Companions of the Prophet.
Taqwa	تقوى	:	Piety.
Tawakkul	توكل	:	Trust in God.
Tawḥīd	توحيد	:	Islamic Monotheism.
Ummah	أمه	:	Nation, People.
Zakāh (Zakāt)	زكاة / زكوة	:	Poor Due, one of the pillars of Islamic tenets.

TRANSLITERATION CHART

أ	a
ى . آ	ā
ب	b
ت	t
ة	h or t (when followed by another Arabic word)
ث	th
ج	j
ح	ḥ
خ	kh
د	d
ذ	dh
ر	r
ز	z
س	s
ش	sh
ص	ṣ
ض	ḍ
ط	ṭ

ظ	ẓ / <u>dh</u>
ع	ʿ
غ	gh
ف	f
ق	q
ك	k
ل	l
م	m
ن	n
ه‍ – ه – ـه‍ـ	h
و	w
و (as vowel)	ū
ي	y
ي (as vowel)	ī
ء	ʾ
	(Omitted in initial position)

	Fatḥah	a
	Kasra	i
	Ḍammah	u
	Shaddah	Double letter
	Sukūn	Absence of vowel